Belfast's Halls Of Faith AnD FamE

Photos on front cover:

Victoria Memorial Hall around 1920
Templemore Hall around 1965
Albertbridge Road Gospel Hall around 1950
Interior, Albert Hall around 1905

Back cover:
The Sunday School 'Trip'

J. Douglas.

BELFAST'S HALLS OF FAITH AND FAME

BY
VICTOR MAXWELL

AMBASSADOR

Belfast Northern Ireland **Greenville** South Carolina

BELFAST'S HALLS OF FAITH AND FAME
© 1999 Victor Maxwell

ISBN 1   84030 051 5

Ambassador Publications
a division of
Ambassador Productions Ltd.
Providence House
16 Hillview Avenue,
Belfast, BT5 6JR
Northern Ireland

Emerald House
1 Chick Springs Road, Suite 203
Greenville,
South Carolina 29609, USA
www.emeraldhouse.com

CONTENTS

FOREWORD

The impact of a holy life and dedicated service to Jesus Christ cannot be eroded by the passing of time. During the forty-three years of my Christian life I have been greatly influenced, encouraged and inspired by many of God's servants whose names have never hit the headlines. They were ordinary people who knew the Saviour and dedicated their lives to serve Him in various parts of our city. In recording the history of many of the Halls of Belfast I have been refreshed and challenged by the work of faith and labour of love of many of these people. Furthermore, I have had the privilege of not only being acquainted with many of the people of whom I have written, but I have had the added blessing of visiting their works and preaching in many of these Halls.

This is not an exhaustible record of all the Halls of Belfast nor is it too detailed in defining the history of each Hall. Rather, it is a record of those who had vision and faith to reach their generation in the city for Jesus Christ. The decades of sowing in faith the Good Seed of God's Word has already realised a great spiritual harvest in the city but eternity will give a fuller picture.

My sincere thanks to all those who helped and aided in conversations about the halls, those who provided publications of local works and to my son-in-law and my daughter, Tomm and Heather Knutson, for their painstaking work in editing yet another manuscript.

Victor Maxwell
Banbridge, Co. Down.

Chapter One

TEMPLEMORE HALL

The founding of Templemore Hall was very much centred around the life and ministry of an extraordinary man who did not hail from Northern Ireland. At the early part of the twentieth century W. E. Tocher and his wife arrived on Ulster's shores from their native bonnie Scotland. He was converted as a young man and had identified himself with the gospel hall in Broughty Ferry near to Dundee. It was there that he cut his teeth in preaching and evangelistic endeavour. In Ulster he and Mrs. Tocher traversed the length and breadth of the Province in a horse drawn caravan as true ambassadors for Christ preaching the Gospel in mission halls located in the remotest areas. These evangelistic endeavours were met with considerable success and soon Mr. Tocher was making a considerable impact on the evangelical life of Ulster by his Bible preaching and evangelistic zeal.

In 1916 many brave men of Ulster "went over the top" and gave their lives at the Battle of the Somme; during this time Mr. Tocher engaged in a battle for souls in East Belfast. The position of pastor at the Iron Hall in East Belfast's Templemore Avenue had become vacant due to the departure of Pastor Robert Graham who left to work in the

Glasgow City Mission. Mr. Tocher was invited by the Iron Hall to fill the vacancy.

During the next seventeen years W. E. Tocher became a quite significant figure in East Belfast and beyond. The Iron Hall, so named because it was made of corrugated iron, was located at the corner of Thorndyke Street and Templemore Avenue and was part of a tightly knit community of narrow streets and neat rows of terrace houses. A majority of the men from this part of the city were employed either in the nearby Harland and Wolff ship-building yards where the Titanic had been built in former years or in the Ulster Rope Works. Both of these industries were the largest in the world in their respective fields.

Besides his powerful preaching, Tocher's wit and humour and sometimes his eccentricity made him a compelling character. Since he came to reside on the nearby Albertbridge Road he forsook the horse drawn caravan and replaced it with a motor cycle and side-car that was aptly named "near a car." Early in life Mr. Tocher suffered from polio and often claimed he was like the Bible's Mephibosheth for he was lame on both feet. The motor bike had been custom made for Mr. Tocher who because of his handicap could not throw his leg over a saddle. This vehicle was put to constant use in the continuing evangelistic efforts of this untiring servant of God.

On other occasions he travelled by train to various provincial towns. These rail trips were generally made sitting in a wheel chair in the Porter's Carriage. When he did have opportunity to travel in the passenger carriage he never failed to grasp the opportunity to witness to personal faith in Christ to his fellow passengers. One day several lads filed into the no-smoking carriage in which Mr. Tocher was already seated. They proceeded to light up their cigarettes and soon the carriage was filled with stale smoke. Mr. Tocher with his winsome Scottish accent courteously spoke up and requested that the boys respect the status of the coach and extinguish their cigarettes. The boys were good humoured enough to comply with the request but asked the pastor if he objected to them singing. He told them he had no problem as he enjoyed music. However, he requested that he be allowed to sing first. Tocher started up with all three verses of the hymn, "Since Christ my soul from sin set free." All the boys listened attentively and respectfully to the old Scot as he witnessed in song.

Nothing daunted Tocher. During the General Strike of 1919 some locals tried to force him to cancel the meetings at the Iron Hall. Employees from the Shipyard and the other great industries of East Belfast, downed tools with workers all over the British Isles.   They were demanding a reform of the standard working week from fifty-four hours to forty-four hours. "Work no more 'til forty-four," was their slogan.   In accordance with the strike's organisers, households were obliged to turn all lights off—gas or electric. Mr. Tocher was determined, strike or no strike, the Lord's work must go on. At the appointed time the lights at the Iron Hall lit as usual for the mid-week evening meeting. A deputation of burly union men arrived at the door of the meetinghouse and told the preacher in no uncertain terms, "Put your lights out, or we will put them out for you!"   Tocher was not to be intimidated and although he complied with their directive he sent word to all the people in the locality to bring their oil lamps. The meetings continued unabated.

During Tocher's early years of ministry at the Iron Hall Ulster's renowned evangelist, William Patteson Nicholson, conducted several evangelistic missions in East Belfast and hundreds of people were converted.   Many of these converts found their way to the corrugated iron building at the corner of Thorndyke Street to enjoy the powerful and effective preaching of W. E. Tocher.   Mr. Tocher also reaped an abundant harvest of converts through his own preaching and soon the Iron Hall was packed to capacity and at times bursting at the seams. To be sure of securing a seat it was necessary to arrive at the Hall at least half an hour before the service began.

Much blessing was experienced at the Iron Hall, but the effect of Tocher's ministry was felt further abroad as some of his early converts volunteered for distant mission fields.   Among these were two great stalwarts of the Sudan Interior Mission, Alex Stewart and Alex Ireland who were farewelled from the Iron Hall for training in Buxton's Missionary Training Colony and then they gave a lifetime of devoted service to Africa.

After more than fourteen years of effective ministry in the Iron Hall Mr. Tocher had become quite a household name in East Belfast and throughout the evangelical community in Northern Ireland. In 1933 he withdrew from his position at the Iron Hall and conducted meetings in the Mountpottinger YMCA on the Albertbridge Road where he attracted great crowds to his Bible study. His Sunday evening services were convened in the nearby Willowfield Cinema with hundreds attending.

Encouraged by the response of the Christian public Mr. Tocher and his friends formed a new assembly. Early in 1934 they purchased a site on Templemore Avenue from the Musgrave Engineering Works. No time was lost in erecting a functional building to be the home of the new fellowship which they constituted in June 1934 as "The Templemore Hall Christian Brethren."

Due to the pressing demand for a meeting place the new hall was simple in its design, as big and plain as a hangar with no extra rooms to serve as a vestry or even a kitchen. The only extra room was in a basement to the rear of the building which housed the furnace for heating the hall.

Perhaps the plainness of the building reflected the worldwide economic depression of the early thirties, yet it underlined the dedication of many ordinary people in giving generously and sacrificially to erect the new premises. The foundations were dug early in February 1934, and Mr. George O'Neill and Mrs. Emerson laid memorial stones to mark the occasion. Within six months the hall was ready and the building was formally open on 2nd June 1934. The new building was packed and overflowing, and some were forced to stand in the street.

Mr. Sam Magowan was converted under Mr. Tocher's ministry in the Iron Hall in March 1924. As a life-long member of Templemore Hall he recalls that inaugural service, "The new hall was packed to capacity, and Mr. Tocher preached his first sermon in the new hall. Like his Lord, the common people heard him gladly and he spoke with great authority."

A fine body of men surrounded Mr. Tocher and formed the first oversight of the Templemore Hall Assembly. The oversight was comprised of George O'Neill, John Dunlop, Robert Scott, Joe Hunter,

John Clarke, John McClure and John Walker. These men also became trustees of Templemore Hall. George Erskine was appointed as the Sunday School superintendent, and later he erected a wooden structure at the rear of the main hall to accommodate the increasing number of children at the Sunday School.

Missionary interest at Templemore Hall was a focal point. The foreign missionaries who had been sent from the Iron Hall now identified themselves with the new Templemore Hall Assembly. Just a year after the opening of the new hall Mary Russell was commissioned from the hall to serve the Lord as a missionary nurse in Nigeria with the Qua Iboe Mission where she worked for more than thirty years.

Tocher's Bible class in Templemore Hall was soon recognised as a principal place for Bible preaching in Belfast. Besides the powerful and consistent preaching of Mr. Tocher himself, other evangelists and Bible expositors from across Britain and the United States ministered God's Word at Mr. Tocher's invitation. Among these were the Scottish evangelists Jock Troop, James McKendrick and the Fraser brothers who preached at several of the annual evangelistic missions which were held in February each year. Tocher not only welcomed these colleagues to the pulpit but often vocally accompanied their preaching with his own commentary and was not slow to sum up his frank opinion of the preacher and his message.

The annual Easter Convention became an important date in the evangelical life of East Belfast. Many of the speakers were invited from Mr. Tocher's acquaintances in Scotland. Renowned amongst these were able Bible teachers such as Messers Weston, Moffet, Eadie and R. D. Johnson. Often these special meetings continued throughout the rest of the week after Easter and large crowds attended each night. One great feature of those Easter meetings was the sweet and inspirational singing of Mr. William Mitchell whose son Jack Mitchell would have a very profound and fruitful ministry as Pastor of the Iron Hall in later years.

Even though expository preaching was the emphasis of Mr. Tocher's ministry, music and singing were both also prominent peculiarities of the ministry in Templemore Hall. There was already a very good mixed voice choir at the hall from the earliest days of the work, but it was in 1942 that Mr. Jimmy Baillie suggested that they form a male voice choir.

The first leader of this choir was Joe Nabney, the noted Belfast gospel tenor. This choir of at least thirty voices functioned for fifty years during which time they conducted meetings throughout Ulster and Scotland. In 1955 they organised a Festival of Male Voice Choirs at Templemore Hall. These festivals became an important annual date on the church calendar. The Male Voice Choir also conducted open air meetings all over Belfast and gospel tent meetings or church campaigns in Drumbeg, Culcavey, Raffery, Mallusk, Dundonald, Knocknagoney, Ballinderry Eden, Ballycoan, Skipton Street, Bethel Baptist, Moneyrea and Ballydoughin. They also spent weekends singing and ministering the gospel in Scotland and in England. During these years countless numbers of people were converted to Jesus Christ. In later years Miss Betty Thompson, the Templemore Hall organist, ably assisted the Male Voice Choir to make several records which were greatly sought after by the Christian public.

Pastor Tocher was probably best known for his prophetic conferences in the days leading up to and during the course of World War II. Reading of the political developments alongside his Bible, he made some bold predictions. Some of these were fulfilled in later years, while others were grossly inaccurate. Among the predictions he foretold were the independence of all nations and a European single currency before the second coming of the Saviour. He also anticipated that the British government would "sell out" Ulster. One Monday night of each month was devoted to questions regarding prophetic matters, and Tocher was prolific in his comprehensive answers to all queries. Often when closing some of those prophetic meetings Tocher would shout, "Jesus is coming! No surrender!"

The German blitzkrieg of 1941 was largely aimed at the Belfast shipyards which were near Templemore Hall. Several streets along Templemore Avenue took direct hits from the German bombs, and many families lost their homes, and their loved ones. Many were also maimed severely in the raids; these were dark days in East Belfast. As sirens sounded night after night the lights of Belfast went out. The footpath curbs were painted white; houses were fitted with dark blinds, and people carried torches as a blanket of darkness descended on the city. Many families were evacuated out of town to the surrounding countryside. Tocher never let the conditions interrupt his Bible ministry. As admonished by the Scriptures he continued "in season and out of season" throughout the war years.

One memorable experience in Mr. Tocher's ministry was in 1937 when Pastor George Olley invited him to Newtownards Baptist Church for an evangelistic mission. The meetings were well attended and Tocher preached his heart out every night. However, there were no evident results at the end of three weeks and the evangelist searched his own heart and questioned why no one had been converted.

Seven years later, when Mr. Tocher was ill, he received a visit from a young up-and-coming preacher. In the course of conversation Tocher asked the young preacher to tell how he had been converted. The young man explained to Mr. Tocher that he had been converted after attending that mission in Newtownards. At the time the young preacher had been a wayward prodigal and a virtual outcast of society. He went on to tell Mr. Tocher how he had stumbled into those meetings, and as a result of Tocher's preaching he had received Jesus Christ as Saviour. That convert was the well known Willie Mullan who not only conducted an evangelistic mission in Templemore Hall in 1944 but would also become the pastor at the nearby Bloomfield Baptist Church and in years to come would be instrumental in leading thousands to Christ. Tocher later confessed that the 1937 mission in Newtownards was the most productive mission he had ever had even though he did not recognise it at the time.

Immediately after the war Dr. Torrey Johnson, the founder of Youth for Christ, brought a young evangelist to Northern Ireland. The principal meetings were conducted in Templemore Hall, and that young evangelist preached for the first time in the British Isles. His text that night was "The Lord is not slack concerning His promise." At the end of the service twenty people trusted Christ as Saviour. The world was to hear a lot of that young evangelist in later years—he was a youthful Billy Graham. Mr. Tocher commented, "If that young man keeps his feet on the ground and his eyes on the Lord, he will be a wonderful vessel."

Following the visit Mr. Tocher was appointed as a representative for Youth for Christ in Northern Ireland and was designated to receive their magazines and literature for distribution throughout Churches in East Belfast. After a few issues Mr. Tocher took exception to an editorial in one edition and sent all the literature back to the United States with the instructions to Dr. Johnson not to send any more literature.

Other noted Bible expositors to preach at the hall were Stratton Shoefelt, Dr. Inglis and Dr. Harry Ironside on his only visit to Northern Ireland. Dr. John Wesley White also conducted a special series of meetings at the hall, and through his ministry many were converted.

On Sunday, May 1956, Mr. Tocher preached his last sermon in Templemore Hall. He was in his eighty-sixth year. His health had been failing, and in his latter days because of his weakness he had to be carried to the pulpit and propped up by his two good friends Mr. Dunlop and Mr. McCready, while the aged pastor preached. John Jordan recalls carrying Mr. Tocher in his arms, "He seemed to be so frail and fragile as I carried him in my arms, but when he got into the pulpit he waxed strong and mighty in the Scriptures."

One day after a period of failing health Mr. Tocher collapsed at the hall, and Dr. Caldwell was summoned. The doctor examined him carefully, and soon Mr. Tocher recovered somewhat. Before the physician left Mr. Tocher stood up and steadied himself on the stick and then thanked the doctor for his kind attention. He finished by saying, "Young man, I have one thing to say—No Surrender!" He never did surrender, not to deteriorating physical health nor to changing trends in church life. He was unflinching and unmoveable in his stand for Christ and the gospel, and to the last he abounded in the work of the Lord.

His home call to heaven was sudden and stunning. News of his death made front-page news in the Belfast Telegraph. East Belfast had lost a stalwart for the truth. On the day of Tocher's funeral, Templemore Hall was packed to capacity while hundreds who could not gain admittance lined the avenue. Pastor Willie Mullan led the gathering in prayer, and Pastor Hugh Orr of nearby East End Baptist paid tribute to the beloved pastor. Mr. John Weston, a regular visitor at the annual Easter Convention and a close personal friend of Mr. Tocher, preached from the pulpit formerly occupied by this great man of God for so long.

Mr. Tocher's service stretched for more than forty years of pastoral ministry between the Iron Hall and Templemore Hall. One of his best-remembered quips was "My initials may be W. E. T., and I never want to be D. R. Y." He never was—God greatly used this dedicated servant.

For obvious reasons Templemore Hall had become known as "Tocher's Hall," and his passing left a great void. Finding a man to fill the vacancy was a big responsibility that weighed heavily on the oversight depleted by the home-call of their leader and shepherd. One name recommended to them was Calvin Dobson. Mr. Dobson was a native of the United States but had come to live in East Belfast to be near to his family. He was a member of East End Baptist Church. Mr. Dobson was a local bread-server for the Co-operative Society and had no previous experience in full-time Christian ministry. However, he was a keen student of the Scriptures and was putting his preaching gifts to good use most weekends. In Mr. Dobson's early days he had been a Methodist lay preacher. He later left the Methodist denomination and for some time attended a local gospel hall before becoming a Baptist.

The oversight invited Calvin Dobson to succeed Pastor Tocher—a challenge that he accepted with fear and trembling. However, in a short time Pastor Dobson matured and carried his responsibility with grace as the hall maintained its strident witness for Jesus Christ. His ministry was forthright and evangelistic, and he had a fervent passion to win the lost for the Saviour. He was a steadfast defender of the faith often exposing the errors of the various cults, which were making their door-to-door assaults in the area. In 1961 under Calvin Dobson's leadership a beautiful meeting hall was erected to the memory of Dr. Tocher at the rear of the main Templemore Hall. This became known as the "Tocher Memorial Hall."

The most noted features about the ministry of Templemore Hall at that time were the evangelistic missions conducted during Pastor Dobson's tenure. In 1960 Pastor Willie Mullan preached night after night to a packed hall, and scores were converted. This was shortly followed by another evangelistic campaign by the Coalmen's Mission which attracted so many of the ordinary working class people and many locals were converted by the grace of God. The Coalmen Testimony Band conducted one week of meetings, and these were followed by a week under the responsibility of the Christian Police Association. A member of the band quipped, "The first week we have the thieves and robbers, and then they are chased by the cops for the second week!"

Also in 1960 the Templemore Hall Male Voice Choir hosted their first Male Choir Festival to which Pastor Peter Donald from Glasgow was invited to be the guest speaker. These festivals continued for more than twenty years, and Mr. Donald, with his own Harper Memorial Baptist Male Voice Choir, was a frequent visitor on these occasions. The Harper Memorial Church was named after its former Pastor, John Harper, who went down with the Titanic, his full story is told in the international bestseller, 'The Titanic's Last Hero'.

In 1963 the Templemore Hall Male Voice Choir conducted an evangelistic mission in the hall. Their excellent harmony in song powerfully rang out the gospel message; several of the members also shone forth as very able preachers who in later years became pastors of various churches. The men were required to be ready to testify of their personal conversion to Jesus Christ. The two weeks of meetings at Templemore Hall were very well attended and were crowned with great days of conversions and blessings.

Pastor Dobson's wife was Eileen McKnight from Castlewellan. They had two children, Edward and May who were reared in the family home on the Belfast's Beersbridge Road and attended Grosvenor High School. While Calvin Dobson won many souls for the Lord, his most notable trophy of grace was leading his own son to personal faith in Jesus Christ. In later years Ed Dobson studied at Bob Jones University in South Carolina and Liberty Baptist University in Virginia. Later Ed joined the faculty at Liberty Baptist College and rose to be the vice-president under the leadership of Dr. Jerry Falwell. Today Dr. Ed Dobson pastors the Grand Rapids Calvary Church, which was founded by Dr. DeHann of the famous Radio Bible Class in Grand Rapids, Michigan.

As the years passed many of the founder members and pillars of Templemore Hall passed on to their reward. However, God raised up other like-minded men to ably support Pastor Dobson; among these were Mr. & Mrs. Harvey who opened their home in Ardenlee Parade to accommodate the Dobson family while the oversight looked for a suitable manse. Mr. Harvey was superintendent of the very large Sunday School. Jimmy Bennett and Sam Magowan looked after the day to day running and administration of the assembly. Jimmy Bennett was deputy superintendent of the Sunday School from 1935 until 1955 and then assumed the position of superintendent until 1970. In all Mr. Bennett gave thirty-six years of service to the Sunday School work. Sam Magowan, a beloved and well-respected overseer, was a very faithful and exact secretary for more than twenty-five years. Frank Hunniford was responsible for the resident Mixed Voice Choir which was widely acclaimed in Northern Ireland.

Pastor Dobson and his family left for the USA in the autumn of 1964, and again the pulpit at Templemore Hall was vacant. In later years Calvin Dobson pastored several churches in the United States, and finally he became an associate pastor to his son Ed at the Calvary Church in Grand Rapids with special responsibility for hospital visitation.

The annual Easter Convention continued unabated with great ministry in the Scriptures by Pastors Hugh Orr, Willie Mullan, Jim Irvine, Dr. John Moore, John Robb and many other servants of God. In the spring of 1964 Pastor Dobson visited his native United States of America, and subsequently he received a call to a church in Camden, New Jersey. News of his imminent departure shocked the members at Templemore Hall.

It was during Calvin Dobson's pastorate that Ken Brown, Bob Buckley and Billy McNaughten hit on the idea of a youth camp. These three men felt that it would be good to provide a camp for the young people. The idea was immediately met with a great response from the youth, and fifty to sixty young campers with their supervisors headed off to sleep under canvas for a week. This camp continued for many years in all sorts of weather and at many different venues around the coasts of Northern Ireland. The annual camp became one of the most effective evangelistic tools of the assembly.

Following Pastor Dobson's exit the pastorate at the hall remained vacant for three years. The overseers were faithful in maintaining the continued witness at the hall. However, it was difficult to maintain numbers at the meetings without consecutive Bible ministry. This underscored the overseers' pressing need to fill the vacancy of the pastorate. They were uncertain as to who would be suitable for the position. Nearby the Iron Hall had recently received the young Pastor Jack Mitchell who had come from Scotland and was making a great impact with his Bible teaching ministry. Some of the oversight from Templemore Hall approached Mr. Mitchell to ask his advice and seek a possible recommendation of a suitable pastor. Mr. Mitchell suggested the name of Mr. Ronald Macmillan. Mr. Macmillan was invited to conduct the services on Children's Day in 1966. The members of the oversight were impressed and extended an invitation to Ronald Macmillan to accept the position of full-time pastor at Templemore Hall.

Mr. MacMillan was from Bishop Briggs and was active in Bible ministry throughout the Brethren movement in Scotland. He had a good position of employment with the Shell Oil Company, and therefore it was not an easy decision to uproot his wife and three children to come to live in East Belfast. After seeking God's guidance Ronnie MacMillan accepted the call and commenced his ministry in Belfast on 8th September 1967.

Mr. MacMillan learned the geography of East Belfast by walking its streets and taking buses to local hospitals. The members at the hall recognised the workload and surprised their new pastor by buying him a car, a Vauxhall Viva, in March 1968. This car made his daily trips much easier for him.

Soon Pastor MacMillan and his family had settled into their new lives in Northern Ireland. However, the full impact of this move for the MacMillan family was underscored when in 1969 trouble erupted on the streets of Belfast at the beginning of what became known as "The Troubles." The escalation of violence throughout the Province brought a self-imposed curfew on many people who were afraid to leave their homes in the evenings. Templemore Hall, like many other churches and mission halls, periodically suffered greatly depleted numbers because of the very real fear of violent clashes on the streets.

Mr. MacMillan was a very methodical person, and he systematically preached through the Scriptures. He continued to be active in the evangelistic tradition of the hall both in the Sunday preaching and outreach to the surrounding community. His friendship with Pastor Jack Mitchell prompted him to suggest that both the Iron Hall and Templemore Hall should come together for a United Easter Convention. This suggestion was met with full agreement in fellowships, and in 1968 the two halls on Templemore Avenue came together to promote an annual Bible Conference which continues to this day. Both Ron Macmillan and Jack Mitchell were able to use their good influence in their native Scotland to introduce many fine preachers to Northern Ireland and some of these, like Pastor Gordon Cardwell, accepted invitations to minister in other churches in Ulster.

Ron MacMillan was skilful at poetry and often wrote verse for everything from weddings to retirements. Because of his tall stature he used the pseudonym "Longfellow." Here is a poem he put together for the fortieth anniversary of Templemore Hall:

In 1934 we're told -
Which makes it all of forty years old -
This hall once built in record time;
Becomes the subject of my rhyme.

Its pastors number, only three;
The first of whom was W. E. T.
His fame was known to all around;
A preacher, simple yet profound.

They quote him still, these modern days,
That apt and long remembered phrase;
"He being dead yet speaketh" here;
His name renowned; his memory dear.

A younger man, Calvin Dobson came;
Bearing a great reformer's name;
For seven years he joined the fray,
And then went off to U. S. of A.

And then another Scot appeared,
Without moustache or hairy beard;
He turned his back on Shell/BP,
To sail across the Irish Sea.

Despite the troubles, he's still here;
No surrender. Never fear.
He means to stay a wee while yet,
To see that you keep out of debt.

His pseudonym is "Longfellow" -
That's just a bit the belt below
His doggerel you'll have to bear,
So long as he is here, so there!

Three Pastors then in forty years,
To share your joys and share your tears;
Let's pray that in the years ahead,
The sheep and lambs will be well fed.

Throughout the time Ron MacMillan pastored Templemore Hall the church distributed literature from door to door throughout the East Belfast area. In 1977 he also conducted an evangelistic mission in a tent at Moneyrea in an endeavour to reach that growing community with the gospel.

Morag and Sheila MacMillan, Ronnie and Jean's two daughters, went to serve the Lord as missionaries in Africa—Morag to Tanzania with Missionary Aviation Fellowship and Sheila to South Africa with the African Evangelical Fellowship. Ronnie MacMillan, their only son and the youngest of the MacMillan family, followed a professional career which took him to live in Hong Kong.

After almost fourteen years in Templemore Hall, Pastor MacMillan announced that he was leaving Northern Ireland to accept a call to a pastorate at the Bethel Church on the Isle of Man. After some years there he later became the secretary of the Keswick Convention, a post which he held until his retirement to Scotland where he and Jean now reside.

The vacancy created by Ron Macmillan's departure continued for several years. During this vacancy greater responsibility rested with the oversight not only to provide speakers for the ongoing ministry at the hall, but also to seek God's man to fulfil the role of pastor.

Early in the vacancy an approach was made to Raymond McKeown in Scotland. Although born in Londonderry, Raymond had been taken as a young boy to live in Scotland. In his early Christian life he had been greatly influenced by the ministry of Jock Troop at the Tent Hall, and following the role model of this famous Scottish preacher Raymond developed skills and abilities that made him one of the most gifted open-air preachers in the United Kingdom.

Raymond and his wife Violet set up home in Partick, a district of Glasgow. While working as a carpenter at the Govan Shipyard, he often used his lunch hour to conduct an open-air meeting at the shipyard gates. These open-air meetings were bright and engaging, and often began with Raymond playing an accordion and singing lively gospel hymns. His genial manner and ready wit were greatly enhanced by speaking the plain man's language; these combined qualities soon captivated his listening audience. Those who knew Raymond will always remember his famous Saturday night and Sunday afternoon gatherings at the Toll Cross and the Glasgow market commonly called "The Barras."

Quite a few Glasgow musicians were converted, and many joined Raymond at the accordion with their trumpets, clarinets and saxophones. The tempo was upbeat, but the message was clear and dynamic, and many passers-by were converted as a result of those open air meetings.

His involvement with the Revival Centre in Glasgow also underscored Raymond's passion for revival. He truly was a man of God and the oversight at Templemore Hall was sure this was God's man for East Belfast.

Because of some disappointment during a previous experience in Belfast, Raymond was reluctant to consider the call to Templemore Hall. The oversight respected his hesitance to accept the call. However, their pursuit for an alternative servant of God drew a blank, and this convinced them that Raymond McKeown was the man God had laid on their hearts.

On second approach from the oversight Raymond was persuaded to accept the call to pastor the fellowship at Templemore Hall. He began his ministry in November 1982, and as well as all the normal duties of a busy pastorate, he immediately embarked on a vigorous open-air gospel campaign in many unlikely places around Belfast. On Friday mornings he led a small group of men to the Short Strand. This was considered "off limits" for Protestant preachers, yet they were greatly accepted by the local people who enjoyed listening to "the wee Scotsman with the accordion." Raymond conducted open-air meetings in many places: in front of Belfast's City Hall, at the gates of Harland and Wolff Shipyard, at Mackie's Factory, at Gallagher's Cigarette Factory and anywhere else he could muster up a crowd to listen to the gospel.

He imparted to the congregation at Templemore Hall his burden for revival and passion for prayer. Sadly, his effective ministry at Templemore Hall was abruptly interrupted after two short years. While his wife was on a visit to Glasgow, John Jordan found Raymond dead at the manse in May 1985. The funeral services were conducted in Templemore Hall with large crowds in attendance. The funeral procession followed to Scotland where Raymond's remains were buried.

Although Raymond McKeown had gone to be with Christ, his drive for evangelism and desire for revival lived on at Templemore Hall. Many caught the vision and became more active in reaching out to the district.

Just a few months after Raymond's decease Victor and Audrey Maxwell arrived home from Brazil where they had been serving the Lord with the Acre Gospel Mission. The Maxwells planned to remain in Northern Ireland to provide further education for their children. On learning of these plans Robert Caldwell, the secretary of Templemore Hall, approached Victor and enquired if he would consider the possibility of becoming the pastor at the hall. After several months of deliberation and prayer, the members at Templemore extended an invitation to Victor to accept this new challenge in his ministry. The induction service for the new pastor took place on Saturday, 6th February 1986.

East Belfast was a big contrast to the jungles of the Amazon, but for the next nine years Victor Maxwell ministered in Templemore Hall, and like his predecessors, he experienced the Lord's blessing on his work. Besides maintaining the tradition of Bible exposition at Templemore Hall, various evangelists conducted evangelistic missions, and these resulted in numerous conversions. Several of those converted came from para-military backgrounds, and others who formerly had been slaves to alcohol experienced the transforming power of the gospel. Some of these eventually became full-time workers among alcoholics and drug-addicts.

One notable evangelistic enterprise was a tent mission at Orangefield Park in June 1988. This evangelistic mission was shared between the Iron Hall and Templemore Hall—Denis Lyle and Victor Maxwell being the evangelists.

Extensive renovations were performed on the hall in 1993. Included in these renovations were a new kitchen, vestry, and store room. A new entrance was also built, and this added a new dimension and appearance to the main hall.

Although he was pastor at Templemore Hall, Victor and Audrey kept up their involvement in Acre Gospel Mission. Audrey was the secretary of the mission and Victor and Audrey visited the mission's various fields to preach and teach the Word of God. This involvement finally led to them returning to Brazil in March 1995.

The departure of the Maxwells to Brazil once again created a vacancy in the hall and added much responsibility to the oversight in difficult times. Church attendance throughout the city continued to be adversely effected by the continuing trouble on the streets. Templemore Avenue was a favourite hunting ground for joy riders who caused misery by stealing cars during church services. Added to this, some charismatic churches creamed off many young people from the hall's more traditional form of worship. It was not an easy time to call a pastor to East Belfast.

After consultation and prayer the oversight issued a call to Mr. John McFarland to become the pastor of the hall. John originated in

Fermanagh. He and his wife Dawn were converted while living in Newtownards and were members of Newtownards Baptist Church during the ministry of Pastor Sam Carson. After showing development in preaching ability John forsook his secure job to accept a call to be pastor of Coagh Baptist Church in County Tyrone. He laboured there with great blessing for nine years. John was inducted at Templemore Hall on 1st November 1996 and remains as the current pastor. His move to East Belfast brought new challenges for God's servant.

Templemore Hall has always been recognised for its strong emphasis on Bible ministry, its keen evangelistic fervour and the far-reaching missionary enterprise. Preachers and pastors such as Leslie Campbell, Billy McNaughten, Eric Magee, Noel Kearny, Ken Brown, Allen Wells and Lawrence Kennedy cut their teeth in gospel preaching at Templemore Hall. Eric and Ina Wells were associated with the hall for many years and served the Lord in Europe with CEF and also worked with Ireland Outreach. Pamela Brown and Elaine Price who were converted through the ministry at Templemore Hall, work with Stauros fellowship in Northern Ireland. Ron and Pat Heywood were supported by the Hall (Pat was a member of Templemore Hall) for years while they laboured with the Japan Evangelistic Band. Alan and Ruth Forsythe were commended from the Hall (Ruth was a member of Templemore Hall) for their work with A.I.M. in Tanzania. Other Christian workers went to distant regions and to other places not so far away to serve as missionaries.

It is impossible to measure the influence of a work like Templemore Hall. It is sufficient to say that the contribution made to the witness of the gospel in East Belfast for the greater part of the twentieth century will be made known one day. The Scriptures say, "The day shall declare it." And that is enough for us.

Chapter Two

THE VICTORIA
MEMORIAL HALL

On a cold and brisk Saturday night in 1958 I was distributing gospel tracts at the front of Belfast's magnificent City Hall. Many people received a copy of La Tournei's leaflet, "Gods Simple Plan of Salvation." While I was waiting for the next passer-by I spied a tall, well-dressed gentleman approaching. He carried a neatly folded umbrella in his hand and wore a three-quarter-length camel hair coat and what looked like a Stetson hat. At first I hesitated to stop the refined looking gentleman to offer him a copy of my literature. However, his eye caught mine, and I felt I could do no other than speak to him as I had to others. "Would you accept a gospel tract?" I asked.

The stranger interrupted his steady stride; he stretched out his hand, and without speaking a word he took a copy of the tract. While he scanned the contents of the leaflet, I asked, "Do you know the Lord Jesus as your Saviour?"

"I most certainly do." he replied in a very deep tone of voice. He then began to gently question me about my own conversion. When he seemed satisfied that I was truly converted, he further enquired if I would like to attend a meeting he was speaking at that night. I apologised and said I had already arranged to meet some other young people to go to the Help Heavenward meeting at Victoria Memorial Hall to hear Dr. Herbert Lockyer. A broad smile came on the gentleman's face and he said, " I'll see you there. I am Herbert Lockyer."

The meeting that night was great. The Victoria Memorial Hall at the corner of Arthur Street and May Street was packed to capacity with young people from all over Belfast. The acoustics of the old music hall greatly enhanced the inspirational singing which was accompanied by Mr. William Hill at the grand piano. Mr. Noel Jordan enthusiastically led the meeting and eventually introduced the internationally known Bible expositor, Dr. Lockyer. As I listened to Dr. Lockyer I couldn't help be amused by how I had tried to "convert" the famous preacher just an hour before the meeting.

Conversion and change are perhaps the most appropriate words when speaking of Victoria Memorial Hall. Since the beginnings of the work in the 1870's until its present location the assembly has changed its meeting venue several times.

The Victoria Hall housed an assembly of the Brethren movement and had its beginnings in the aftermath of the 1859 Ulster Revival. In the wake of the great spiritual revival the Brethren movement had rapid growth throughout the British Isles and beyond. As the movement spread several Brethren evangelists from Scotland and England visited Ulster and were instrumental in founding various assemblies. Initially they encountered some opposition to the new and simple form of worship introduced by the Brethren.

Among those who came from Scotland were James Clarke and James Smith. They met up with Martin Shaw, Francis Moore and John Marshall who with some friends and their families had initiated meetings in a private home in King Street and Christopher Street where they conducted Bible studies and celebrated the Lord's Supper. Others were attracted to join with them, and as numbers increased they rented the Abercorn Rooms at 101 Victoria Street.

The first speakers at those early meetings were Mr. James Campbell and Mr. William Matthews. Of those first meetings one wrote, "Here the Lord wrought mightily, convicting and converting sinners. The truth of believers' baptism was taught fully, and many, both young believers newly saved, and older believers who had never before heard the truth of God, obeyed the Lord in being baptized."

The newly formed group suffered some verbal criticism even from other Christians who didn't agree with the new movement. "We just go according to what we find written in God's Word, and He looks after us and sees that we lack no good thing" was their reply to critics.

It is not clear exactly how long the newly formed Assembly of believers remained at the Abercorn Rooms. However, it is known that these founding members moved to the nearby Victoria Room at No. 63 Victoria Street in October 1874. During the first year at this new meeting place the numbers increased from around fifty to well over one hundred souls.

Campbell and Matthews conducted special meetings in various locations near to the centre of the city, and at these many people were converted. The growing assembly at Victoria Room welcomed many friends, and the earliest roll book records amongst others, the visit in 1877 of one, Annie Housmin of London, who was commended by the better known Dr. Thomas Barnardo, founder of the renowned homes for orphaned and destitute children. Evangelist David Rea of Portadown and a number of other evangelists also regularly preached at the Victoria Room. Visitors came from the surrounding countryside to join in worship, and others came from as far away as Norwich, Glasgow, Stranraer, Cork and Tipperary.

Missionary interest in Victoria Hall Assembly was keen right from the beginning of the work in the 1860s. Mrs. Martin Shaw was saved during the '59 revival in Ireland. After her marriage in 1863 to Martin Shaw, they went to live in Dublin. During a serious illness the following year she prayed that if God spared her life she would dedicate herself to His service. This promise that she gave to the Lord she faithfully kept for fifty years until 1914 when, at the age of 78, she entered into the presence of her Master and Saviour.

Mrs. Shaw was a wonderful needle women, and she used this gift in helping missionary mothers and others by making clothing and underwear suitable for the particular climate and needs of the missionary. Mr. and Mrs. Shaw returned to Belfast in 1866, and Mr. Shaw became a well-known accountant. They met with the earliest assembly group, and Mrs. Shaw continued with her service of sewing. She took orders from friends for garments, which at that time were usually made at home or by dressmakers; she used this money to finance her own mission work.

Gradually her service increased and she invited other sisters to assist her. They met every Monday in a small house in Ballymacarrett which was used by an assembly for meetings. Often by the light of an oil lamp, they planned, cut out and sewed garments and made tea for those who joined them after their day's work. A hand sewing machine was carried to this meeting from Mrs. Shaw's home at Eastleigh Drive, Knock.

Mrs. Shaw was greatly assisted by Mrs. Pentland, Mrs. Blyth (nee Trimble), Miss Parkinson, Miss Susan Maxwell and others. The faithfulness and zeal of these dear women can be realised by the example of Miss Susan Maxwell—the eldest of a large family early left fatherless. Leaving her work in Academy Street at 6p.m. she walked to Ballymacarrett, helped with the work and then walked home to the Shankill Road. It should be remembered that public transport at the close of the nineteenth century was by horse-drawn train or cab. However, at that time the horse tram went only as far as Carlisle Circus. On the night of 15th September 1886, Susan did not return home until very late. Her route home took her across the old Ha'penny Bridge which was the predecessor of the Albert Bridge. It was on that night the bridge collapsed.

This ladies group later moved from Eastliegh Drive to a room in the Mountpottinger Orange Hall. It was around 1887 that the Women's Missionary Sewing Class became part of the activities of the Victoria Hall Assembly. Many of these sisters also formed the Missionary Work meetings which engaged ladies in needlework skill, and with the sale of their goods, they sent thousands of pounds to the missionary cause.

Many sisters who helped in the missionary sewing class throughout its existence eventually went to mission fields around the world.

The late William Gilmore recalled his attendance at the first Easter conference meetings held in the Victoria Room when some 400 people were present. He continued to attend the Easter conference for seventy-three years and saw the numbers attending exceed four thousand people with Bibles in hand. Because of the increasing numbers it became obvious that the Victoria Room was too small to contain all who wanted to attend.

It was on Sunday 18th November, 1888, the assembly "came into occupation" of Victoria Hall, a second floor room at 20 Victoria Street, on the corner with Queen's Square and near to the famous Belfast landmark known as the Albert Memorial Clock.

The Victoria Hall had been a public hall, and for a number of years it had been used by musical and choral societies for practice and performance. Jenny Lind, the celebrated Swedish Nightingale of that time is known to have sung there. Charles Dickens also graced its platform in 1858 to give readings of his works to a packed house. Recounting the experience in a letter to his daughter Dickens wrote: "The room will not hold more than from eighty to ninety pounds." Arthur (his business manager) was in the deepest misery because shillings got into stalls, and half-crowns got into shillings, and stalls got nowhere, and there was immense confusion. It ceased, however, the moment I showed myself and all went most brilliantly . . ." (Belfast Telegraph, 27th August 1937). There was obviously more concern for the listeners' money than their literary meditations.

During the course of the 19th century Belfast emerged from being a town of around 20,000 at the beginning of the century to a registered population of 208,122 in 1881. However, poverty was rife, and outbreaks of Summer Cholera were all too common. The housing situation was desperate, and sanitation in most working class areas depended on the flow of the nearest river. Municipal consciences were sensitive to these problems, and as a result, the celebrations of Queen Victoria's Jubilee Year in 1887 were curtailed because of the social emergency.

Notwithstanding, Belfast was developing; educationally, culturally, commercially and industrially. Almost inevitably Queen Victoria's Royal Charter conferred on Belfast in 1888, and it passed from the status of town to become a city.

Although the assembly of believers at Victoria Hall was also growing in numbers and maturity, its leaders were not without their problems. In these problems the Word of God was always the final arbiter on matters of doctrine, practice and church order. As one of the first assemblies to be established in Belfast, they were constantly called on for advice and counsel from those who were forming similar local churches throughout Belfast and beyond.

Even in those early days the Assembly at Victoria Hall engaged in a full measure of local assembly activities. The Sisters' Missionary Sewing Class developed largely during this period. The first missionary conference was held in Victoria Hall in 1913, and Alexander Hamilton introduced the Sunday School that same year. His earlier meetings for children in the old King Street Hall represented the first Sunday School amongst the Brethren in Belfast. This Sunday School took place before the morning meeting.

With the growth of the assembly many workers engaged in reaching out with tract distribution. Much of this was done under the leadership of W. H. McLaughlin and resulted in the establishment of a number of new assemblies including Kings Moss Gospel Hall.

In his book Irish Evangelists now with the Lord, James G. Hutchinson records that a number of evangelists were associated with Victoria Hall. Thomas Lough, James Marshall, William McKelvey, John H. McKnight and David H. Oliver, all active in the Lord's work at the turn of the century, were in fellowship at Victoria Hall. David H. Oliver had just bought his discharge from the Army and on returning to Belfast was walking in the area of the Customs House. Although it was raining, an open-air meeting was in progress, and the preachers greatly impressed him. "These men must have something I haven't otherwise they would not stand here and preach in such weather." He stopped to listen, was invited into Victoria Hall and later surrendered his life to

Jesus Christ. "Think of the rich mercy of God to me;" he wrote later, "A week ago in jail for fighting, tonight saved by the Grace of God." (28.5.1877)

After nearly twenty years at 20 Victoria Street those attending the services at the Victoria Hall had outgrown the capacity and safety of the premises. Mr. W. H. McLaughlin was not only an ardent worker in distribution of gospel literature, he was an experienced builder and son of the co-founder of McLaughlin & Harvey, a leading building contractor in Northern Ireland. In March 1916 Mr. McLaughlin initiated the discussions regarding new premises. He also made a generous offer of £500 towards a new hall in another location. The majority in fellowship at Victoria Hall favoured the continuance of the assembly effort in a central city position if such could be procured.

After some inquiries about the availability of city centre properties, it was learned that the Music Hall in May Street was on the market. Immediately interest was shown in acquiring these premises as a new home for the Victoria Hall Assembly. Others added generous donations to that of Mr. McLaughlin's, and the building fund was well established.

The Anacreontic Society of music quickly grew to a large organisation which soon required a large facility in which to house their functions. From this need, the Belfast Music Hall was built to seat 800 people.

Besides the many secular uses for which the Music Hall was used it was also the location for the great Evangelical Union Prayer Meetings which developed out of the 1859 Revival. One historian recorded, "The meetings were held each Wednesday from 1:00 p.m. to 2:00 p.m. so that many of the business community could attend during the dinner-hour. The secretaries of this united prayer meeting were the Revs. James Morgan of Fisherwick Place and Charles Seaver of St. John's on the Laganbank Road. Leaders in both the churches and in the town enthusiastically and energetically supported them. The chair was taken by such outstanding people as William Ewart, Esq., Jun., the Lord Bishop of Down, Connor and Dromore, the Rev. Dr. Henry Cooke, the Earl of Roden and George A. Thompson, Esq. The services took the usual form. Praise (never many verses), prayer, reading of Scripture; brief comments on the reading were sometimes made, but there were no lengthy addresses. The prayers were passionate and to the point, and it was soon found that brethren who could not see eye to eye about certain ecclesiastical matters, were able to agree together about the salvation of souls."

With the rapid development of the Anacreontic Society, interest in music grew in the city, and a number of similar societies sprang up. The opening of the Ulster Hall in 1862 provided better accommodation for over 1500 persons and thus overshadowed the much lesser capacity of the Music Hall. As a consequence the Anacreontic Society sold the Music Hall in 1863. Shortly afterwards the society disbanded, and they, with other lesser-known groups, were incorporated into the Belfast Philharmonic Society in 1874.

The Music Hall at this time became the property of brothers Charles and Adam Duffin. An Independent church used it for a while. Later the Original Secession Church under the Rev. G. McMahon met here, prior to moving to Botanic Avenue around 1879.

The Church of Ireland Young Men' Society (CIYMS), which was formed in 1850, occupied the Music Hall for approximately three years from 1882. In 1885 the Ulster Constitutional Club, with great intentions, purchased the building from the CIYMS and conducted their political activities before declaring themselves bankrupt in September 1886.

The CIYMS owned the Clarence Place Hall which was next door to the Music Hall. This they used as library and reading rooms. They decided to re-purchase the Music Hall which they had owned some years earlier. Their renovations coincided with the Golden Jubilee of Queen Victoria, and they duly named their new acquisition as the Victoria Memorial Hall. They added a plaque high up under the entablature which read:

MEMORIAL HALL
JUBILEE YEAR OF HER MAJESTY
QUEEN VICTORIA 1887

"My son, fear thou the Lord and the King,
and meddle not with them that
are given to change.
Proverbs 24 :21

Although the renovated Victoria Memorial Hall was the property
of the CIYMS they sub-let the premises to many other groups before it
became the property of the Victoria Hall Assembly. Besides the
gymnasium on the upper floor, there were also bagatelle rooms, baths
and a variety of recreational facilities. The remaining parts of the
building were sub-let to different tenants at various times before the
Victoria Assembly took possession in 1916. These included:

> The Belfast Philharmonic Society
> E. J. Dowdall, Accountants
> Church Missionary Society
> Cavehill and Whitewell Tramway Company
> Belfast and Ligoniel Tramway Company
> Sydenham District (Belfast) Tramway Company
> Griffith's Cycling Academy later known as Belfast Cycle School
> Forster Green Hospital for Consumption and Chest Diseases.
> Belfast City School of Music.
> M. W. Kay & Company, Fancy Linen and Handkerchief
> Manufacturers.
> Belfast Glass Merchants Association.
> Belfast Battalion Headquarters of Church Lads Brigade.
> Registered Offices of Belfast Paper Stock Company.

Within weeks of Mr. McLauglin giving his generous gift towards a
new location a building fund was begun. At the same time inquiries
were made regarding the availability of the Memorial Hall in May Street
and the terms of purchase. The ground rent was reported to be £27 per
annum. It was also calculated that for another £200, the building could
be made into a most suitable meeting-place.

The acquisition of the May Street was a big step for the Victoria
Hall Assembly, and much prayer went into the matter. To purchase a
new building and move location during the dark days of the First World

War was a big step. Only by the help and guidance of an Almighty God could they have contemplated such a transition. It was by no means smooth sailing; however, there was unity among the membership that this was the right way forward.

R. D. Gordon, Alexander Hamilton and W. H. McLaughlin were three outstanding brethren who had shown great vision and competence in leading the local church in all matters. They were appointed as trustees with the responsibility of negotiating the purchase of the property for the assembly and the signing of the deeds. With the approval of the assembly this negotiating committee made an offer of £4,000. To the surprise and delight of all this bid was accepted.

In October 1916 the Victoria Memorial Hall became the possession of the new owners. The superb location of the newly acquired premises suited the needs of the assembly membership and their activities and served as home of the assembly for more than fifty years.

After the purchase of the Victoria Memorial Hall many renovations had to be carried out, and these took more than six months to complete.

On Sunday 6th May, 1917 the first meetings were held in Victoria Memorial Hall, May Street at which the guest speaker was Brother Charles Hickman of London. He stayed to minister the Word for the remainder of May and thereafter was a frequent visitor to the assembly.

In 1919 the number of trustees of the Victoria Memorial Hall was augmented to twelve with the appointment of nine brethren to the trust to supplement the responsibility of the original three trustees. They were Samuel Spence, Robert Vogan, W. R. Johnston, R. Robb, James Hillis, William J. Moody, George Templeton, Robert J. B. McKeown and Robert Verner.

During the next two decades prior to World War II, hundreds of different speakers preached at Victoria Memorial Hall which became Belfast's leading Brethren Assembly. These included William Gilmore, J. McAlpine, Harold Wildish, Harold St. John, James Marshall, G. Goodman and many others too numerous to mention.

These visiting brethren mostly ministered at the Sunday afternoon ministry meeting at 4 o'clock. This meeting was greatly attended and particularly helpful to converts of the W. P. Nicholson campaigns during the two decades of the twenties and thirties.

Besides the on-going ministry of the Word of God there was always great evangelistic outreach from the Victoria Memorial Hall Assembly. Often this outreach took the form of evangelistic campaigns in tents that held in excess of 1,500 people. Other Belfast assemblies co-operated in these evangelistic meetings in the canvas tents. Evangelists G. T. Pinches from England and J. F. Spink from the United States held a memorable mission in a large tent on a site at the corner of Grosvenor Road and Fisherwick Place. Bill Wilson was one of the many converts at these meetings. Later Bill and his wife Isa went to serve the Lord in China and Malaysia.

In 1933, Fred Elliott of Birmingham preached the gospel in the same tent nearby to Barry's Amusement Grounds at Fisherwick Place. Three years later, in August 1936, R. Scammell (London) and J. F. Spink (Chicago) were responsible for the evangelistic campaign in Garfield Street on the site where the Castle Court Shopping complex now stands. The final crusade in this series was held in 1939 in the same well-used tent on the Annadale Embankment. The speaker on that occasion was Mr. J. P. Lewis from Wales.

In all these campaigns there were tremendous times of blessing. Christians were stirred and many people came to know Jesus Christ as Saviour.

Following the war the evangelistic zeal of the members of the Victoria Memorial Hall continued with guest evangelists teaching and preaching the Word of God. These included C. E. Stokes, George Harpur, Montague Goodman, Herbert Lockyer, William Freel, G. C. D. Howley, Peter Brandon, R. E. Pettifer, Donald Wiseman and Roger Forster.

The Annual Missionary Convention was first held in the Victoria Hall in Victoria Street in 1913. During those early years missionaries from China, British Guyana, India, Mexico, Bolivia, Central Africa and Italy and elsewhere brought interesting and challenging reports.

In June 1917 the first Missionary Conference Weekend was held in Victoria Memorial Hall, and this convention continued every year until 1971. Although it was originally held in June, a change to the autumn took place later.

Writing of those early days Ernest Wilson recalls, "My earliest recollections of the assembly was in a large upstairs room in a building in Victoria Street beside the Albert Memorial Clock. Mr. W. H. McLaughlin and Mr. Hamilton were two of the elders." In those days many distinguished servants of God including Mr. John Ritchie of Kilmarnock and David Rea the evangelist who had large gospel meetings in the nearby "Chapel Fields," visited and preached in the assembly from time to time.

Those were happy days, and many were being saved, and new assemblies gathered in the Lord's name were planted in various parts of the city. At the same time, Victoria Hall was a centre of missionary interest. Mr. Fred Stanley Arnot had visited the city telling of the need in Central Africa. As a result two brethren, Mr. H. B. Thompson and Mr. James Johnstone volunteered to join the pioneer party which accompanied Mr. Arnot on his return to Africa in 1889. Mr. Johnstone, an experienced evangelist died of fever before landing on the West African coast, the first casualty in that noble band of pioneers who opened up Central Africa to the gospel. This caused a wave of sympathy and interest in missionary work among the assemblies in Northern Ireland.

The missionary study class in Victoria Memorial Hall was commenced to stimulate that interest and to provide information of the needs and the open doors for service in the mission fields of the world. It met in the minor hall and was attended by leaders of many assemblies in the city. Mr. J. E. Johnstone from the Adam Street Assembly had gone to India in 1905 and Mr. Tom Rea to Central Africa in 1911; both were commended by the assemblies in Victoria Hall and in Ormeau Road and in Bangor. Since then a steady stream of devoted men and women, called by God and commended by their brethren have gone out from Northern Ireland to the mission field with the glorious gospel.

In 1971 the Missionary Convention was subject to another major change. Due to the lack of parking and to the threat of terrorism in the city centre the conference had to find a new location. It was then that the friends at the Holywood Assembly sent an invitation to convene the Missionary Conference at the Holywood Gospel Hall. The large attendances at Holywood constrained the organisers to use the municipally owned Queen's Hall in Holywood where the missionary meetings were held up until 1976.

In such an atmosphere of missionary interest, it was not unexpected that folk connected with the assembly would hear the call to service overseas and join the growing band of pioneer missionaries. There is not room in this record to detail the names of all those who went to many lands with the gospel of the Lord Jesus. Some like Tom Rea went in 1911 to serve in Central Africa and remained until 1960. Besides his evangelical work, he had a printing press and with Jack Prescott printed various books of the New Testament in Lunda. Later at Kasaji, Singleton Fisher translated the remaining New Testament books and the Old Testament. After these were checked and revised Tom Rea printed the whole Bible in the Lunda language.

Willie McKee was a member of Victoria Memorial Hall Sunday School and later he was the first member to be commended for service abroad from the assembly. He went first to Australia and then to China. In 1934 he had an operation for sinus trouble.   Sadly, he contracted smallpox which was very prevalent in China and died in 1934.

In 1949 Maureen Hull became engaged to William Walker who was commended from Cregagh Street Hall to the work in North India. Willie followed on to the sub-continent while Maureen took a midwifery course to help her in the medical work in India.   Commended by the Victoria Memorial Hall, Maureen joined William in 1949, and after they were married they served the Lord first at Karmahar and later in Delhi. After they returned home William continued to serve the Lord as Dean of Residence at Queen's University, Belfast. He also did a very active work amongst overseas student.

From 1954 until 1967 Frank and Margaret Maconaghie worked in Nigeria at the Qua Iboe Mission Hospital School of Nursing at Etinan, amongst the Ibo and Ibibo people. In April 1958 they moved north where Frank took up an appointment with the Northern Nigerian Ministry of Health, and they served in both Kano and Makurdi.

Dorothy Gould was commended to Murchison Hospital in South African in 1962. She later married Dr. John Fisher, the senior doctor at the hospital. Due to his severe heart condition he was obliged to retire from so active a life. They took up residence some distance from the hospital from which they ran a medical service.

Alex Farrell had Japan very much at heart, and the oversight and the assembly had every confidence in recommending him and his wife Ella to the work. Alex was much used of God in the conversion of many people and in ministry in the assemblies in Japan.

These are but a few of the many missionaries commended and supported by the Victoria Memorial Hall Assembly over many decades. Besides this, members of the assembly have supported numerous missionary and Bible societies prayerfully and practically over the years.

In the 1920s Mr. W. R. Johnston, Mr. J. W. Lannon, Mr. Stephen Thompson, and Mr. William Hill (Senior) began a Saturday night meeting that became an institution at Victoria Memorial Hall. It became known as "Help Heavenward at the Vic!" This youth meeting was to prove a watershed in the experience and lifestyle of many young and older Christians in the fifty years of its existence.

On Saturday evenings throughout the winter months hundreds of Christian young people folk attended the Help Heavenward Rally. A feature of those occasions was the hearty singing, led for many years by Stanley Mawhinney, W. G. Hill and George Wilson. After some years other assemblies and church groups followed the example of this youth meeting at the Victoria Memorial Hall. The civil unrest caused by the outbreak of the "troubles" in 1969 imposed a virtual curfew on the Belfast city centre, and this contributed to the decline in attendances at the meeting and the final closure of the Help Heavenward Rally in 1970.

Another important feature of the development of the work in Victoria Memorial Hall was the Youth Camp work. These camps go back to the first experience of the boys sleeping under canvas in 1934. This first camp was held in Kilkeel and was led by Albert Rea. It was such a success the camps continued each year at Kilkeel and then in Lord Antrim's Estate at Glenarm, until the intervention of World War II in 1939.

The girls were not content to sit idle either. In 1935 Miss Eileen Hamilton and a team of willing ladies began what was to prove an equally successful camp. This was also under canvas; they continued to camp each year at Kilkeel and Glenarm until 1938.

In 1952 there was a revival of interest in camp work. It was the girls who took the initiative and in July 1952 held their first V. M. H. Girls' Camp. However, instead of under canvas they booked into Shimna House in Newcastle. They preferred the guaranteed shelter from wind and rain rather than the rigors of living under canvas. Other venues visited for "camps" were Drumalla House, Carnlough; Mourne Grange School, Kilkeel, Sligo, Isle of Man, Helensburgh and Prestwick all of which echoed to the sounds of groups of chattering, singing girls enjoying their holiday.

The boys were quick to recognise the success of the rejuvenated girl's camp. Members of Jim Buckley's Bible class had been on holiday together in caravans for a few years. Many of these lads trusted the Saviour, and once again the value of taking young people on holiday was realised. In 1956 Victoria Memorial Hall Boys' camps recommenced. Drumalla House at Carnlough was their first choice. Thereafter they varied the location of the camp to Bushmills Grammar School; Heswall, Cheshire; Mourne Grange School, Kilkeel; Ramsay, Isle of Man, Helensburgh, Prestwick, Ayr, Edinburgh, and Southampton. Jim Buckley and Billy Flannigan were two of the prime movers in this great work.

The children's work at the Victoria Memorial Hall was also a very strategic programme. Alexander Hamilton introduced the Sunday School to the Victoria Assembly in Victoria Street at the turn of the century. It proved to be a seedbed which contributed substantially to the growth of the assembly throughout its entire existence.

There also was the Happy Hour which was convened on Friday nights. It was in 1932, after a successful children's mission at Merrion Hall in Dublin, that Albert Rea brought Billy Maybury and a team of enthusiastic workers to start children's meetings in the minor hall. It was some time later at the suggestion of Billy Maybury that it became known as the Happy Hour for boys and girls.

A number of assemblies in Belfast originated from work begun by members of the Victoria Hall assembly: Oldpark, Joseph Street, Roslyn Street, Cregagh Street and Broadway. The Iron Hall Assembly also had its beginnings through the outreach of the Victoria Memorial Hall. Sisters maintained a witness among women at Rathmore Street.

Campbell Street Mission Hall until its demolition for redevelopment in 1969 accommodated the work among women and girls, and then the Andrews sisters and others carried it on at Glencairn Estate. W. A. Agnew ran the Crimea Street Children's Meetings in the heart of the Shankill Road area, and others were an inspiration and a blessing to many.

On special evangelistic endeavours the stage of the Grand Opera House, the Plaza and Maxim's Ballrooms, the boxing ring at the Ulster Hall, Queen's Island Shipyard, Crumlin Road Prison, were all extended pulpits to Victoria Memorial Hall.

Opportunity was also taken to broadcast on BBC's Morning Service. Speakers at these included Thomas Elwood, Albert Rea, Robert White, Dr. David Gooding, Annesley Logan and David Bloomfield.

Much of the other outreach over the years included work among the soldiers during World War II. There was visitation to the seamen at the docks who were welcomed and introduced to the gospel for the first time. Open-air meetings, which were held across the road from the city hall, were a feature of the outreach from the Victoria Memorial Hall for over half a century. Only eternity will reveal the full story of what was accomplished by these various outreaches.

It was a shock to the oversight at the assembly when in 1966 an architect's report revealed a weakness in the structure of the Victoria Memorial Hall building. The west wall (on Upper Arthur Street) had developed a bulge. As other major repairs were also required in other areas of the building, it seemed that the old hall's days were numbered.

As the implications of this began to sink in it caused no little concern. It was a major upheaval for the assembly, and it occupied much discussion and negotiation for the next ten years. Would the home of this vibrant church have to be demolished? Would this mean the end of the Victoria Memorial Hall Assembly? Was there not a great need for a down-town church? Could the assembly afford to rebuild? Why not split up into two or three smaller units? Why not postpone a decision until after the troubles? Surely the Lord is coming soon. These were only a few of the questions that were raised. There was discussion, debate, uncertainty and much doubt.

A building committee was formed and a building fund was opened. Possible sites and premises were visited, but nothing seemed to be suitable for the assembly. Public and private prayer was focused on this matter. The future seemed so uncertain and the task so enormous.

Early estimates for a replacement building on the same site, offering the kind of facilities the existing programme demanded, were astounding. How could such a sum be raised and even if it could, was this the best way to spend over £250,000, which was a colossal amount of money at the time.

In 1975 planning permission for a new building on the same site was refused. The former Music Hall was listed as a building of historical and architectural interest by the Department of Environment and could not be demolished without consent. These legal and technical problems seemed impossible to untangle. Only the Lord could show a solution to what seemed to be insurmountable obstacles. The assembly continued to pray.

Soon the answer came. News reached Victoria Memorial Hall Assembly that the congregation of the Crescent Presbyterian Church sited on Belfast's University Road was moving to other parts of the city. As a result, they needed to dispose of the building as soon as possible. Ensuing discussions with their elders revealed a sincere desire to sell to Victoria Memorial Hall Assembly.

The inevitability of major changes affecting the assembly and the possibility of the Crescent Presbyterian Church coming on the market presented a tremendous challenge to the oversight and indeed to all members of the fellowship. This great undertaking plus the almost unbelievable potential of moving next door to Queen's University seemed to be the right way forward.

The Crescent Presbyterian Church, was first opened on Sunday 11th September 1887 by Rev. W. S. Swanson, Moderator of the English Presbyterian Church assisted by Rev. W. J. Patton of Dromara and the then minister of the church, Rev. Dr. John McIlveen. Built at a cost of over £8,000 it was designed by a Glasgow architect, John Bennie Wilson, to whom is attributed six other church buildings in Glasgow. The premises offered great alternative accommodation for the Victoria Memorial Hall Assembly although a complete refurbishment of the building was necessary.

By Christmas 1975 the General Assembly of the Presbyterian Church in Ireland received the confirmation needed from the Victoria Memorial Hall Assembly, "We want to buy the Crescent Church." Subsequently at an extra-ordinary session of the General Assembly of the Presbyterian Church in Ireland at Church House on 9th December 1975 an agreement was reached that the Crescent Presbyterian Church building should be sold to the Victoria Memorial Hall Assembly.

Much work was needed to equip the building to meet the needs of the new owners. The building committee entered into discussions with leaders of youth work, church meetings, women's groups, and representatives of various assembly activities. Everyone had an opportunity to put forward his point of view, suggestion or criticism.

Plans were drawn up and then improved upon. Every consideration was made to ensure that the renovations were compatible with the architectural design of the Crescent Church while also providing a facility that was both comfortable and serviceable for the needs of the new occupiers. The major changes included the removal of the railings and heavy gates on University Road to give a more welcoming aspect to the church. At the side of the church the grounds were landscaped to provide car parking for approximately forty cars.

The two doors of the old church were comparatively narrow and were replaced by a more inviting double glass door and screen with handles of glass mosaic. The famous Greek text "Till he come" above the entrance was removed and replaced by a mosaic panel bearing the name of the Crescent Church.

The former Victoria Memorial Hall Assembly moved into their new premises on Saturday 15th January 1977. The Crescent Church was born, and a new chapter began in the life of this assembly which had its beginnings back in the 1859 revival.

The first public services were held on Sunday 16th January with great crowds in attendance. Derick Bingham from Newcastle was the invited speaker for the month of January. He preached morning and evening, and there was an obvious sense of the presence of God in the midst.

During the next twenty-one years the Crescent Church matured and multiplied. Gifted men within the assembly and invited guest speakers from other assemblies continued to enrich the ministry to make the Crescent one of the principal churches in Belfast. Dr. David Gooding, a noted Bible scholar; William Walker, a former missionary to India and for some time a Dean of Residence at Queens University, and Val English were men of exceptional gift.

Derick Bingham, a graduate in English and English Literature from the nearby Queens University and a Keswick speaker, maintained a strategic ministry at the Crescent Church for the next twenty-one years. Tuesday Night at the Crescent, a weekly Bible Class, became the largest such midweek meeting in United Kingdom with over a thousand people in attendance, the majority of these being young people. Many were students from the university campuses and medical staff from the local hospitals.

The great missionary conferences continued with the same emphasis as before with visiting missionaries from all around the world reporting on their work. Other missionaries continued to be sent from the church to many mission fields.

Bible conferences and evangelistic campaigns also formed a large part of the on-going ministry of the Crescent Church. Renowned Bible teachers such as Warren Weirsbe, Josh McDowell and Dr. Stephen Olford made visits to the church.

The Crescent Church was not only strategically placed near to Ulster's largest university and biggest hospitals but is also adjacent to what has become known as Belfast's "Golden Mile." From the door of the Crescent Church straight into the centre of Belfast is an avenue of clubs, restaurants and hotels that make it the busiest nightlife in town. The members at the Crescent caught the vision of a mission field that was literally on their doorstep. For some years teams of believers from the church provided soup and coffee late on Friday and Saturday nights in their witness to the passing crowds.

Victoria Memorial Hall like the Crescent Church has stood for the "Scriptural principles of open brethren even when to do so meant standing alone." The uniqueness of the open brethren tradition has altered somewhat in recent years, with the emergence of other assemblies who shared this same position.

Mr. William Agnew, an elder at the Crescent, a trustee and the chairman of the building committee back in 1977, wrote these words, "The future lies before us, and we pray that we may be obedient to the leading of the Holy Spirit in all things. There is much land to be possessed. There will be Jerichos on the way, but if we go forward in His Name alone, we can claim the promise given to Joshua : 'Be strong and of a good courage, be not afraid neither be thou dismayed; for the Lord thy God is with thee whithersoever thou goest.' At the Crescent Church, we will continue to meet according to New Testament principles, owning no other Head than the Lord Jesus Christ. To our Breaking of Bread meeting we welcome all those who are born again Christians and who love our Lord Jesus Christ in sincerity and truth."

Chapter Three

EARLY BRETHREN ASSEMBLIES

William Gilmore, a great man of God among the assemblies in a former generation, was born in Newtownards in 1867 and was converted as a boy of thirteen under the powerful preaching of Mr. Walbran. Even as a teenager William showed early signs of zeal for obeying his Lord when he got out of his sick bed to be baptized in the sea at Ballyholme, near Bangor. Perhaps it could be said that there was a measure of zeal without wisdom for the baptism not only was in the sea but in the midst of a snowstorm on the 10th January 1883. He suffered much ridicule for being so foolish, but the reason he was prepared to face the hostile elements was that the doctors had disclosed to his family that his illness was terminal, and they calculated he had approximately three months to live. There are no known medicinal virtues in the salt water of Ballyholme Bay, but Willie Gilmore lived beyond the three months and survived into his nineties.

Following his baptism he was received into fellowship in the Newtownards Assembly. It was there that he began to exercise his preaching talents, and within ten years of his conversion Willie Gilmore was preaching along with his father-in-the-faith, Mr. Walbran.

When William Gilmore began to preach there were only three Brethren Assemblies in all of Belfast, and during the seventy-three years of his ministry he witnessed the growth of the Brethren movement. In 1953 William reminisced about the early days of the Belfast assemblies at a special meeting in Ebenezer Gospel Hall.

The first three assemblies which I referred to were Old Lodge Road, Sandy Row and Victoria Rooms. Before these assemblies were formed Bible readings were held in 8 Christopher Street and in King Street. There was one thing about the Old Lodge Hall which was a little bit amusing to me, the seven overseers were all named Sam. I don't remember them all now, there was Sam Heany, Sam Nesbitt, Sam McCracken, Sam McCullough and Sam Miller.

Sandy Row Hall leads me to think of Mr. R. M. Henry. He is the man who started what is now Apsley Street Hall. Mr. Henry was a "fully qualified minister" as they are called. He had an "M.A." At a meeting of ministers he asked the clergy present if they could produce a command in the Bible for infant baptism or give an example of it being done anywhere in the scriptures as he had never been able to find it. They refused to debate with him, so he withdrew from that ministry and published a very good little book called 'The Form of the House'. After this he became a Baptist pastor and on leaving this he published another booklet called 'Why I left the Baptists'.

Mr. Henry then took a few Christians like-minded with him and held the first meetings in a room in the Ulster Hall. As the meetings grew he applied for Sandy Row Orange Hall. After being there for some time he got the hall in Apsley Street. From then till now that assembly has gone on well in the things of God.

The meeting in the Victoria Rooms commenced in the Abercorn Rooms, Queens Square. These were meetings held by Mr. James Campbell. The Victoria Rooms were afterwards taken over by the Eglinton and Winton Hotel. It was in these rooms that I first attended the Easter meetings. We had four hundred present, and I was just up from the country and thought it was a great crowd but now we have four thousand on an Easter Monday. Some don't understand me when I talk of being seventy-three years at the Easter meetings, but I attended these meetings before I was into fellowship in Newtownards. The brethren then moved to Victoria Hall.

Mr. James Campbell's preaching partner was Mr. Wm. Matthews. In my judgment they were two of the greatest preachers in that time. On Campbell's last visit to this country I came with him and Andrew Fraser on the top of a tram car from what is now Ballyhackamore to Victoria Hall. I said to Campbell, "I think Victoria Hall is not so strict now as when you started it." He answered, "No, but you should never run from an assembly when difficulties arise, that is not the way to help; so long as the assembly is open for the truth of God let us embrace the opportunity. Time enough to cease when they won't receive the message." I don't think any assembly in this city has reached that stage yet.

Let me mention a remarkable thing about the preaching of Campbell. I have never known him to speak without sinners being aroused, convicted of sin, and converted to God. He had a tent at Donegall Pass in 1874, which was the year of Moody's meetings. Many were brought into the Apsley Hall meeting. There was an incident about Campbell's movements that some did not quite understand. He had meetings at Knockbreda, and they were so successful that the Presbyterian minister invited him to preach in the church, which he did. He preached the gospel faithfully and then gave a stirring address on baptism and separation to God. The next Sunday he was noticed out. It was said concerning him, "He was a man who would have made you afraid of sin if he looked at you." I think that was true. He had a wonderful testimony.

I once gave an address in Apsley Hall on "The Life of James Campbell". The place was packed. There never was a man so much used of God in this country. He started about forty assemblies here. The memory of Campbell and Matthews is sweet to this day. Now don't you think the young people should hear these things, I think they should.

There was a place in East Belfast called Campbell's Row, about six houses together. Some local brethren started a gospel work in one of the houses, and a few people were converted. Amongst those responsible for the work was Mr. Kane of Larne.

Another worker was William Jamison, the man who formed the acrostic from John 3:16 on the front of the Gospel Hymn Book. In later days he was ill for a long time, and I visited him often and spoke at his funeral in the Knock graveyard ever so many years ago. Mr. Jamison lived in a place called Henryville Street off the Woodstock Road. In the Henryville grounds he had a baptistery made out of a lake and many were baptized there including Mr. W. H. McLaughlin of Victoria Hall.

After the meetings in Campbell's Row the brethren took the Mountpottinger Orange Hall and had meetings there. David Rea was the preacher. From these meetings in the early days the assemblies grew. They grew out of gospel work and they should do that still. It is not good to have assemblies made up of people from other assemblies. Spurgeon called that; "Fishing from the basket instead of from the sea."

The meeting in Mountpottinger Orange Hall moved to Mourne Street There were some good elders there: Martin Shaw, a chartered accountant, Charles Ritchie, a builder, Johnny Jordan and James Hedge. The meeting continued to grow and is known now as Albertbridge Road Hall.

I remember another meeting which was held in the Orange Hall in King Street. It developed into Matchett Street Assembly. I was with Mr. Agnew the day he went to search for a piece of ground to put the wooden hall on. It is on that piece of ground the present hall still stands. A good while after that I had twelve weeks meetings in a tent in Tennant Street. I wish I could do that now, but I could not. The meetings were crowded out.

My most noted hearer in those meetings was Billy Spence. He was just a short time saved, and afterwards he told me, "Those meetings put me on my feet." Billy had only one theme—himself and Mary Ann. Often I heard him telling the story of his conversion at the corner of Agnes Street, and he always ended up by saying, "If you don't believe me 'axe' Mary Ann." Bill and Mary Ann's bodies sleep in the Old Shankill graveyard. The week that Billy died brought a great loss to Belfast.

In the same week came the home call of Billy Hutton. I was at his funeral and there was the biggest turnout I have ever seen since the Prince of Wales was here. From the Custom House steps to Dundonald cemetery the streets were lined and people carried gospel banners along the way. Billy Hutton led many to the Saviour. He belonged to the Iron Mission Hall.

There was a little hall in Byron Street where a meeting was carried on. Most of the people came from Matchett Street Hall. It was a small meeting to start with, and I remember having two weeks meetings there shortly after it commenced. It was there that I first heard the name of Bob Weir, when his mother told me one night that prayer had been answered and Bob had been saved. She told me how he was saved through someone preaching and then getting into an argument with him.

That hall was removed in 1911 to Comber Place on the Old Lodge Road. It was there that the Ebenezer people, as they are now called, first thought of having Sunday afternoon meetings. I started those meetings with forty people. After sixteen Sundays without a break we finished with two hundred and forty. There were many that attended those meetings who did not belong to the assemblies. Many of them joined the assembly. We would like to see more of that now, and if we were what we ought to be, we would. Often we sing Revive thy work, O Lord, and I think it is possible. If the coming of the Lord is delayed a little longer God may send a time of revival. It is not at all likely that God would allow the Church to end in defeat.

The old elders, one by one, have been removed, but we have quite a lot of young people. The brethren were successful in obtaining a larger place in Manor Hall. They bought that hall, and it is a very good one. I think I am safe in saying that the most active man in connection with it was Bob Weir. He lived for that meeting and worked for it. There is a little room at the back of the platform where I had many long talks with him. Sometimes he sent for me to talk over things that were troubling him or difficulties that had arisen. I never enter that room, but I think of Bob Weir. His special gift was conducting open-air meetings, and no one has been able to take his place. Many a soul Bob brought to the Lord in his own way. We were all sorry when strength and health failed him, and he had to give up. The assembly in Ebenezer misses him, and for years to come his name and his work will be remembered.

Another meeting which must have been one of the early assemblies is Adam Street. I mention it because it is like myself—it has kept to the middle of the road. Though I cannot remember them building that hall I had the privilege of being present at the opening meeting. There was a large attendance and Halyburton spoke. Adam Street is one of the assemblies that has kept in touch with me since the beginning when I set out in the Lord's work.

I remember Abraham Matthews building Donegall Road Hall. Many thought it was a waste of time and money for there was nothing but fields all around it. I said to him, "I think you are making a mistake as there are no houses near nor people to gather in." He said, "Well, we are building it in faith, we expect all these streets will be built up in a few years." So they were, and the hall is now in a good place, and I have had many happy meetings there. The little assembly prospered very well largely due to the Sunday School work, children's meetings and open-air work.

The Ormeau Road Hall began in a little hall in a place called Fulton Street where Apsley Hall had their open-air meetings on Sunday nights. Some brethren thought they should use the wooden hall to start a new work on the Ormeau Road. These brethren went, and quite a number followed them from Apsley Hall, including Mr. D. W. Alexander and his daughter and three aunts. William Campbell and Mrs. Campbell and quite a number of others all went there and they had a fairly good sized meeting and a nice hall. I have had meetings in it many a time. The first meetings I ever had on the Tabernacle were in that hall, and we had the place packed for the Tabernacle was a sort of new subject then. It is not new now.

We now come to Kingsbridge Hall. The assembly there has grown, and they have a nice hall, one of the nicest halls I think in the city. Possibly Ballyhackamore and Kingsbridge hall were built from the same plans. Then I would mention Cregagh Gospel Hall which had a very small beginning. I remember when the meetings were in a little wooden hall in Roslyn Street. It was small, and I think most of those who were in that meeting have passed away. However, when the meeting was brought up to Cregagh Street there was a great improvement in the attendance, and Cregagh, though beginning as a very small meeting, is now quite a large one and one of the most successful in the city, especially since they opened their

new hall. I had the pleasure of having meetings there too.
I had a whole week on the one hundred nineteenth Psalm
and another week on King David.

With regard to another little hall—Parkgate Avenue
Assembly, it is one of the newer meetings. It has grown
well too, and then we have Ballyhackamore. I really could
not tell you very much about it. I know that some came
from Baptists on the Sandown Road. They have a Baptist
church there, and some came from this Baptist place to
Ballyhackamore. There is a large meeting there, and some
very good elders too including Mr. Robinson and others
who have been a great help in keeping that assembly going.

Since William Gilmore gave that report forty-five years ago there
have been great changes to the assemblies in the city. New assemblies
such as Ballysillan, Dundonald, Castlereagh, Broadway, Carryduff and
Glenburn Gospel Halls have flourished because of outreach. Several
assemblies have closed, and others have relocated. The inner city
assemblies have suffered with the shift of population to the outskirts of
Belfast or outlying other towns. This has resulted in decreasing numbers
in some of the oldest assemblies. However, this displacement of people
has also been to the benefit of various halls such as Bethany Hall at
Finaghy, Lockview Assembly on the Stranmillis, Newtownbreda Gospel
Hall, Clarawood Assembly and Brooklands Gospel Hall.

Chapter Four

ThE BelfasT CitY MissioN

A brisk knock came to the front door of a small terraced house in Rathmore Street on the Ravenhill Road, and the visitor then quietly opened the inside door and called, "Are you in Mary?"

"Come on in," was the reply from the narrow kitchen, known in Belfast as the scullery. Mary Wardlow was glad to see her unexpected caller, Billy Anderson. He needed no invitation to sit down for Billy immediately made himself at home in any of the houses he called at on the Ravenhill Road. He was the missionary at the Boyd Endowment City Mission founded in 1897 as a religious and educational school in the heart of the old Lagan village.

Billy Anderson knew every family in the area, and he was on a first name basis with all their relatives from granny and granda down to the great-grandchildren. He shared in their joy and excitement when young couples were married and when their children were born. He was present in their grief when sickness and death were unwelcome intruders to their homes. Billy Anderson was nothing short of an institution on the

Ravenhill Road where he served his Lord as the city missionary for more than fifty years.

Across the city Bob Anderson, Billy's brother, fulfilled a similar role at the Great Northern Street City Mission and he served there for as many years. Between the two they provided more than one hundred years of Christian service in the city and even today some in their immediate family still continue in Christian work in Belfast.

Billy and Bob Anderson, converts from the Nicholson meetings in the early twenties, were typical of the devotion, zeal and diligence of hundreds of city missionaries in Belfast. Certainly no history of Christian work in this city should ever be written without due mention made and recognition given to the work of the Belfast City Mission. At the end of twentieth century the mission will complete one hundred and seventy-three years of gospel work in our metropolis.

It was not always known as the Belfast City Mission. When first established in 1827 it was named the "Belfast Town Mission," and its objective was "the promotion of Christ's cause, among the poor, the careless the Christless and the churchless".

Belfast at the time was a misty damp and backward town, which had a population of about 40,000 and was growing rapidly with the influx of many people from rural areas of Ulster in pursuit of work. Ironically, their arrival in Belfast resulted in higher unemployment rates because the local industries could not absorb the swollen workforce.

Social depravation and high unemployment resulted in increased crime, vice and drunkenness. Police and court records from that period indicate that juvenile delinquency was rife and increasing to an alarming extent. Some believed that so many parents were addicted to drinking and gambling that they were unfit to look after their children.

It is difficult for us in the present to visualise what Belfast was like back in 1827, since it has expanded rapidly and altered greatly during the past century. As the name suggests, Townsend Street really was the end of the town, and Boundary Street was on the northern boundary between the town and the country. The whole area which is now the

Shankill Road and Crumlin Road mostly consisted of green fields. York Road was practically devoid of houses, and the terminus of the Midland Railway was on the verge of the country. Newtownabbey was not heard of and Whitewell, Whitehouse and Whiteabbey were just small villages removed from Belfast.

Green fields stretched from the south side of Donegall Square, then the site of the old White Linen Hall. Donegall Pass was a pleasant country lane, and the few residents were subjected to a foul aroma that emanated from the Paper Mill Dam, which covered most of what is now Ormeau Avenue. Cromac Street was densely populated, as was the district leading to Peter's Hill. Sandy Row consisted of Tea Lane and a few buildings leading to the Malone Turnpike, which today is the junction with the Lisburn Road. Donegall Place was the home of the gentry. Victoria Street was a new development, and a very narrow Queen's Bridge led to the small industrial suburb of Ballymacarrett. The "Cuts," the straightening of the course of the river to form the Victoria Channel, was in progress, and the material from the excavations created a new island. This island, first known as "Dargan's Island," after the name of the contractor that constructed it, was later named "Queen's Island." For many years Queens Island was one of the beauty spots of old Belfast with decorative gardens, amusements and bathing facilities.

Life was arduous in the eighteenth century. Generally speaking housing was poor. Men and women started their days early in order to survive. Amenities such as running water, light and sewage were primitive. Water for household use had to be carried from local water fountains.

The gasworks were established in 1823, but the gas produced was only for lighting, and its price was set far beyond the reach of what most ordinary people could afford. Many burned candles, and the very poor used the rush light, which consisted of rushes dipped in grease and clamped in an iron holder. Matches, a reasonably new invention, were so unreliable that most people kept a tinder box in the house. Some of these tinder boxes, with their pistol-like holder for the flint, were very beautiful and many times they would be handed down from father to son.

Life was miserable for many. A report was written of one lady of the time: "In a house I found a poor woman sitting picking among cinders. That was her daily employment. She said, 'I go out in the morning to gather them. Then I come home and clean them and sell them. That is just the way I get a morsel of bread.'"

Public transport at the time was limited to horse drawn carriages on the cobbled streets of the city, and large barges were slowly towed by horses along the canals and rivers near to Belfast's linen industries. Rail transport was not introduced until the middle of the nineteenth century; therefore, inter-city transport was either by foot or on horse drawn stagecoaches.

Wages were so low that a working man with a family to sustain found it difficult to purchase the bare necessities of life. The highest paid workers at that time were the engine drivers for the Ulster Railway, which connected Belfast with Armagh, and they received £2.50 per week. Firemen were paid £1.20, while porters, signalmen, and guards received a mere seventy-five pence per week.

Possibly the working classes from that era put up with the long hours of employment because they had so little to do in their spare time. Most were debarred from the enjoyment of literature by reason of illiteracy, and the opportunities for amusement, leisure and sports were non-existent at that time. Perhaps it is not difficult to understand why drunkenness was deplorably common, in spite of the energetic Ulster Temperance Society founded in Belfast in 1829 by the Rev. Dr. John Edgar.

In spite of the depressing circumstances that have been outlined Belfast was a thriving, bustling town of one hundred thousand people, steadily increasing in population wealth, and industry.

It was at the turn of the century that a variety of evangelical bodies devoted their efforts to the spread of the gospel both at home and abroad. The principal organisations among these were the British and Foreign Bible Society established in 1804 and the Hibernian Bible Society established in 1806. In addition vigorous evangelism among Roman

Catholics throughout Ireland took place by clergymen and workers of the main denominations of the day.

The Rev. Reuben John Bryce, a Presbyterian minister and principal of Belfast Academy, was regularly faced with the great needs of the underprivileged. He shared his deep concern for the many unchurched and indifferent people in the city of Belfast with a few of his fellow Presbyterian colleagues and friends. He challenged and motivated his contemporaries to join with him to form the Town Mission, otherwise known as The Society for the Religious Improvement of the Poor of the Town of Belfast. They teamed together and formed an executive committee, called the Directors, that affirmed the Town Mission was to be undenominational in character. In one of the oldest documents issued by the Directors of the mission they stated their objectives: "The Town Mission was first established to meet a very crying evil. Its earliest promoters were urged by the voice of strong necessity to bring into play a moral engine for the benefit of the poor, the untaught and neglected population of our town. They looked for difficulties and encouragements. They were aware that merely because the machinery was novel it would be regarded by many as worse than useless. It was felt, however, that a society of some kind was absolutely needed—that people were living and dying without God, for no man cared for their souls—and therefore, in the name of God, the society was formed."

At that inaugural meeting of the Town Mission they also drew up a set of rules to define the character of the work and set out the principles on which its ministry would be exercised. Of the eight rules, which were unanimously adopted, the first five clearly set forth their early objectives.

- The society will endeavour to procure, in different parts of the town which appear most destitute of the means of grace, a number of places in which, once or twice a week, religious exercises may be conducted with the people. As soon as one suitable place shall be procured, the work shall be begun.

- To each station there shall be at least one agent appointed, who shall meet with the people that may attend, on some part of the Sabbath, and on any week-day evening that may be found convenient and conduct with them religious exercises.

• Together with such an agent, another shall be appointed to each station, whose duty it shall be to visit the poor in their own houses adjoining the places of holding meetings: to converse with them plainly and affectionately on their spiritual concerns; to distribute or read to them religious tracts, or portions of the Holy Scriptures; and to invite them to the places of meeting, or to places of public worship and to try to get their children sent to the Sabbath School. Both these agents are to be qualified according to the first part of the next rule.

• The agents employed by the committee shall be persons in full communion with some religious denomination, and shall be of approved evangelical sentiments, and of exceptional moral character. In conducting religious exercises, those alone shall be considered qualified to preach to the people who are authorised to preach by, the religious body to which they belong, or who are regular ministers of the Gospel.

• The committee alone shall have the nomination of the agents, the removal of them from station to station, as they may find convenient, or as it may serve the interests of the society, and the providing for them of all necessary accommodations.

The first workers of the town mission were instructed to put great importance on house to house visitation. They were diligently encouraged to seek out families and individuals that were without the advantages of public religious instruction, and who in some instances might be indisposed to receive Scripture knowledge. The missionaries were earnestly encouraged to read the Scriptures and pray with the families and to keep a detailed journal of their daily visits.

These early missionaries with the town mission were referred to as "agents" and were looked upon as auxiliaries to the churches. The preaching of the gospel was restricted to those specially authorised by the respective church authorities, a requirement generally accepted in those times.

The first agent of the town mission was William Cochrane who came from the Lisburn area. The quality of his life and service were characteristic of the devotion of those early workers. Dr. Killen described him as "an eminent, gifted and pious man . . . who had been brought to a saving knowledge of the truth under the ministry of the Rev. James Morgan." In a subsequent tribute by Dr. Morgan, minister of the new congregation at Fisherwick Place, it was said of William Cochrane:

> It is questionable whether any minister in Belfast was the means of more conversions than this agent of the town mission. Certainly among the poor no man ever had the same influence. He ought to have been ordained a minister, and perhaps could have been had he lived; but in his incessant visits among the poor he was worn down and seized with fever under which he succumbed, though he had been a man of Herculean frame and constitution.

The first anniversary meeting of the Town Mission was convened on February 11, 1828 in a church in Donegall Street. The meeting was reported by the Belfast News-Letter as "very numerously attended by persons of various conditions of life." Among the speakers who took part was the Rev. J. Seaton Reid, the historian of the Presbyterian church. In the course of his address he said, "I feel there are 15,000 or 16,000 people in this town who must be excluded from Sabbath services for want of accommodation. Therefore I rejoice that an organisation has arisen to carry religious instruction into quarters where it is unknown and unregarded. I wish to speak earnestly on its behalf for I have felt the necessity of it, and I trust it will be fostered."

During the first year they endeavoured to enter two needy spheres of outreach. One was to rent rooms in the poorest and most thickly populated districts for two evening gatherings addressed by ministers, reading the Scriptures and distributing tracts. Already there were five such places with no fewer than five hundred in attendance. The other concerned visitation and the reading of the Scriptures. Mr. Cochrane was the only agent employed to carry out this heavy workload, and with the large and ever-increasing population the committee decided that at least three more missionaries were needed.

The following year the annual meeting was presided over by the Rev. Dr. Samuel Hanna. The attendance of the Sunday evening meetings was good, but unfortunately the numbers were down at the Thursday night gatherings.

The town mission had agents working in five areas of Belfast. In Brown Street the prevailing social conditions were not conducive to attending a house of public worship hence the missionary visited the locals in their houses. Another mission was established in Sandy Row where "there was no school and not one place of worship for all that extensive district." A third work was in Cromac Street—"a neighbourhood generally inhabited by people from the country. The majority of these also are Presbyterians who may in a certain sense, be said to be "strangers in a strange land for they have few connections with the town. The station was opened only a short time ago. It is hoped that it will be of use to poor persons who have now left the care of their former minister and to whom no minister has yet made his way." The work in Little Donegall Street was held in a small meetinghouse known by the name of Bethel. The final main work was in Mill Row on the New Lodge Road. Apart from these, there were several minor meetings during the week attended by the agents of the society.

Initially the agents were received at the homes with some caution and suspicion. However, as the work became more widely known the agents of the mission were welcomed as they visited people in their homes and more agents were employed.

In its second year the town mission had great difficulty obtaining sufficient funds to maintain the work and support the increased number of full-time agents. An agent received a salary of approximately £50 per year. A request was made to Dr. Henry Cooke to preach a sermon on behalf of the mission, and this resulted in a substantial offering which enabled the work to continue.

In 1836 there was a terrible outbreak of cholera, and the epidemic wreaked havoc in Belfast. Sheds were erected near to the fever hospital to accommodate and treat hundreds of cholera victims. The mission faced a great crisis during that time, but they remained faithful to their work. "When cholera was committing its ravages the agents of the society were unremitting, even vigilant in their labours, and at no period did they meet with a more cordial reception. While this fact shows the steady zeal of the agents it proved that their services were doubly acceptable when sickness and death threaten. At other periods the Scripture readers' visits may be received with comparative indifference ... but in the painful moments of distress, and in prospect of approaching dissolution, they are welcomed with gladness as unassuming and faithful friends and messengers of truth, mercy and peace."

In the second decade of the work of the town mission the population of Belfast had increased by more than fifty per cent. This was largely due the increased industrialisation and the improvement of transportation. In 1839 the Ulster Railway inaugurated a line between Belfast and Lisburn, and the NorthEastern Railway opened another line between Belfast and Ballymena.

A new transport network gradually took over from the stagecoach and horse-drawn vehicles for all but short journeys. The transfer of the textile industry to factories where machines took the place of the handloom, and steam power became the symbol of the new industrial Belfast attracted increasing numbers from the country.

The building of houses was unable to keep pace with the increase in population, so in many cases two or even three families had to share their accommodation in one house. Overcrowding added to the already sordid conditions under which so many had to live and crime and vice were further encouraged by these factors.

From a spiritual point of view the rapid increase in population further emphasised the need for more churches and more ministers and missionaries to attend to the needs of the people, especially as many of them had been uprooted from their usual environment. Within the main Presbyterian body eight new congregations were formed and churches were built within a relatively short period. The town mission also opened several new centres during this period of expansion in Belfast.

Prior to the great revival in Ulster in 1859 the town mission came through some difficult times and many re-adjustments were made to the society. Student ministers and licentiates joined with agents to expand the work of the mission among the needy people of the city.

Although the beginnings of the 1859 revival were traced to the prayer meetings in the schoolhouse in Kells, Co. Antrim, the outpouring of blessing from the great spiritual awakening was experienced in Belfast where tens of thousands of people were converted. The revival gave fresh impetus to the agents of the town mission. "The Town Mission was never so honoured as during the past year. While most of the congregations of the town have shared in the blessing, we believe it has fallen in greatest abundance on the class who come under the care of the mission. For many years we have been sowing the good seed, breaking up the fallow ground, and looking and praying for the harvest."

This was reported in the Belfast News-Letter in October 27, 1860. "During the revival of the past year this (Belfast Town) mission was signally blessed. The number of persons drafted from the mission into the churches may be reckoned by thousands. The missionaries effected the work of excavation and preliminary training so that, when the quickening and refreshing grace was given as a plenteous shower, a rich harvest was gathered. There is still, however, a vast work to be accomplished."

Joy and sadness were mixed in the daily experiences of the missionaries. In their rounds they came into contact with every class of life and were able to see at a glance the needs of a situation. Mr. Elliott, a missionary, was an indefatigable man of God and he wrote in February 15, 1868:

> Social reformers meet in congress and devise methods for alleviating the sorrows of fallen humanity. Our mission supplies an answer and works out the problem. The only sovereign antidote for the moral epidemics of our town is the gospel. Nothing but the Bible can excavate the masses from their pollution and degradation. Give us the Word of God—there is no sword like that—give us it, and we fear not to beleaguer the citadels of vice and enter the dark caves and low dens of infamy and wretchedness. We heartily accord to education a work and a place. But it is

not enough. It opens festering sores but brings no balm. It fills the head but leaves the heart like ice. It dispels the thick mists of superstition and ignorance but cannot wash away the defilement that is encrusted upon the sinner's conscience.

There is much sickness at present. I visited one very bad case of fever. The woman has since been removed to the hospital. Her husband tells me that his wife in her ravings makes frequent allusions to my meetings and me. My wonder is that contagious diseases are not more prevalent. Take the example just mentioned. The house in which this woman lived is a type of others. It is a wretched hovel in Meeting House Lane. Three families are crowded into two rooms. The heavy atmosphere is sickening and oppressive. In places such as these hundreds drag out a degraded existence, and in places such as these the messenger of the Cross goes to preach Jesus and seek the lost.

Last week a woman requested me to give the pledge to a person whom she would bring to my meeting. Great was my surprise tonight when I found that the individual was her very own daughter—an exceedingly pretty and very youthful girl. I have been frequently in the house, but I never for a moment suspected that one so young and fair, and apparently so mild and gentle, could be the slave and victim of this soul-destroying habit. As I administered the pledge she sobbed as if her heart would break, and with hanging head, touched the pen (for she cannot write). Were anything wanting to complete my hatred and detestation of this abominable vice, that spares neither age nor sect, this occurrence has filled up the measure of my indignation.

The combined result of the reorganisation of the town mission followed by the blessings experienced during the months of the revival not only brought an increase in the attendance at meetings but also an influx of workers. It was thought that as many as one third of the ministers from the Presbyterian church came through their training days as missionaries with the town mission. The increase in numbers demanded better organisation, therefore the administration divided the town into twelve districts for the work of the mission. There was a great sense of stewardship from the churches, and several churches from various areas combined to support an agent working in their area.

Between the Revival of 1859 and the end of the century, the work of the town mission continued to grow. This growth was greatly enhanced by the visits of Dwight L. Moody and his song leaders to Belfast in 1874 and 1892 when they conducted evangelistic missions in the city. Their visits to these shores stimulated much evangelistic activity throughout the city, and many missionaries engaged in evangelistic tent missions and other endeavours.

In referring to the effects of the Moody mission of 1892, leaders of the town mission stated: "Though it only touched the fringe of the class among whom our agents operate the wave of divine awakening which swept over our city reached some of our centres and crowded meetings. Anxious inquirers waited to be spoken to, and professed conversions and reformed drunkards were all told that the power of the Lord was present to bless. At some of these meetings Roman Catholics attended, and professed to accept Christ as their Saviour, while men, long hardened through drink and sin not only made a new start in life but became also most zealous helpers."

In that same year Mr. John McNeill conducted a very successful evangelistic campaign and many were saved as a result. The work of the mission continued to grow. In areas where no town mission work existed Christians were prepared to open their homes for cottage meetings. One such meeting took place in the home of Miss Fanny Hunter in Weaver Street. Very soon the work outgrew her home and a hall was opened in Milewater Street in 1874. Over the next twenty years the work there increased until it was necessary to find larger premises. A bequest from Mr. John Getty provided funds to purchase a site on the corners of Mountcollyer Avenue and North Queen Street and a new hall was erected in 1897. Mr. Bell was the first missionary commissioned to this new work.

Most of the years of the Mission's work was conducted against a background of political strife and sectarian violence in Belfast. Periodically street riots erupted in various districts and made the work of the Mission difficult but vital.

The transition from being known as town mission to its present name, "The Belfast City Mission" came as a consequence of Belfast receiving the Royal Charter of city status in 1888. For the mission the transition took place at a meeting held on April 17, 1895. A resolution was submitted and carried in the following terms:

> Whereas Belfast in 1888 having by Royal Charter been raised from the rank of a town to that of a city, and is now by common consent so designated, be it resolved that in the title of this mission the word 'City' be substituted for that of 'Town' and that in future the name of the mission be the Belfast City Mission, formerly called the Belfast Town Mission.

A new constitution was also adopted at this time and this incorporated a number of changes which included the following:

> That the mission districts should as far as possible be co-terminus with the parish areas arranged by the local presbytery; that a missionary should be attached to each congregation with an outlying population to be brought into church connection; that the mission might appoint either a lay missionary or a licentiate, as the particular congregation might prefer.

The turn of the century was an appropriate time to measure the population explosion in Belfast. From the inception of the Belfast Town Mission in 1827 to 1900 the city had multiplied more than seven fold from being a town of 40,000 people to having a population of over 300,000. This increase was largely due to the continual migration from rural areas to find employment in the increasing industrial development in the city.

The measure of influence the missionaries made on the growing community is perhaps hinted at in a report presented on February 20, 1908.

> Visits paid to the homes of the poor totalled 51,915, to the sick and dying, 9,830, and to public institutions 623. Moreover, meetings and Bible classes held in different districts numbered 8,712, those attending the meetings aggregated 181,226, and families brought into connection with congregations made a total of 95. Because of losses and financial strain the number of missionaries was twenty and these had undertaken this really stupendous amount of work and nobody had ever heard them murmur or complain. Truly, sacrifice lay at the foundation of the whole enterprise and formed the governing principle of all its operations.

The evangelistic work of the Belfast City Mission continued to be very effective. Their endeavours were greatly strengthened by the visit of two great men of God—Dr. Reuben Torrey in 1903 and later by the famous evangelist Gypsy Smith in 1906. Two city missionaries went to visit Evan Roberts in Wales, and as a result the impact of the Welsh Revival was felt in Belfast. The combined effect of these events produced a great stirring in the city during which hundreds of people were converted and many believers were awakened to be more devoted to prayer and Christian service.

Although Belfast was putting together hulls of great ocean going liners—the Titanic, the Olympic and the Britannic—the city was not a healthy place to live and the mortality rate was high. Diphtheria, tuberculosis and typhoid were almost endemic. The population did not enjoy the protection that vaccines and antibiotics would provide decades later.

When the Great War came in 1914 hundreds of men from Belfast were enlisted to serve King and country in the defence of liberty. Boat loads of young men left Belfast's docks midst tears and fond farewells from wives, children, parents and sweethearts. Alas, thousands of these young men never returned.

In 1916 Belfast suffered a double blow. First, there was the Ulster Uprising at the Post Office in Dublin, and this brought a foreboding shadow over the city when thousands of her young men were at war in France and Belgium. The shadow cast over Belfast loomed darker in July when the tragic news came through that thousands of Ulster Volunteers had been killed at the Battle of the Somme.

Dr. Henry Montgomery, Minister of Albert Street Presbyterian Church and founder of the Shankill Road Mission, was Honorary Secretary of the Belfast City Mission in 1916 and summed up the mood of the time.

> Amid events unparalleled in the annals of history, when to many the very foundations seem to be shaken, the agents (missionaries) have been at work, full of hope, and ever rejoicing in the triumphs of the Cross and the message it has for the broken and bleeding hearts of men. They have visited the shadowed homes of sorrowing parents and fatherless children. They have come into contact with hearts ploughed by bereavement and stricken with the sense of irreparable loss. All reports go on to show that the people are not only thinking deeply today but also evidence a readiness to speak freely about the things that belong to their eternal peace. It is gratifying to record that in response to our country's call, the men associated with our mission have nobly responded. The city mission roll stands at the high figure of 800. Our prayer is that God will be very gracious to each of them, and so far as it is in accordance with His divine purpose cover their heads in the day of battle.

In 1915 Mr. J. C. Cunningham was appointed as a Missionary and began to work in the Sandy Row district. He continued there for five years and later was transferred to Canton Street in East Belfast, where he served for the next fifty years.

Following the Great War of 1914-18 the political unrest and strife which had been increasing in many parts of Ireland, spread to the city resulting in riots and bloodshed. Consequently, due to the drastic political changes which followed, a parliament was established in Dublin for the whole of Ireland except for the six counties comprising Northern Ireland. They opted out and established a parliament of their own in Belfast. This eventually led to the founding of Northern Ireland as a part of the United Kingdom. The new government faced bitter strife and violence, and the city of Belfast suffered much in the loss of life and destruction of property in the years that followed.

It was at this time that Ulster experienced another spiritual wakening through widespread evangelism by the evangelist W. P. Nicholson. Mr. Nicholson was born in Bangor and converted in his early twenties. For some years he had been engaged in evangelistic work. He commenced a series of campaigns in the early summer of 1921, beginning in Portadown, then moved to Lurgan, Newtownards and Lisburn. Many were saved as a result.

Dr. Henry Montgomery, the Honorary Secretary of the Belfast City Mission for more than forty-six years, engaged Nicholson as an assistant at Albert Street Presbyterian Church where he was the minister. It was at Dr. Montgomery's invitation that W. P. Nicholson first came to Belfast in February, 1922 to conduct a mission at the Albert Hall, the home of the Shankill Road Mission which Dr. Montgomery founded. There was a great response to the mission from the many city mission halls of the area. Thousands of people attended Nicholson's meetings each night, and over two thousand people passed through the enquiry room seeking counsel about salvation.

The blessings that were poured out on the Shankill area was only a foretaste of what was to follow in other districts of the city. Similar evangelistic missions were held in the year that followed, and the remarkable impact of W. P. Nicholson's preaching was felt throughout Belfast. These special evangelistic campaigns had a powerful effect on the whole community, and nowhere more than the districts in which the city missionaries carried on their work.

The measure of how wonderfully God worked in Belfast during those years was well expressed by the report of one city missionary who wrote:

> At no time in the past sixteen and a half years has the tide
> of blessing risen so high. Meetings, Sabbath School and

Bible classes have been crowded, and the revival spirit has pervaded all. Many of God's people have been lifted to a higher plane of Christian living and are now filled with a passion for souls. Sinners have been saved and backsliders restored. The work among the youth is growing steadily and is of a most encouraging character. The men who were led to Christ in the opening months of the year are growing in grace, and are most anxious to gather the godless and careless men of the district into the men's own meeting on Sabbath afternoon.

Another said of the time:

The Revival has come to our hall, and many which for years have not been to a religious service, are attending regularly. After the usual meeting is over, crowds remain for prayer and testimony until a late hour. One evening four young men about eighteen years of age, five women, and one man who was just a short time out of prison, all professed conversion.

Following the wave of blessing throughout the city there was an influx of new workers to the mission, and many of these gave long years to the work. Mr. Samuel Haslett was appointed to the hall in Havelock Place in 1926 where he served the community for nineteen years. From there he served for another seven years in Bellevue Street and later worked in the Sandy Row district for sixteen years. Mr. David Magill was appointed to be the missionary in the Island Street district in 1927, and he remained there for forty-one years and became one of the best-known Christian workers in the Newtownards Road area. Mr. James Cassidy founded the work at Kilburn Street in 1927 and continued as missionary there until his retirement in 1967. Mr. James Leetch was appointed to Lord Street district in 1933 where he maintained a work over a period of thirty-five years. Many other missionaries gained their early experience in the Belfast City Mission before becoming licentiates and then ordained ministers in the Presbyterian church. Others followed to become ministers in other denominations.

The great depression of the early thirties brought another period of high unemployment to the city, particularly in the two major industries—

linen and shipbuilding. In 1932, for example, there was not a single ship launched from Queens Island, and most of the men employed in shipbuilding had to be paid off. During the depression, many were forced to look for relief, which at the time was on a scale which scarcely allowed a moderate subsistence. Welfare organisations were among those who sought for adequate standards of relief and the board of superintendents of the mission advised an improvement in this respect. In such a period of need and distress, the workers of the mission were heavily involved in relief work, as the various halls were usually located in the areas most affected by unemployment.

However, as in the times of blessing many new works were pioneered and new halls such as Kimberly Street and Donegall Road were opened, and the work of the mission continued unabated even during the days of high unemployment and economic distress. Someone remarked, "When the dole queues are longer, the churches are more full." This was the experience of more than thirty city missionaries in the years running up to World War II.

The Mission Report of 1938-39 was very encouraging and detailed the missionary's intensive labours of the year: 75,448 visits in the homes of the people; 16,942 visits to the sick and dying; 3,252 visits to hospitals of the city; 671 Sunday School teachers in forty-two schools with an average attendance of 5,865 scholars; 204 families brought into church connection; and weekly Bible classes held in twenty-nine mission districts with an average attendance of 2,309.

With the outbreak of war in September 1939, the enforcement of the black-out and other restrictions affected public meetings in general and the work of the city mission was not excluded. Many of the residents of Belfast were evacuated to rural areas due to the threat of air raids on the city. This evacuation left whole districts denuded of population.

For those who remained in the city meetings were held in street air-raid shelters. On one such occasion, the missionary visited various shelters after the siren had sounded and led the people to sing choruses, then he sang a solo, preached for five minutes, and concluded with a brief prayer. One old woman, over seventy years of age, said that she had not been in a place of worship since she left Sunday School and had been greatly impressed by the service in the shelter. In another shelter containing about fifty people, mostly Roman Catholics, he sang 'Jesus, Lover of my Soul', then spoke for five minutes and ended with prayer. One related to him later that the audience was greatly impressed, many wept and said it was the best shelter they were ever in for nobody had ever done that before.

In 1939 Andrew Orr, a former blacksmith from near Ballymena, became the missionary in Kimberly Street where he zealously served the Lord. Mr. Orr completed forty years of service in the mission with periods spent in Derg Street, Roden Street, and Canton Street. Andrew Orr was persistent in his witness to those for whom he felt he had responsibility. On one occasion while engaged in door-to-door visitation he encountered a very big man who invited Andrew into the house. After a long conversation the missionary came to the point and asked the man if he could pray with him. This seemed to trigger hostility within the man's mind. He stood up, his large frame towering above the city missionary, and with some threats he ordered Andrew out of the house. He acted as if he would strike Mr. Orr who managed to escape unscathed from the house. In no uncertain terms the man told the missionary never to return. Mr. Orr was always gentlemanly in his manner, and he felt great concern for the enraged man. In spite of the threat of being browbeaten he returned to the man's house. With subsequent visits he was able to build a good relationship with the man and eventually had the joy of leading the man to faith in Jesus Christ.

As the war continued, it brought with it both difficulties and opportunities. More people seemed to be aware of their spiritual needs. Various missionaries found that there were increased attendances at the various meetings, and people had come to terms with the black-outs which did not prevent them from going out in the evenings.

One particularly sad event for the city mission during the war years was the death of Dr. Henry Montgomery in February, 1943. He had been Honorary Secretary of the mission for forty-six years and his association with the society covered a period of fifty-nine years. Few people had promoted the interest and expansion of the Belfast City Mission so much as this one man who had an intense love for Christ and a passion for the souls of the people of Belfast.

An ambitious housing programme marked the post-war years to meet the desperate need for new accommodation in the city and its environs. The building of new houses had virtually ceased during the war years, and in addition many houses had been destroyed or damaged beyond repair in the air raids of 1941. This expansion of the population intensified the work and strategy of the mission throughout the city. New city mission halls such as Ligoniel and Shore Road were opened, and new workers were recruited for the work.

In the beautiful summer of 1955 the Jack Shuler Crusade at the King's Hall in Belfast brought a season of concerted evangelism in the city. Workers of the Belfast City Mission and the thirty of its missionaries acted as counsellors, advisers and stewards, at the Crusade, and busloads from many of the mission halls travelled to the King's Hall each night. Thousands of those in attendance at the Crusade made profession of faith in Christ. The impact of the month long Crusade gave another boost to the numbers attending the various mission halls throughout Belfast.

During the latter half of the sixties there were great changes that took place in Belfast. A large number of old, inner city houses were demolished and the area was prepared for redevelopment. The work of the mission in these areas was adversely affected. Halls such as Cromac Street City Mission, the Hutchinson Street City Mission had to close. Roden Street, Cuba Street, Ardglen, Lime Street, Havelock Place and McClure Street were also casualties of the changing times in Belfast. As this programme advanced parts of Belfast that were once familiar disappeared.

The demolishing of houses in the centre of the city was balanced by the building of new housing estates on the outskirts of the city. The reallocation of the population gave opportunity for some halls to be improved upon and some new halls built. In the autumn of 1962 building commenced on a new hall in the Ballysillan district to serve the people in the new housing development of that area. The hall was opened in April, 1963. In addition a modern hall was opened in connection with the Boyd Endowment School on the Ravenhill Road, as the old building was unsuitable for the work. Three years later a new hall was erected in Mayo Street to replace the previous property there.

The new Rathcoole housing estate on the northern outskirts of Belfast presented a challenge to the mission, hence a site was acquired for the erection of a hall and the development of a new work in this fast growing area. Roy Graham rose to the challenge and pioneered the work there. The hall was built in 1970 and the work developed quite rapidly. After twenty-eight years Roy Graham continues in Rathcoole as the missionary, and the work there is possibly the strongest of city mission at this present time.

The Glencairn housing estate on the Ballygomartin Road grew out of the redevelopment on the lower Shankill. Brian Clenaghan was commissioned by the Belfast City Mission to establish a new work in the estate. The response from the local residents was very favourable, and a new hall was constructed and opened in 1973. That work has been a gospel beacon throughout the years of Ulster's troubles. George Lunn is the missionary in Glencairn today and, plans are afoot for a new building to replace the present hall.

Ernie Shooter pioneered the work of the City Mission in the Ballybeen housing estate at Dundonald on the eastern outskirts of Belfast. A new hall was built there in 1976 and Ernie Shooter has continued with that work since its inception. During these years the mission in Ballybeen has been a centre of evangelism and many people trusted the Saviour through Ernie's ministry. Many gospel missions have been organised and the hall has both a Boy's Brigade Company and a Girl's Brigade Company.

Mrs. J.C. Buick, wife of the Superintendent of the Hall, officially opened a new City Mission Hall in the Ballyduff estate on 22 September, 1995. Rev. Jackson Buick was the special speaker. Some three hundred people were present at the opening service, many of which came from the surrounding area. Mr. Raymond Hume is the missionary in Ballyduff. The beautiful and spacious hall has ample room for the various meetings as well as for youth organisations such as the Girls' Brigade Company, which has over eighty girls attending. Since the official opening the numbers attending the various meetings and activities has increased, and there is a great sense of anticipation as to what the Lord is going to do in the new hall. This was confirmed at the first box-opening meeting when a lady was gloriously saved.

In 1987 the old Island Street City Mission Hall which stood for over one hundred years was demolished in the redevelopment of the area. As the bricks tumbled down it seemed they were laden with the memories of former years and times of great blessing. Mr. Samuel Bill, founder of the Qua-Iboe Mission, first began his Christian service for the Lord at the Island Street Hall in 1887. David Magill served in that same district for over forty years and quite possibly wore out more shoe leather than any insurance or rent collector. Someone penned these words in tribute to Mr. Magill:

"He's shown the way of life to those
Who needed it, both friends and foes,
And many here still bless the day
That David Magill came past their way."

A new hall was built just across the road from the site of the old hall and it was opened on 29th October, 1988. The work of the city mission continues on Island Street near to the Belfast shipyard and under the shadow of the famous Samson and Goliath cranes.

In 1991 the hall in Great Northern Street was demolished to make way for a housing development, and for four years the mission was without a proper hall to continue its work there. The workers found a vacant warehouse farther down the same street, it was purchased and work began in May 1995 to convert it into a mission hall. That work was completed and the new hall was officially opened on the 11th November, 1995 by Mrs. Robert Anderson, the wife of a former missionary who had served in the area for fifty-two years. Mrs. Anderson's son, Rev. Trevor Anderson, was the special speaker and the soloist was Mr. Mervyn Black, the mission's architect. Despite it being a very wet day almost two hundred people were present at the opening. Mr. Ronnie McCullough is the missionary at the Great Northern Street Hall, and the number of new people now attending the meetings encourages him.

In 1995 the Bellevue Street City Mission merged with Mayo Street which also underwent extensive renovations. The Old Woodvale Mission Hall, which had been an outreach from Woodvale Presbyterian Church, was incorporated as Disraeli Street City Mission. Currently a new City Mission work is being established in the Clarawood estate in East Belfast

Mountcollyer City Mission hall was completely altered and renovated in 1995. Mrs. Nell Cooke, wife of a former secretary Mr. Billy Cooke, re-opened it on 9th March 1996. The special speaker on that occasion was the Rev. John Dickinson. The opening was attended by almost two hundred people. Mr. Brian Smyth, missionary at the hall, was encouraged by this.

With many city centre churches uprooting to other locations the City Mission concluded that a missionary was needed in downtown Belfast. John Miskelly was commissioned to this work and there Mr. Miskelly seeks to evangelise taxi drivers, bus drivers and people who work in the city. He visits foreign ships that anchor at Belfast docks and makes contact with the crews. Strategically, he conducts lunch hour meetings in various city centre locations and meets with vendors and buyers at St. George's Market.

Mr. George Ferguson, the current executive secretary of the Belfast City Mission, and Robin Fairbairn his assistant, are active in organising mission summer teams to help in various districts of the city. During 1998 teams went to the Ballyclare Fair and to the Edinburgh Festival.

Dr. John Girvan, former moderator of the Presbyterian Church in Ireland, began his Christian service in January 1946 as a missionary with the Belfast City Mission. He was led into the Presbyterian ministry in 1950 and became the assistant minister to Rev. David Porter who also had been a city missionary. Both Rev. Porter and Dr. Girvan would afterwards become Presidents of the Belfast City Mission. In the Belfast City Mission annual report of 1996 he reminisced and contrasted the work of the mission in his early days to what it is today:

> The years I spent on the staff of the Belfast City Mission were undoubtedly among the happiest of my entire life. Having been brought up in a rural setting, I experienced some misgivings and even fear as I embarked on the work of knocking doors in the streets of the Donegall Road district, introducing myself as the Belfast City missionary

for that area. However, in a matter of days those fears had evaporated as at almost every door I was greeted with warm friendliness and invited into the home.

Exciting conversations and discussions took place as I got to know some of the conditions and circumstances that made up the lives of the folk who lived in those streets. There were stories of bereavement occasioned by the effects of the war recently ended—bereavement not only in regard to servicemen and women killed in action, but also those who had become victims of air raids on the city. I met men who had been discharged from the Services because of war wounds or impaired health and were no longer able to work; some were resentful and bitter as they felt they had been tossed onto the heap of forgotten things.

Another thing that played havoc in many homes and families at that time was the dreaded disease, tuberculosis. I remember several houses in which two or three and even four members of the same family had fallen foul of that scourge and had been admitted to hospital where they remained for six or nine months, and even in some cases for more than a year. Indeed, not a few failed to recover at all as, for example, a woman of thirty-six years of age who passed away in the City Hospital, and just a few weeks later, her son, sixteen years old, stricken with the same disease, died in Whiteabbey Hospital.

Naturally, such circumstances provided opportunities for the missionary to get close to the families and show understanding and sympathy for their plight and give what practical assistance he could. This opened the door for the sensitive introduction of the gospel, assuring the people of the love of God for them whatever their circumstances and encouraging them to put their lives as well as their problems into the hands of the Saviour. I saw ample evidence of the power of God to transform individuals and even families as Jesus became real through their simple trust in Him. This did not necessarily change their physical and material circumstances, but their attitude to those circumstances was certainly tempered by the knowledge that God cared for them and gave them the courage and grace to accept whatever might be their lot. It has been thrilling to meet some of those people in recent days that have survived the years and are still seeking to live for the Lord.

Of course there were homes into which it was difficult to gain access. Sin, perhaps expressing itself differently from today was no less real, and the message of the gospel was not always accepted as the good news it was proclaimed to be. As I engaged in door-to-door visitation, there were those who told me in no uncertain terms that they wanted neither my message nor me. However, being present in the streets and making use of the opportunities for showing care and giving help where possible contributed toward breaking down barriers and even disarming those who were inclined to be hostile.

An interesting and encouraging feature of the work of the mission in those days was that the Sunday Schools were packed with children. Dedicated teachers were usually forthcoming, and in the main parents were co-operative in seeing that their children's attendance was reasonably consistent. The annual outing was a great event when five or six buses were required to take the children and parents to Ballywalter or some such place for the day. This provided another means of contact with the adults.

In those days attendance at a place of worship on Sunday was observed by many. The churches in our district were well attended, especially the evening services. In fact, the number present at the evening services exceeded that at the morning hour of worship. Those who came along to the meetings in the City Mission Hall were faithful and indeed were instrumental in bringing with them many who had otherwise little interest. One very encouraging aspect of the work in our hall was the interest shown by men. In particular, we had a weekly Men Only Meeting when on Friday evenings from 10:00 to 11:00 p.m. about two dozen men came together to pray for the blessing of God on the work of the mission. I could tell of incidents of which I have no doubt were answers to those prayers. All that was fifty years ago. What changes there have been since those days.

In spite of the present rate of unemployment there is an affluence today that did not exist at that time. The television set had yet to become part of the furniture of the home, and few of the people in the district had motorcars. In the main, they lived in kitchen houses— there were few homes fitted with bathrooms or inside toilets, in many cases the families were too large for the available accommodation, and the mother often experienced frustration as she tried to cope with the domestic needs of the family. When the father came home from work—if he was employed—there was little hope of an evening's relaxation in the house because of all the coming and going. In too many cases he would make his way to the local public house where it was all too easy to become a victim of the drink habit. There were, alas, many men and women who became slaves to intoxicating liquor, and as cheap wine was available, we were saddened to see some sink into the gutter from which only the power of God could rescue them.

As I try to compare those days with the present time, I would have to say that in spite of all the physical and material limitations in which the people had to live, there was, nevertheless, a contentment in hearts and homes which is sadly missing today. True, there were families that were broken up because of the irresponsibility of one or both parents, but be it said that in many of those situations the missionary was able to get things sorted out without recourse to any marriage guidance organisation. Divorce was a rarity, homosexuality and lesbianism were terms unknown to the vast majority—there was a standard of ordinary simple decency in accordance by which most people tried to live.

Another thing that used to impress me was the great neighbourliness in the streets. When the front door was opened in the morning, it was customary to leave the key in the outside of the door without concern about it being used by any unwelcome intruder. When trouble of one kind or another happened in a home, all the neighbours rallied to the support of that family, and that support was given often to the point of sacrifice.

The missionary today is working in a vastly changed world. Material improvements have made the God he seeks to present appear less necessary than in days gone by. His message is bedevilled by the cynicism that is the hallmark of today's society. Sunday observance is fast ebbing out of the weekly programme. The great majority of our children are not being taught basic Biblical principles by their parents—in too many homes there is only one parent. All in all, the missionary in today's world is operating in a vacuum as far as spiritual things are concerned because the elementary knowledge of those things which we used to take for granted no longer exist.

There is no doubt that there is a vast difference between the social conditions that prevail today in Belfast compared to those of the early nineteenth century when the Town Mission was founded. Robin Fairbairn, assistant secretary of the Belfast City Mission, stresses that there are still great social needs in the city. There is a proliferation of one-parent families. In one school in East Belfast sixty percent of the children are from single parent homes. Hundreds of men and women are caught up in the political unrest and terrorism and have had to serve lengthy jail terms. Pubs and clubs still generate a great problem with alcoholism, which still brings a heavy toll on many families. Immorality, drug abuse and increased crime are all immense problems at the end of the twentieth century. Added to the affluence which generates materialism, apathy and indifference toward spiritual issues are widespread.

Robin Fairbairn wrote in the Presbyterian Herald of December 1998:

> Society has changed, it is no longer unusual for the Missionary to find children from the same home attending Sunday School yet all having different surnames. To one such single parent home gifts have been left for the children who are faithful attendees at Sunday School.
> Happy homes are not always the reality for every child. A father who had been in prison for some time, when released, only stayed with his wife and three children for six weeks and hasn't been seen since leaving the mother to cope with the demands of home and family life. Christmas provides the missionary with an opportunity to be able to help in these difficult situations. At one home, where a father was ill and unable to work, parcels left at Christmas made an impression on the family which started them thinking about the gospel resulting in a number of conversions, with a member of that family today engaged in full time Christian ministry.
>
> Unemployment can and does have an adverse effect upon the lives of people. The father of the family who lived next door to a mission hall was made redundant just before Christmas last year. The assistance given by the missionary was a great help. Recently the man got another job and said to the missionary, "Thank goodness I won't be needing help this year." Sadly just a few weeks ago he was once more paid off.
>
> While one of the founding principles of the Belfast Town Mission, as it was known in 1827, was to 'Reach the Poor', it was to be done in the context of seeking them for Christ. The greatest human need is not clothes, food, or even presents for children at Christmas but the Lord Jesus Christ.

As Rev. John Lockington says in an article on biblical evangelism in "The Reformer", 'Many Christians rightly have compassion for the hungry and poor, homeless and abused and take action to alleviate that need. Yet Christ requires a similar compassion for the spiritual needs of multitudes, and a willingness to give ourselves to the same extent to point them to Him. What greater need have people than to know Christ? What greater good can we do than tell them about Him?' It is for this very reason the Belfast City Mission exists to tell people about the Lord Jesus Christ.

There are two things that never change—the need of the human heart without Christ, and the message of the everlasting gospel about the ever-living Saviour. Today we may have affluence and better conditions, but there is also greater apathy and more corruption than in the past. When human need is married to the fullness of Christ's love and mercy through His atoning death, then salvation is experienced and transformation takes place.

D. L. Moody said, "The measure of a man is not in how many servants he has, but how many men he serves." The Belfast City Mission has been servant to God and the church. It has kept true to its original aim, namely, bringing the gospel to the poor and the non-churchgoing in Belfast. The evangelisation of the great masses of this large and ever-growing city is an imperative duty laid on all of God's people, a duty which the Belfast City Mission has taken up, and for more than a century and a half has carried on with many tokens of divine approval. The work of the mission is to Belfast as a cleansing stream passing through the waste and dark places and wherever its operations extend lives are changed, homes purified and souls saved through the endeavours of the missionaries. The influence of the missionaries moving in and out among the people is doing much not just to elevate the community but also to continue to bring Christ to the careless, the Christless and the churchless.

Chapter Five

THE COALMEN'S MISSION

Belfast's City Hall is one of the most beautiful and graceful public buildings in all of the British Isles. For the official opening of this magnificent edifice in 1906 the celebrated artist, Sir Robert Porsonby Staples, was commissioned to paint scenes typical of Belfast that would be displayed in the splendid corridors of the building. One of the outstanding features of life in Belfast at the turn of the twentieth century was the ferryboat that travelled from Queens Quay on the River Lagan down the Belfast Lough to Bangor. This boat trip gave the theme of the enduring jingle sung by Belfast children, "The Bangor Boat's away." Sir Robert decided that he must capture this famous ferryboat on canvas for posterity.

A visit to the quayside gave him some idea of the ambience of life at the Belfast docks. Scanning the area he saw pretty ladies in their rich finery boarding the ferryboat for a days outing along the County Down coast. Crewmen were in a busy frenzy preparing to sail. Men on horse drawn carriages waited for their fare. At the edge of the main gangplank he noticed a young barefooted boy. The boy called out, "Tele! Tele! Belfast Telegraph!" Some passengers dropped a coin into the boy's grubby hand and took their copy of the local daily newspaper. Sir Robert looked at the lad, clothed in tattered and patched frazzles, and felt he must include him in the painting of the Bangor boat.

Sir Robert called the young boy and asked, "Can you come down to my studio this week? I would like to include you in a painting of the boat."

The little boy's name was Sammy Spence, and he couldn't believe that an artist would want to paint him. He agreed to go and they set up a time. When Sammy got to his house later in Newfoundland Street he told his mother about the artist's request. Mrs. Spence felt Sammy would have to make a good impression for the artist so she borrowed some of his brother's clothes and shoes to clad Sammy appropriately for the sitting with the artist.

When they got to Sir Robert's studio on the prearranged day the artist didn't recognise Sammy and asked who they were. Wee Sammy, never lost for a word, spoke up, "I met you down at the Bangor boat. I'm the wee fella that sells the newspapers. You said you wanted to paint me."

The artist was embarrassed. "Son, I didn't want you to get all dressed up for the painting. I wanted you to come just the way you were down at the docks."

Sammy was disappointed, and Mrs. Spence dragged her son home to change into his old duds and then they returned to the studio. When the painting was completed in 1906 it was presented to the city fathers to adorn the walls of the city hall. That painting is still on display at the Ulster Museum and one can see the ten year old Sammy Spence dressed in rags clasping a bundle of newspapers. His anxious face is partly hidden under an old cap and a grubby hand is at his mouth as he calls out, "Tele! Tele! Belfast Telegraph!"

In later years Sammy Spence was to use this true and personal experience as an illustration of how many people try to reform their lives before coming to Jesus Christ. "You don't need to dress up to come to Jesus. He wants you to come just as you are."

Sammy Spence certainly did not try to clean up his life before his conversion. He led a notorious life. Sammy was a diminutive figure of about five feet tall which for obvious reasons earned him the name Wee Sammy.   In spite of his small stature he gained employment as a stevedore at the busy Belfast docks. Everybody there knew him, and many avoided his company for Sammy was a tough wee nut. It is reputed that on one occasion Sammy was caught red handed leaving the docks area with something stuffed up the inside of his coat. The Bulkies, as the harbour police were colloquially known, stopped him and wanted to search him. Sammy was defiant and told them that there was no way they would search him. He said, "In the street where I live there are hard men. The farther you go up the street the harder the men are, and I live in the last house!" Sammy walked off with the goods still stuffed up his coat and left the Bulkies standing there.

Sammy was a typical Belfast man through and through. Sadly he drank excessively, and often under the influence of alcohol he often got into brawls and fights that sometimes landed him in jail.

During the political upheaval following the Easter Rebellion in Dublin and the partition of Ireland, Sammy was not behind about entering into the fray of street fights, riots and shootings to defend, what he felt was the right for Ulster to remain British. It would be wrong to say he was a terrorist, but Sammy certainly was a terror on the streets agitating and inciting mobs to violence. These activities not only endangered his life, but frequently resulted in Sammy being incarcerated in the Belfast jail.

Sammy Spence gained such an infamous reputation that he became the best known docker in the Belfast jail. In later years Sammy related that one day as he walked along a Belfast street he passed a crowd of fellows who were tossing coins towards a gable wall playing "pitch and toss."   This gambling game was illegal and often the police would unexpectedly swoop on the gambling party and whisk them off to the police station. Just when Sammy was passing the group playing "pitch and toss." a police patrol swooped on the gang and arrested them all, Sammy included. Sammy later admitted, "I was in jail sometimes when I shouldn't have been and at other times when I should have been in jail I was walking free on the streets of Belfast." Sammy estimated that he had a police record that few could match with sixty-four charges processed against him.

Sammy and his wife lived in a small terrace house in Newfoundland Street at Bridgend in East Belfast. It defies imagination to understand how they raised their twelve children in such a small house. Added to this difficulty Sammy admitted that he made life even more distressing for his wife and family because of his drunken escapades. Before his conversion Sammy was only sober during the weekends he spent in jail. He was completely irreligious, but his wife attended meetings in Memel Street which were convened by Rev. Redmond, the Rector from St. Patrick's Church of Ireland.

One Friday night in 1927 Sammy arrived home stociously drunk and enquired for the whereabouts of his wife. When his daughters told him she was down at the church meeting Sammy replied in slurred tones and told them he was going there for he needed some religion. Sammy often spoke nonsense when he was drunk so no one really expected him to go near the religious gathering. When Sammy staggered into the meeting Mrs. Spence blushed for she thought Sammy had arrived to take her out of the meeting or to disrupt it.

Mr. Redmond knew Sammy and all about his reputation and took the situation in hand. He quickly befriended the drunken man and disarmed him of his befuddled chatter. Before the night was over Sammy Spence was on his knees and called upon God for mercy and forgiveness. One of Belfast's most notorious characters of the time was converted by the grace of God.

The transformation in Sammy's life was radical and immediate. Sammy was in his mid-thirties at the time of his conversion. On the following Saturday night he was sober for the first time since he had got married. He returned to the docks on Monday to tell his friends of his conversion. Because of his tough reputation not many people made fun of Sammy, and his conversion made an immediate impact on others at the docks.

Prior to Sammy's conversion he was constantly busy and involved with friends at pubs or at work. After his conversion he found he could not sit still. He felt he needed to be busy for his Saviour. Because the Rev. Redmond was the first clergyman that Sammy knew he immediately went to work for St. Patrick's Church of Ireland and raised funds for their church activities. Sammy collected jam pots and sold them.

He started cottage meetings every Monday night in his home. Every chair in the house was filled, and people sat on the floor or stood in the hallway as wee Sammy led the singing and an invited speaker preached. Quickly the house became too crowded, and Sammy spoke to Alex Keenan, Secretary of the Wolff Dart Club, and asked for the use of the club hall in Memel Street for his meeting. Sammy had been a regular drinker with Alex at the club before his conversion and on many occasions had raised funds by selling tickets for dances and social nights. Alex and the friends at the club assured Sammy that he not only could use the hall, but they would help set it up. Some of his old drinking partners came to the meetings and trusted the Saviour. The meetings continued for many years until the outbreak of war in 1939.

Sammy worked on the county Down side of the River Lagan. Just at the entrance of the Harland and Wolff Shipyards, the coal boats from England and Scotland berthed at the quay to off load tons of coal. Kelly, Kingsberry, Craig and Harcourts were the principal coal importers at the time. These companies employed hundreds of men who, by the nature of their work, were often as black as the material they handled. Mountains of dirty and dusty coal rose up from quayside as horse drawn carts lined up to draw the precious fuels to homes all over the city.

Just as the Lord had worked in the heart of Sammy Spence so there were others at the coal quay whose hearts the Lord had opened. Mick Martin, Sam Dunnon, Alex Small, Pop Stewart, Sam Dunlop and Sammy Spence combined to maintain a vital witness for their Lord at the docks. They conducted open-air meetings and travelled to various mission halls to testify of their Saviour. They soon became known as the Coalmen's Testimony Band. Their witness was very effective wherever they went. They had the privilege of leading some of their work colleagues to trust the Lord, and they won souls for Christ in many other meetings.

With the outbreak of War in Europe in 1939 and the emergency conditions imposed on all British ports, the activities of the Coalmen's

Testimony Band were suspended. In spite of the restrictions, which were imposed on the city's population, the men continued to serve the Lord individually.

In 1947 several Christians at the Coal Quay approached Sammy Spence and Pop Stewart and asked them to revive the former testimony band. Sammy Dunlop, Billy Hamilton and Eddie Higginson joined Sammy and Pop Stewart and began to speak and testify at cottage meetings as opportunities were presented. Each day at lunch break they met in the tea hut for prayer times. As the men removed their caps and bowed their heads they were encompassed by implements and tools used by the work men at the coal boats. Although the surroundings inside the hut were most unconventional the Lord's presence was there.

Over the next two years the Coalmen's Testimony Band's reputation began to spread, and soon the men were almost swamped by invitations to testify and preach in many places. Sammy Spence and Pop Stewart met with Mrs. Harcourt and requested the use of the weighbridge shed at the entrance to the Coal Quay to hold prayer and fellowship meetings on Wednesday and Thursday nights. The request was readily granted, and the meetings proceeded. The meetings in the old shed were lively and bright. Prayers were offered freely, fervently and sincerely. People sent prayer requests for diverse needs. Marvellous answers to prayer were obtained. There were no airs nor graces with these Christian coalmen. A spade was called a spade. They spoke the common man's language and were gladly heard because of it. Although they had no theological training the coalmen were able to communicate the gospel in such a way that the ordinary people grasped exactly what they meant.

Numbers at these meetings increased rapidly. People from all over Belfast, most of whom had no connection with the docks nor the Coalmen, attended the weeknight meetings because of the warmth of the fellowship and their admiration for these dedicated working men. The growing numbers forced the Christian coalmen to look for somewhere else to convene gospel meetings for the general public.

Their attention was directed to a larger shed that had been used by His Majesty's Custom and Excise when American ships dropped anchor in Belfast Lough during the war. The St. John's Ambulance used the building when the Customs and Excise vacated the shed. Sammy Spence, ever an opportunist, appealed to the brigadier of the St. John's Ambulance at Bryson House, for permission to use the shed on Saturday nights for a gospel rally. Sammy's request was granted and at the end of 1949 the first Saturday night rally of the Coalmen's Mission began. The shed was the property of the Harbour Authorities, and they charged a nominal fee of one shilling per year for the use of the building. The old shed accommodated about four hundred people and very soon it was packed also and people could not gain admittance. It became so difficult to obtain a seat that people had to queue in a line outside before the hall was opened.

Fellow docker and crane driver, Bob Moffet, and Billy Stewart, who delivered coal on his horse and cart, joined the original group of coalmen. David Sinclair volunteered to be the pianist. Tommy Hunsdale on his violin became a permanent weekly feature of the meetings at the Coalmen's Mission. Evangelists and ministers from all over Northern Ireland were invited to preach each Saturday night. Week after week people were converted and lives were transformed.

Aside from the meetings the coalmen worked eight to ten hours per day, six days each week. Work at the Coal Quay was strenuous and was certainly not a white-collar job. Three nights of each week after work was finished the men, covered in dust and grime, would rush to their simple terrace homes in east or south Belfast to get ready for the evening activities. Luxurious or fancy bathrooms were virtually unknown, therefore the men had a quick wash in cold water at a sink. After a hasty meal they rushed back to the hall for a meeting. On the weekends they held a meeting on Saturday night and then travelled to meetings every Sunday night. When they conducted evangelistic missions they went through this rushed routine six nights of the week.

God used the Coalmen's Testimony Band as they travelled all over the city and beyond conducting meetings indoors and out. Blessings were poured out on many of these meetings and scores were converted.

George Neill, Sammy Spence's son-in-law, tells of his own conversion at the end of 1948:

The Coalmen's Testimony Band conducted a meeting in Foundry Street Mission Hall one Saturday night. Sammy Spence never liked to go home early, and after the meeting finished he and Tommy Hutton with a group of friends headed round the Sammy Mawhinney's house in Central Street. Sammy was terminally ill, and when they all arrived I was already there visiting my sick friend.

The believers sat around Sammy's bed encouraging him in the Lord with news about the meetings and what was happening in the various halls and churches. They burst into song with some of their favourite hymns. After a time of singing Sammy Spence spoke up and said he would like to sing a special song for Sammy Mawhinney.

Wee Sammy was no singer but with gravel-like tones he started up,

Is there anyone can help us,
One who understands our hearts,
When the thorns of life have pierced them till they bleed;
One who sympathises with us,
Who in wondrous love imparts
Just the very, very blessing that we need?

Yes, there's One,...only One...
The blessed, blessed Jesus He's the One!
When afflictions press the soul,
When waves of trouble roll
And you need a friend to help you
He's the One.

Wee Sammy sang all three verses with great passion and feeling and everyone including Sammy Mawhinney joined in the chorus. He may not have been much of a singer, but by the time Sammy Spence finished that hymn my heart was broken and tears coursed down my cheeks. Sammy Mawhinney saw my condition and from the sick bed he asked 'Geordie, would you not come to the Saviour tonight?' Thank God I did. Sammy Spence led me to the Saviour in Sammy Mawhinney's home that night. He not only became my father in the faith, but he also became my father-in-law in later years.

George, like many other of the Coalmen's new converts, threw his weight into the work of the mission, and he became part of the evangelistic team. Such was the measure of blessing that on one Saturday night at the rally Mr. Davidson, the Missionary at Cuba Street City Mission, invited the men on to conduct an evangelistic mission in his hall. That first mission continued every night for six weeks, and fifty-six people from the Newtownards Road were converted at those meetings.

Pastor Evans of the Iron Hall attended the meetings at Cuba Street, and was so greatly blessed he invited the Coalmen's Testimony Band for an evangelistic campaign at the Iron Hall. The Iron Hall mission also continued for six weeks and again over fifty people were converted to Jesus Christ. The congregation at Templemore Hall invited the team to conduct a mission at their hall, and it was a mission with a difference. Throughout the first week the Coalmen's Testimony Band sang, testified and preached the gospel every night. This was followed the next week by similar meetings conducted by RUC Sergeants Baxter and Fitzimmons and Chief Inspector Kennedy from the Christian Police Association. At the time it was commented, "Thieves and robbers preached the gospel for the first week and then came the cops!" Marvellous grace was upon all of God's servants, and many sought the Lord at those meetings.

A six-week mission followed at Nixon Street on the Shankill Road, and then for another two weeks in Shankill Baptist Church. Rathmore Street Mission Hall followed next for another two weeks of evangelistic meetings. During the meetings at Rathmore Street Sammy Spence went visiting homes in the area. At one home Sammy spoke to a good living woman who protested her innocence when it came to a matter of sin. Sammy stressed that we are all sinners and all need salvation. The woman replied to Sammy, "Mister, my name is on the church roll, and that is good enough for me."

To this Sammy replied, "Missus, you might as well have your name on a sausage roll as on the church roll. Without Jesus Christ you can never get to heaven."

Invitations for evangelistic missions piled up, and the meetings had to be planned at reasonable intervals. Scores of people were saved during this great time of evangelistic fervour and activity.

After the meetings a cup of tea was provided either at the venue of the meeting or in a friend's home. Invariably Bob Moffet was invited to give thanks for the refreshments. Bob predictably prayed,

As Thou did'st bless the loaves and fishes,
So bless the food upon our dishes,
And as the sugar dissolve in the tea,
So let our lives dissolve in Thee.

The men were as zealous for the Lord at their work place as well as at the meetings. Billy Stewart delivered coal all over Belfast and never missed an opportunity to witness for his Lord. One day while delivering coal on Belfast's Antrim Road he became aware that the family to whom he was delivering coal were Jewish. As he walked back and forward from the coal cart to the coal house and threw in the sacks of black coal, he not only counted the number of bags, but he prayed that the Lord would give him an opportunity to witness to the man of the house. After the last bag was thrown in Billy wrote the man an invoice for the coal.

No obvious opportunity had opened for Billy to speak about the Saviour so he made his own opening. Deliberately turning to the unsuspecting Jew Billy said, "Sir, I promised my Saviour I would speak a word of testimony for Him wherever I went, and I would like to tell you about Him. Do you remember when you fellas were going through the desert and snakes came out from every place?"

The Jewish customer incorrectly assumed that the event Billy was referring to had happened in the recent World War when Rommel was locked in war with Montgomery in North Africa. Billy continued unabashed, "There was no healing for you Jews until Moses made a serpent of bronze and lifted it up to the people and whoever looked at the serpent was saved. Jesus said that just as Moses lifted up the serpent for the salvation of the sick and dying so He also was also lifted up on the cross as Saviour and He is able to save Jews and Gentiles." The stunned man hardly answered a word.

A feature of the Saturday night meeting at the Coalmen's hall was Sammy Spence giving out the prayer requests which could only be understood by Ulster people. Quite innocently Sammy announced, "Mrs. Smith requests prayer for her husband who is in bed with the doctor!" That brought a roar of laughter. Another night he read a short note, "Prayer is requested for a brother up the country who has a very bad pain in his leg, and he takes it on and off every day." At times he would ask prayer for some young people who had gone to Bible College, "We need to pray for the young people who are passing through the walls of the Bible Colleges." It sounded like a very painful experience for the young people.

At times when no musician was available to accompany the singing Sammy called out "We've no piano tonight so we'll just fut it." Sammy burst into song and kept the timing of the music by loudly stamping his foot on the platform as the people heartily sang the gospel.

With so much travelling involved to the various meetings it was reasoned that the Testimony Band would be wise to invest in a vehicle that would enable them to travel together rather than in separate cars. Sammy Spence, a great innovator, always had a great ability to pick up very good bargains. He could quite easily make money, spend money and give his money away. He considered the transport predicament of the Coalmen's Testimony Band and contacted an undertaker in East Belfast. After some negotiation Sammy bought a hearse.

The hearse was stripped of its more sombre frills and trimmings and in their place the men installed bench seats where the dais for the coffin once filled the long rear part of the vehicle to convert it into a makeshift mini-bus. Eddie Higginson who had been with the testimony band since it was reconstituted in 1947, was skilled at painting banners for Orange Lodges and he employed his expertise in painting appropriate texts on each side of the former hearse. On one side he painted, "Passed from death unto life," in fancy calligraphy lettering, and at the rear he adopted a slogan which read like a route shown on a public transport bus and it read: "Heaven via the Cross."

It was with great enthusiasm that the men embarked on their first journey in the converted hearse. As they travelled all over the countryside people at the side of the road in deference to the approaching hearse stood still, and men respectfully removed their caps. Imagine their reaction when instead of a coffin they saw a hearse full of singing men.

Perhaps a hearse was the most appropriate name for the old vehicle, for it was a virtual death trap. When ten burly men and Wee Sammy piled into the vehicle it became top heavy and as they drove over the bumpy roads the old vehicle rolled and swayed as Billy Stewart, the driver, tried to hold it on the proper side of the road. There was many a close shave with oncoming traffic even though the roads were not very congested with traffic in those days.

It was concluded that the team should invest in a means of transport which would be safer and perhaps more comfortable. Sammy kept his eye open for an appropriate vehicle. With his deftness for a bargain, when he was at an auction he spied a single decker bus that had been used during the war. He alerted the dealers not to bid for it as it was required by the Coalmen's Testimony Band for their meetings. On the day of the auction there were no opposing bids, and Sammy and Billy Stewart drove away in their newly acquired bargain which was secured at a ridiculously low price.

The blue and white bus was a great asset for not only could the men travel to the meetings in safety, but their wives and other invited guests could accompany them. This was by no means a luxury coach. The seats were made of wood and there was no heater on the bus. In cold weather long icicles often had to be broken on the inside of the bus. The men had to scatter straw on the bus floor to help keep their feet warm and the passengers often had to wrap up in heavy clothing. Notwithstanding the discomfort, with Billy Stewart at the steering wheel, trips were made all over Ireland in all sorts of weather as the men pursued their evangelistic enterprise.

While these outreach meetings were going on all over the Province the work continued unabated at the Coalmen's Mission Hall at the docks. The St. John's Ambulance Hall soon proved to be totally inadequate for the crowds attending. In 1953 the Coalmen encouraged people to pray that the Lord would provide them with a bigger building. An appeal was made to the Harbour Authority for permission to renovate and extend the former Customs and Excise shed. The Authority granted permission but strictly on the terms that the extended and renovated building would retain it original form and still remain the property of the Harbour Authority.

People generously contributed to the building programme and soon the materials were purchased. Mr. Bertie Scott, a close friend of Sammy Spence at Templemore Hall, supervised the construction work, much of which was done by voluntary labour. The Coalmen and other friends rallied round to help. One lady from Bangor who passed the building every morning en route to her business in Belfast city centre, noticed the construction work at the quayside. The progress of the building fascinated her. One day her curiosity compelled her to enquire what the building was for. When she was told it was the Coalmen's hall to be used for the preaching of the gospel she offered to help. She instructed them to lay laminated floor tiles instead of the cement floor they were planning on and send the invoice for the material and labour to her. Mrs. Campbell, who owned a clothes shop in Ballyhackamore, paid for all the lighting at the new hall. These gifts were typical of the generosity of many who wanted to show their support for the Coalmen's Mission.

A new roof replaced the old one. Brick walls were built in place of the corrugated iron siding. The capacity of the refurbished building increased from four hundred to six hundred, and the opening of the new building took place in June 1955. A gospel accordion band played Christian music to the crowds outside. Lady Kelly, of the Kelly coal family, cut the ribbon and officially declared the new hall open for the glory of God. A great praise meeting followed.

From the outset the new hall was packed every Saturday night. People came early and lined up along Station Street and over the Queens Bridge in order to gain admittance. Many who failed to get into the hall stood outside to listen to the meeting over loudspeakers, which were erected above the entrance. Sailors often sat on the decks of their boats that were berthed in the harbour, and they listened to the testimonies and singing.

Many great preachers conducted Saturday night meetings at the Coalmen's Mission Hall. Willie Mullan preached for an evangelistic mission at the hall. The hall was packed every night and dozens of men and women came to know the Lord. Ian Paisley captivated a packed congregation on many Saturday nights as he thundered out the gospel message. Archie Barr of the Brethren was another favourite preacher with the Coalmen and he often preached for them on the Saturday night meeting.

Various singers came also. Hubert Brown of Lisburn thrilled the hearts of many with his rendition of the old gospel hymn, "Ship Ahoy". Johnny Floyd of Rathmore Street was another favourite singer on Saturday nights, and he often travelled with them to their meetings in different locations.

No matter who the preacher was, Pop Stewart, who was a foreman at the coal Quay, always made the closing appeal for sinners to come to Christ. Pop may not have been the most fluent preacher of his day but his ability to make a warm, persuasive and sincere appeal could not be bettered.

Undoubtedly, the secret of blessing for these Saturday night rallies was the night of prayer that followed when the prayer room was packed with Coalmen and friends on their knees calling upon God for souls until three or four o'clock on Sunday morning.

Lily Boal who was raised in the dock area of Belfast was adopted as the missionary from the Coalmen's Mission. Lily as a teenager was converted in Mountcollyer City Mission Hall. She knew many of the testimony band members from their early days before they were converted. In 1939 Lily devoted herself to a life of devotion and sacrifice as a missionary with Worldwide Evangelisation Crusade in the Northwest Frontier of Pakistan and India. She only returned home twice in the twenty-four years she spent in that distant land. Throughout that time the Coalmen took an active interest in Lily and her work. As well as supporting Lily Boal other missionary societies greatly benefited from the generosity of the Coalmen's Mission.

The work continued to grow and be blessed week by week both at the Coalmen's Mission Hall and at the meetings around the country. Sammy Spence continued to do a lot of individual work with needy people on the Streets of Belfast.   He provided meals and clothing for the down and out paupers, and he visited known criminals in the local jails and led many of them to faith in Christ. Sammy would scan the classified columns of the newspapers and pick up bargains to pass on to the poor and needy. He even bought a few unwanted grave plots and reserved these for prisoners who died in jail or for the poor who died without next of kin to bury them. On several occasions only Sammy, the Governor of the prison and the undertaker stood around the grave to bury the remains of some unknown prisoner who died after years in jail.   Sammy knew most of the long-term prisoners, and when they were released they came to the Coalmen's Mission looking for their former inmate and friend.

Summer time was a great opportunity for witness. Sometimes the Coalmen would visit a seaside resort and conduct open-air meetings. One lasting personal memory was taking part in the Coalmen's annual witness at the Belfast Orange Procession to "the Field" on the 12th July. Half an hour ahead of the procession Bob Moffet, George Neil and many other friends wore vests with gospel texts painted on the front and rear.   Armed with thousands of evangelistic tracts they followed the five mile route from Clifton Street in North Belfast to 'the Field' at Finaghy on the edge of South Belfast. Sammy Spence and Pop Stewart followed behind their group on a pony and trap with Billy Stewart at the reins.   These Belfast characters were known to thousands and all the way to the "Field" waving bystanders called out, "Hello Sammy. Hello Pop!"

In August 1969 political troubles spilled over unto the streets of Belfast. Street fighting, shootings, fires, car bombs and car highjacking became an all too common scene on the streets of Belfast. People who had once travelled to Belfast from the surrounding countryside to enjoy the Coalmen's meeting on Saturday nights, were now afraid to come to the city. Even though the numbers attending the meetings started to diminish, the testimony band continued their work both at the hall and travelling round the country to churches and mission halls.

In 1972 came the end of the Coalmen's Mission fruitful era. It was marked by one of the worst tragedies of Ulster's troubles. A car bomb exploded near to the bus station in Oxford Street, and a greater part of the remains of the blown up car landed on the roof of the Coalmen's Mission Hall and caused severe damage. When the men met to consider the future of their work they appraised their future role and they reluctantly concluded that the damage to the hall was a turning point for them. Most of their principal workers were now advanced in years, and others had passed on to be with the Lord.

As the testimony band had been generous and zealous during their thirty-three years of existence so also in their demise they displayed the same benevolence. The furnishings at the hall were donated to various churches and mission halls in Belfast. The trustees distributed the remaining funds to missionaries and missionary societies.

After the Hall was vacated the Harbour Authority demolished the building to make way for a new fly-over and road layout. Today the site of the old Coalmen's Mission is unrecognisable as it is covered by a maze of roads and overhead passes. For thousands of people the spot still remains precious in their memories as the place they met the Saviour.

Sammy Spence and Pop Stewart remained active for their Saviour even after the Coalmen's Mission was formerly closed. Sammy Spence went on to be with his Saviour in May, 1974. He had attended the wedding of Bertie and Grace Scott's daughter on the Saturday, but because of the restrictions imposed on travel due to the Ulster's worker's Strike Sammy stayed at his daughter's house overnight so he could attend Templemore Hall the following morning. After breakfast on Sunday morning Sammy went to get dressed for the morning worship service. As he was fixing his tie he felt unwell. His daughter came to his aid, but no one could hold Sammy any longer. In his daughters arms he passed on and went home to be with Jesus. A few years later

Pop Stewart followed Sammy into the Lord's presence. Since then all of the original Coalmen's Testimony Band have gone home to heaven.

These theologically untrained men were greatly skilled in winning souls to the Lord, and because of their devotion and zeal many had entered into heaven before them. Only eternity will reveal how great the harvest was.

Mr. S. Boyd wrote in a tribute about his friend Sammy Spence :

Well known, especially in Memel Street,
At Coalmen's Mission we all did meet,
He led the Coalmen' s Testimony Band,
Sammy offered to all a welcome hand.

In the Coalmen's Hall at Queen's Quay,
Many souls were saved we all did see,
Other Coalmen helped, too many to name,
But they all played their part just the same.

Sure our loss was heaven's gain,
And we know one day we'll all meet again,
The Lord buries His workmen it is true,
But carries on the good work by me and you.

How we will miss you dear brother
In all the good work that you've done,
In the Coalmen's Mission and elsewhere
But the Crown of Life you have won.

No doubt you were a Friend indeed
A very good Friend to all in need.
With the Lord's work so much at heart
Now at the end from us you part.

Gone to be with the Lord you love,
To join with the saints up above,
To bask in the sunshine of God's love
From world of sorrow to Heaven above.

You led our meetings in the Testimony Band,
You visited the sick and lent a hand.
You were loved by all, a leader indeed,
You did what you could to sow the Good Seed.

Sure it's only goodnight brother Sammy,
We will see you in the morning.
The Day Thou gavest Lord is ended,
But for Sammy a new day is dawning..

Chapter Six

THE WELCOME HALL

Amy Carmichael from Dohnavur Fellowship is a name well known and respected in Christian circles all over the world. As well as her many years of work in Japan, China, Sri Lanka and India, her devotional writings and poems have touched and inspired Christians for many generations. However, long before her departure for the mission field or the employment of her pen in her literary classics, Amy left a lasting work in the hearts of the working class populace of the Shankhill Road in West Belfast.

The Carmichael family were traditionally Scottish Covenanters and originally came to Ulster from Ayrshire. They were a family of means and were dedicated to their Saviour and to the witness of the Presbyterian church. In 1773 they built the Millisle Presbyterian Church and in the same year gave ground for the erection of the Ballycopeland Presbyterian Church. Both of these churches continued as separate congregations for 130 years until they amalgamated in 1911 to form the Millisle and Ballycopeland Presbyterian Church, which continues to this day.

Amy's father managed one of the family's two flourmills which had been owned by the Carmichael's for generations. Millisle itself derived its name from the larger mill which was situated near the shore, and a stream forked round both sides of the mill to provide the power for the water wheel to drive the mill's machinery. The family home still stands on Millisle's Main Street, which runs parallel to the shore on the North Down coast.

Amy Beatrice Carmichael was born in Millisle, Co. Down, on 16th December 1867, and was the first born of David and Catherine Carmichael's seven children. Her birth was registered in 1888 at the Ballycopeland Presbyterian Church.

In the same year that Amy was born the Carmichael's contributed a large sum of money for the building of a school on the opposite side of the street from their house, although Amy had a private governess for her elementary education. The school continued to function in the same building until 1959 when the growing population brought demands for larger premises. The old school house still stands on Millisle's main street and today is the home of Millisle Baptist Church.

As well as learning reading, writing and arithmetic, Amy attended Sunday School so she could learn spiritual truths. The early initial Christian influence on Amy's life was nurtured at the local Ballycopeland Presbyterian Church where her family had their own private pew. Theirs was truly a happy and prosperous Christian home. From her earliest years Amy manifested her potential for leadership, even if it was in mischievously leading her brothers and sisters in playing many pranks on the family.

Although raised as a Presbyterian when Amy got older she was sent to a Wesleyan Methodist Boarding School—Marlborough House, in Harrogate, Yorkshire, England. The combined influences of her Christian family, her home church and the meetings of the Children's Special Service Mission which she attended while in England led Amy to personal faith in Jesus Christ when she was fifteen years old and still a student at the Marlborough House Boarding school.

During her three year absence from Millisle great changes took place in the mill industry, and the Carmichael brothers had to close the mill and leave the small town. When Amy returned to Northern Ireland to complete her education she went to live in the family's new home at College Gardens in Belfast's select Malone Road area. Things did not look good at home, for her father had fallen upon hard financial times, and the family problems got worse when Mr. Carmichael's health began to fail. Shortly after Amy's eighteenth birthday Mr. Carmichael died.

Her father's death had a very sobering effect on Amy's young life. As a Christian the family's tragedy helped her focus on the needs of the many disadvantaged people on the streets of Belfast. On one wet and windy Sunday not long after her father's death Amy was returning with her brothers from the morning worship service in the very respectable Presbyterian church in the centre of the city. Amy saw an old lady who looked very poor and was carrying a heavy bundle. Ignoring the disapproving looks of the other parishioners Amy and her brothers helped the lady carry her load along Bedford Street. When they arrived at the junction of Ormeau Avenue and the Dublin Road Amy noticed a newly constructed fountain. In spite of the continuing rain driven by the wind Amy gazed at the new landmark, and as she did she seemed to hear a voice saying, "Gold, silver, precious stones, wood, hay stubble, every man's work shall be made manifest for the Day shall declare it, because it shall be tried by fire, and the fire shall try every man's work of what sort it is." Amy turned to see where the voice had come from, but through the driving rain she could only see the muddy street and the passing people and nothing else. At the time Amy didn't speak to any one about what had happened, but that incident changed her life, and it changed her attitude to life's values—nothing could ever be the same again. The longing of her heart was expressed in a hymn that came into her possession at that time:

Upon a life I did not live
Upon a death I did not die,
Another's life, Another's death,
I stake my whole eternity

It was at this time that Amy decided to dedicate her life to help the poor and needy of Belfast.

Amy started by conducting children's meetings in her home at College Gardens. She was encouraged by Dr. Henry Montgomery of the Albert Hall and the Belfast City Mission, to become involved in evangelistic outreach on Saturday evenings. This activity helped her to see how the "other half" lived in Belfast. Zealously Amy extended her Christian service and initiated various meetings for boys and girls in various homes and led a weekly Bible study for the staff and students of Belfast's Victoria College at Cranmore Park. She worked at the local YWCA and introduced a special class for Belfast's mill girls at Rosemary Street Presbyterian Church. Because these mill girls were too poor to buy fashionable hats they used shawls to cover their heads when they attended church services. This practice earned them the name of Shawlies.

Amy's ongoing work among Belfast's crude and common Shawlies invited disapproving comments from those who felt Amy should respect her proper upbringing instead of going to the city's slums after these girls. Dr. Park, minister of Rosemary Street Presbyterian Church, was quite an innovator and often shocked the respectable members of his church by what some considered as being outlandish methods. He readily consented to Amy's request for the use of the church hall on Sunday mornings to evangelise and teach the Scriptures to these unsophisticated and underprivileged girls. Five hundred girls attended Amy's weekly class at the church

Amy's mother supported her in her endeavours to reach and to help the underprivileged. In spite of many verbal objections and contemptuous looks from other parishioners, the work continued to grow and at times overflowed the church hall. Finally, it was to the relief of many at the Rosemary Street Church that Amy finally intimated she would need to look for other premises to accommodate the growing numbers that were attending her classes.

In a local magazine "The Christian", Amy's attention was drawn to an advertisement offering the sale of a corrugated iron building which would accommodate five hundred people and could be erected for £500. The Carmichael family's assets had dwindled to virtually nothing, and Amy with no fixed income didn't have the means to purchase the building. Amy remembered that when she was a child in Millisle she was asked to collect donations for the Bird's Nest, a Christian orphanage in Dublin. When she visited her grandmother in Portaferry she took her collecting card with her and asked some of her grandma's friends and neighbours to contribute to the cause. Amy remembered that one man who had just built a new house refused to donate anything to the fund. Amy felt rebuffed and disappointed by the response and never forgot the incident. As a result of that experience Amy reasoned, "Why not ask God to speak to those who love Him and motivate them to help those whom He loves, rather than ask help of those who don't love God?"

During her few years of work in Belfast she had learned to pray and trust God for every situation. Enthusiastically she imparted to the girls her vision to purchase the iron hall, and their burden of prayer at the regular meetings was for God to meet this need and send them £500.

One day soon after the girls began to pray Amy and her mother were visiting in a friend's house. The hostess showed an unusual interest in Amy's work with the Belfast Shawlies. Subsequently, this lady told an older friend, Miss Kate Mitchell, a lady of considerable means, about Amy and her zeal and vision to provide a hall for the growing number of the city's mill girls. Miss Mitchell was very interested in what she heard and desired to know more about Amy, so she invited her for lunch in her opulent home which was named Olinda. After that visit, when Amy shared the burden of her heart to Miss Mitchell, she received a letter from the wealthy lady who offered to buy the iron hall for the growing work. This direct answer to prayer was a tremendous lesson in the life of faith that Amy could never have taught the Shawlies in a meeting. Their joy was unbounded.

With the money to purchase the building in hand another hurdle had to be cleared—they did not have a site to put the building on. Amy encouraged the girls once again to make this a matter of prayer. Amy had learned that faith without works was dead so she went to the office of Mr. Ewart, the owner of one of the biggest mills in Belfast, and asked if he would sell her a site where they might erect their building. For an absurdly low price, Mr. Ewart offered Amy a piece of ground in Belfast's working class area at Cambrai Street which runs from the top of the Shankhill Road through to the Crumlin Road. The location was perfect.

The prefabricated iron hall was duly erected on the site, and for obvious reasons Amy named it The Welcome Hall. The mill girls helped make curtains for the windows, and the hall was completed in good time. Invitation leaflets were printed and sent out to many people for the opening of the hall on 2nd January 1889.

The new venture, however, was not without its critics who disdainfully labelled the hall The Tin Tabernacle. Notwithstanding the criticism, Amy's invitation leaflet described the new hall as being the mill and factory girls branch of the YWCA. The underlying reason for this work was perhaps reflected by a little composition Amy included on the invitation:

Come one. Come all.
To the Welcome Hall
And come in your working clothes.

Dr. Park, Amy's minister at Rosemary Street Presbyterian Church and a great encouragement to her in the work, spoke at the dedication service. During the opening service Amy sat on the platform and repeatedly read the hand painted text on the wall above, "That in all things He might have the pre-eminence." Colossians 1:17. When she rose to speak Amy simply said, "As truly, as truly I knew how, I wanted those words to be fulfilled."

The dedication of the Welcome Hall was followed by a two week evangelistic campaign by two of D.L. Moody's evangelists from the USA. The two evangelists introduced a new hymn to the friends at the Welcome Hall:

I know not why God's wondrous grace
To me He hath made known,
Nor why unworthy as I am
He chose me for His own.

But I know Whom I have believed,
And am persuaded that He is able
To keep that which I've committed
Unto Him against that day.

It was at these meetings that the hymn was sung for the first time in the British Isles, and instantly it became a favourite with those who attended the Welcome Hall. In the weeks that followed one could hear it's tune being whistled or someone singing the chorus in the streets around the newly constructed hall. Each night during those first weeks many souls were won for the Saviour.

After the inaugural evangelistic meetings the enthusiastic congregation at the Welcome Hall settled down to a busy weekly schedule.

Sunday	4:30 p.m.	Bible Class
	5:30 p.m.	Sunbeam Band Meeting
Monday	1:20 p.m.	Dinner Hour Prayer Meeting
	7:30 p.m.	Singing Practice
Tuesday	7:30 p.m.	Night School
Wednesday	1:20 p.m.	Dinner Hour Prayer Meeting
	7:30 p.m.	Girl's Meeting
Thursday	4:00 p.m.	Mother's Meeting
Friday	1:20 p.m.	Dinner Hour Prayer Meeting

This was a great work and a heavy responsibility for a young girl of twenty-two years to sustain. However, Amy did not stay there long.

In 1989 Mrs. Carmichael left Belfast and took Amy and one of her sisters to live with a family friend in England. Other fields beckoned Amy and after several years in England she left the British shores for her life's calling in Asia. During the next fifty years of her missionary career she did not return again to the Welcome Hall or to her native Northern Ireland.

After an initial period in Japan Amy finally went to India where she founded the renowned and highly esteemed work of the Dohnavur Fellowship. This work was established to reach and rescue many of the exploited "temple children," the abused and neglected waifs that lived on India's streets. Like her work among the Shawlies in Belfast, the mission to the needy street urchins grew rapidly and became very effective and efficient.

In 1931 Amy suffered a major health crisis and subsequently was confined to bed for the rest of her life. From her bedroom Amy directed the work of the Dohnavur Fellowship, and with her enforced seclusion she put her pen to good use. She wrote letters of encouragement to many of God's servants and authored thirty-five books—many of which are considered Christian classics. Her devotional writings became well-known all round the world. Amy Carmichael passed away in 1951.

God's work is always greater than any of His workers and there was a great future for the Welcome Hall.

After Amy's departure the work of the Welcome Hall took on a different character and it had more emphasis that belied the text Amy had chosen as her personal objective: "That in all things He might have the pre-eminence." The evangelistic zeal abated and soon the premises were being used more for social and educational purposes. Sewing classes and demonstrations of goods and wares were given the pre-eminence. The Welcome Hall that had once been a burning and shining light in the area lay idle, and its flame and influence were almost extinguished.

In 1926 Canon Warren of St. Silas Church of Ireland was challenged when he noticed the neglected Welcome Hall. He mused, "This place could be used to touch many people in the area, and there is no better person to do it than Jack Johnson."

Jack Johnson was born in Tunney, Ballinderry in 1886. After leaving school he found employment as a textile engineer with Combe Barber Textile Engineering Works. He left his home in the country and lodged with one of his sisters, Mollie, in Palmer Street which was adjacent to the Welcome Hall. During his apprenticeship in Belfast Jack was converted to Jesus Christ.

From the earliest days after his conversion Jack Johnson was out and out for his Lord. He repeatedly put his all on the altar in full and glad surrender to unconditionally serve the Lord and follow Him wherever He might lead. Jack's motto for fellowship was, "Keep short accounts with God."

With enthusiastic zeal he engaged in soul winning both in and out of the pulpit and seldom lost an opportunity to witness to others of his faith in Christ. He would approach a person on the street and politely ask if they could answer a question for him. On agreeing to his request Mr. Johnson posed this query, "If the righteous are saved with difficulty, where will the ungodly and the sinner appear?" Many were startled at the question but often an opportunity was then given to discuss the individual's need of salvation through Jesus Christ. On other occasions when travelling by train or coach with fellow Christians Mr. Johnson would inquire from one of the party, "Tell me where you were saved." Subtly the opportunity to give a word testimony to all the unwitting passengers was provided. Jack Johnson was always alert to the need of the lost all around him, and his passion was to win them for Jesus Christ. His integrity in daily life and private devotion in prayer balanced Jack's zeal and public witness.

Jack met Miss Elizabeth Barrett McGee, a Faith Mission Pilgrim, and fell in love with her. Elizabeth was a gracious and gifted girl who was also dedicated to serving the Lord. Once they were married they made a great team. Although they didn't know what God had planned for their lives they were well equipped for the Lord's service.

They set up home above a baby needs retail shop on the Shankill Road where Mrs. Johnson worked. Jack continued his job at Combe Barber. In the evenings they were given opportunities to employ their talents in the Lord's work at various meetings.

When Canon Warren first approached Mr. Johnson about the neglected hall and its potential he declined the initiative as he didn't know any of the trustees. When he told his wife about the opportunity she encouraged him to give it a try. They consulted with Mr. McClean of the Faith Mission who said he knew Miss Kate Mitchell who had first donated the money for the purchase of the Welcome Hall. They asked permission of Miss Mitchell if they could conduct a Faith Mission Prayer Union in a small room at the rear of the hall. Mrs. Lowry had held the prayer meeting in her home in Cambrai Street, however, she was happy to move it to the old hall and supported the endeavours of the Johnson's. This was the beginning of the resurgence of the work in the Welcome Hall, which for too many years had fallen into decline.

Once the prayer union was established Jack started a Sunday Bible Class for boys. It was well attended and several girls asked if a similar class could be started for them. Mrs. Johnson agreed to their request with the condition that they could bring fifteen girls along. Seventeen young girls attended the first class. That was the beginning stages of a Sunday School, which blossomed and grew into a large school with many teachers.

The small prayer group Bible classes continued meeting at the rear of the Hall until one day a man who worked in the Springfield Road Post Office challenged Mr. Johnson, "Why don't you open the big doors at the front of the hall?" Jack told him he thought the small room was big enough, but the man persisted. Mr. & Mrs. Johnson, open to the Lord's prompting, gave the matter prayerful consideration. They finally felt this was the Lord urging them to enter a new phase in the work.

One step at a time the work grew from a prayer meeting to a Sunday School and now a Sunday Evangelistic Service. It wasn't long until a full programme of meetings was complete with the addition of a Saturday Night fellowship meeting and a Sunday morning Breaking of Bread Service. These developments were supported by the Trustees who were led by Mrs. Brownrigg of Seapatrick, near Banbridge, a niece of Miss Mitchell.

From Jack Johnson's earliest days at the Welcome Hall he laid great emphasis on issues that were important in his own life: evangelism of the lost, holiness of personal life and full surrender to the will of God. The effect of these qualities was soon reflected in the growth of the hall. Jack became the pastor and superintendent of the work in the Welcome Hall, a honorary position for which he refused any salary or payment. It was through the business at Johnson's Baby Shop which provided Jack and Elizabeth with a living.

Jack's emphasis on evangelism led to many fruitful evangelistic campaigns that were held regularly, and through their success the work grew. In 1932 Julius Lipton, a converted Jew, came to the Welcome Hall for a special campaign. After three weeks of the mission seventy souls were saved. This was the beginning of a move for God in the area. Dr. George Guest Williams, a great expository preacher and Bible teacher who belonged to the Christian and Missionary Alliance, came to the hall in 1934. As a result of his ministry a joint Bible class for men and women was started at the hall. These were just the early rains, a foretaste of better things to come.

In 1935, under the ministry of Mr. Fred Brown, God broke in in a mighty way. This may be described as the best and most powerful evangelistic mission the Welcome Hall ever experienced. Fred was a young man who had just graduated from college. Prior to entering college Fred worked on the United States' railroads. The Rev. Harold Brown of Lurgan Presbyterian Church introduced Fred to Jack and Jack arranged for him to come to the hall for a period of special meetings. From the moment he came, the seal of God was on his ministry. The church was packed to capacity with every available seat occupied, and people were even sitting on windowsills, and crowds thronged outside the door. Jimmy Johnston was the soloist at the meetings and on a few occasions he even preached.

God moved in with great power and blessing, and souls were saved every night. There was a great air of expectancy as people seeking Christ were counselled until midnight. Jack Morton, for whom they had been praying for many years, came out for the Lord at those meetings but had a great difficulty in getting through to the place of assurance. There was great rejoicing when the news came late one night that Jack had come right through for the Lord. He became one of the pastor's right hand men in the Welcome Hall. He was a stalwart during times of difficulty and a steadying influence in every crisis that the pastor passed through.

Bill Black was also converted in these halcyon days of blessing. Like many other men from the neighbourhood he had spent most evenings at one of the many pubs on the Shankill Road and too soon he fell into the evil of booze and was soon following in the accompanying evils that often follow. Liquor blocked his mind and was destroying his body. He took casual employment in Wilton's Funeral Undertakers. One day when the firm was short of pall bearers Bill was asked by a lady in the office to put on a long black coat and top hat and go to a funeral in a home. When Bill arrived in the house of mourning he moved to put the lid on the coffin and was startled to see his own name on the lid. It was as if he had been hit by a thunder bolt. He tried to drown God's voice speaking to him but, before midnight that same night, intoxicated with drink, Bill staggered into a home in Ottawa Street, and there an ill lady quoted John 3:16 to him and faced him with his need of Jesus Christ. That night Bill was gloriously saved. Bill Black not only went on with the Lord but soon went into training at the Faith Mission and eventually became a superintendent of the Faith Mission.

Sometime after his conversion he encountered a moment of weakness. Bill always kept a five-glass bottle of spirits in a narrow wall recess in the shop where he worked. He decided to have a drink from the bottle, and very carefully he tried to lift the bottle only to graze the corner of the recess. It was as if the bottle had been cut by a glazier for the bottom fell out of the bottle, and the contents spilled on the floor. Bill was sure it was God who stepped in and delivered him from the liquor. He never did touch another drop of alcohol again.

Bill trained at the Faith Mission, and he and his wife Tilly served the Lord in the Mission. Bill became the district superintendent for the Faith Mission in the Highlands of Scotland, and later in Ballymena where he worked until the Lord called Bill home.

Jim Neill, a former elder at the Welcome Hall, recalled those great days of blessing during Fred Brown's visit, "Those were times of heaven on earth. Hundreds were saved during that mission and are still going on today. Fred had great ability to paint word pictures to the extent that when he spoke of Peter stepping out of the boat to go to Jesus you could almost sense the lap of the water against the boat."

In 1935 a gospel quintet of black musicians came from Cleveland, Ohio for special meetings at the Welcome Hall. In the United States the quintet attracted large congregations, yet they were humble enough to come to the Welcome Hall in Cambrai Street. The group's leader, Brother Lacey, and his wife, faced one another on the platform and sang many songs to the glory of God. One catchy song the people enjoyed was The Grumbler's Song. They brought great gladness to the people who bubbled over with the joy of the Lord and were greatly blessed as they listened to these gifted singers harmonise their voices.

Fred Brown returned to the Welcome Hall in 1937, and on this occasion he was accompanied by his new bride who was a very gifted musician. In the United States she conducted a radio programme every morning at seven o'clock. During Fred's second visit to the Welcome Hall God again blessed their ministry and many souls were saved.

In 1939 the Rev. Gnania Jos from India paid a visit to the Welcome Hall. Prior to his conversion Gnania had been a disciple of Gandhi and toured India with this famous mentor. He propagated Gandhi's message until one day he found the Lord and He completely changed the direction of his life. His visit to the Welcome Hall was a time of great blessing. The Hall was packed every night with many standing outside the doors and windows trying to see and hear what was going on. One evening before his message he announced the hymn "Who is on the Lord's side? Who will serve the King?" The service was interrupted when a very tall man stood up and said, "I will be on the Lord's side I will serve the King." No sooner had he spoken when many others in the congregation stood to their feet and publicly voiced their allegiance to God. The Holy Spirit swept through the hall. The preaching was set aside that night in order that souls could be dealt with. All over the church people were crying out for forgiveness and asking God for a deeper experience in sanctification. Revival fires had been lit and many transactions were made in heaven during those days of Gnania Jos' visit.

From those early days evangelistic missions continued to be held in the Welcome Hall for many years and God blessed in the salvation of many souls. Much of this work could not have gone on if Pastor Johnson had not had a band of spiritual men and women around him. Charlie Hamil, was one of the Pastor's right hand men. Jim White and Sam Morrow did a splendid job of maintaining the building in first class condition for many years.

Mrs. Johnson died on 16th January, 1948, and Pastor Johnson returned to live in the country. This certainly wasn't as convenient for the work at the hall, living so far out of the city. It was at this time Bobby and Tilly Snoddon opened their home to the pastor to stay there any weekend he needed to. This invitation was accepted, so he would travel from the country every Saturday afternoon and stay with the

Snodden's until the following Wednesday. This proved a great help to the pastor and a blessing to the Snoddons. Jack loved those times of fellowship with Bobby and Tilly. They were people of like mind and just lived for the Welcome Hall.

As well as evangelistic campaigns at home the Welcome Hall always had a vision for the evangelisation of the uttermost parts of the world and was involved in world missions. Jim Grainger, a mighty man of God, went to join C. T. Studd in the Congo in 1927. He was as gentle in character, as he was strong for God. For fifty-seven years he served God in the heart of Africa. He pioneered the southern area of the Congo, where the Name and message of Christ was unknown. Today, there are thousands of believers in that troubled land. Jim was deeply loved by the Africans. After a brief illness in 1984 he died, and his passing was greatly regretted by all who knew him.

Just prior to Jim's home going he was at a meeting when the challenge was given to dedicate one's life to the Lord afresh. Jim, although advanced in age and having spent over half a century in Africa, was the first on his feet, offering himself unreservedly to God. Within a week Jim was at home with his Lord.

Billy Creighton was another early pioneer missionary. He was a teacher in the Welcome Hall Sunday School when he heard the call of God to full-time service. He joined the Baptist Mission and for twenty-three years he served the Lord until he was called home to higher service.

Bobby Milliken went to the Congo also where he spent over thirty years serving the Lord. Owing to the unsettled conditions because of the Zimba uprising in the Congo in 1964, Bobby and his wife Ivy left Africa and went to pioneer a work in Northern France. He had the joy of seeing a work established in the Miners Mission in France. After seventeen years Bobby and Ivy retired to England where they carried on a similar evangelistic work among the coal miners.

Harry Young before his conversion was an international boxer, a gambler, and a "Teddy Boy" from Ardoyne. He became a Christian through his brother Eddie. He joined the Welcome Hall were he was nurtured and guided in his spiritual life under Pastor Johnson. He felt the Lord leading him into full time Christian work. He studied at All Nations Bible College, and in the mid-fifties he went serve the Lord in Arabia. It was there he met and married Joan, an American missionary. They pioneered and established a medical work as well as helping to build up a New Testament Church in the Gulf.

Due to the physical disability of their eldest son they had to return to England and there they started a work among the Arab immigrants in Birmingham. Over the years he has had the joy of leading Muslims to faith in Jesus Christ. Harry went to be with his Lord suddenly in 1998.

Harry's brother Eddie was also a boxer and was a finalist in the Amateur Boxing Association Lightweight Championship of Northern Ireland. He was heavily involved in all the youthful activities and pursuits of his day. Eddie was converted at an open-air meeting, and subsequently the Welcome Hall became his spiritual home. Pastor Johnson looked on Harry and Eddie Young as the Apostle Paul looked on Timothy; they were his true sons in the faith.

Eddie's wife Sadie, nee Cosby, was raised in a Christian home in Cambrai Street. When she was eighteen Sadie came to know the Lord in Keswick Street Mission. Some years later she was invited by a friend to a W.E.C. prayer meeting in the Welcome Hall which was led by Mr. and Mrs. Snoddon. It was through these prayer meetings that Eddie and Sadie heard God's call for foreign missionary service.

After Bible college Eddie left for Senegal with WEC in 1958 followed by Sadie in 1960. They were married in the little church in Ziguinchor. For the next twenty years they laboured extensively in different ministries in that West African country until their circumstances changed and a new challenge brought them back to Northern Ireland— Eddie was invited to be the pastor of the Welcome Hall.

Many others were to follow the challenging example left by these great missionary pioneers from the Welcome Hall during Pastor Johnson's ministry. Billy Davidson went to South America; Alfred Williamson went into the Presbyterian ministry and became the minister of the Nelson Memorial Presbyterian Church, located not too far from the Welcome Hall; Jim White JR., went to Cliff College, then to the United States, where he entered into the Presbyterian ministry. Jim became a chaplain to the U.S. Armed Forces; Betty Young, a sister of Harry and Eddie, went to work for the Faith Mission, where she served the Lord until she was forced to return home owing to her parents' health; Ella Scott trained at the WEC Missionary Training College where she met Brian Butcher who became a Baptist pastor in England;   John Adams joined the Welcome Hall in the forties. He was a founding Member of the Woodvale Quartet.   Later he went to Dublin to serve the Lord where he remained until his home call in 1998; Philip Skelly served the Lord in the London City Mission and then moved to a small Baptist Church on the east side of London.

Pastor Johnson's ability and strength were no longer sufficient for the task at hand because of his age. One of the workers, Mr. Teddy Allen, was asked to oversee the work until a successor was appointed. Before his death, Pastor Johnson had the joy of presiding over the opening of the new building on 5th September 1959. The offering taken that day cleared any out-standing debt accumulated in its construction and the new church was opened free from debt and to the glory of God.

It was a thrilling day for Pastor Johnson. That building stands today as a monument and memorial of this faithful servant of God. Like the demolition of the old building Pastor Johnson also laid aside his earthly tabernacle on the 25th April, 1966 in order to be clothed with his heavenly house. He died in the Snoddon's front bedroom. Bobby and Tilly were with him to the very last when he made a triumphant entrance into heaven

In a wonderful way God planned for the man of His choice to be available at the right time to take pastor Johnson's place. Robert and Isobel Mackey and family were at home after nearly twenty years of serving the Lord in Liberia. They were helping at a Bible college near to Holywood, County Down. They were still in an unsettled frame of mind when a suggestion was put to them to consider the pastoral position at the Welcome Hall.

They both felt the Lord was in this move. Robert Mackey was inducted into the Welcome Hall in 1965. For the next five years Robert and Isobel did a splendid job. It was during their time that the Welcome Hall became a member of the Fellowship of Independent Evangelical Churches, and it's name was changed to the Welcome Evangelical Church.

Jimmy Stewart was one of many men who were saved during Mr. Mackey's time there. Jimmy was born in Oregon Street, and although reared in a Christian home Jimmy sowed his wild oats in his youth. One night Jimmy's mother invited him to a gospel meeting in the Welcome to hear Robert Mackey. God opened his heart to the gospel that night, on 29th September, 1968. In his life he proved God to be a present help in time of trouble.

> Four years had passed of blessed Christian fellowship, when tragedy struck! It was an ordinary day in the month of March, 1972. After some Saturday morning shopping, I was enjoying a relaxing cup of tea in the Abercorn Restaurant. Suddenly there was a terrific explosion. That's all I remembered for some days, until the surgeon broke the awful news, "I am sorry Mr. Stewart, but there was absolutely nothing we could do—both legs had to be amputated above the knees."
>
> I just couldn't believe it. The bottom seemed to be falling out of my world. The thought came, Why me Lord? To have to spend the rest of my life in a wheel chair, a helpless, hopeless cripple! As I lay in the hospital bed, after the surgeon had left, crushed, grief stricken and bewildered, the Saviour drew graciously close. "I'll never leave thee. My grace is sufficient for thee." I reached out in my need, and the joy of the Lord flooded my soul. I felt as though I had been transported to heaven. I knew from that moment all would be well, and the Lord has kept His word.

Two years later Jim was walking. Where? Up the aisle in the Welcome Church to be married to his beautiful fiancée, Miss Florence

Orr. Jimmy was no longer alone—God had provided a help meet for him.

Robert and Isobel Mackey left the Welcome Church in 1970 to return to WEC as international secretaries for the mission.

For the following two years John Galbraith who came from East Belfast pastored the Welcome Hall. John left the Welcome Church when he received a call to the pastorate of the East End Baptist Church on the other side of the city.

When Pastor Galbraith left Mr. Billy Lyttle who had been an elder for several years stepped into the gap and superintended the work along with others until the next pastor came.

Eddie and Sadie Young had returned from Senegal after twenty years of service with WEC International. The Welcome Evangelical Church issued a call to Eddie to be the new pastor of the flock. Eddie Young was inducted as pastor in the Welcome Church in 1980, and he with his wife Sadie faithfully served the Welcome Evangelical Church under God for the next fifteen years.

During those years Eddie Young organised many gospel missions. The evangelists included George Bates, Ivan Thompson, Patrick Kitchen and Sam Workman who held forth the Word of Life in evangelism at the Welcome Church. Eddie and Sadie continued to stimulate missionary interest at the church.

Times have changed since the days of the Shawlies when Amy Carmichael first caught the vision of erecting the old iron hall. The intervening years brought much blessing to the Welcome Hall through the ministry of various servants of God. Thousands of people were brought to Christ through the witness of the gospel. The text that Amy Carmichael chose for the wall still holds true, "That in all things He might have the pre-eminence."

In 1998 Jim and Sarah Thompson were appointed to lead the work at the Welcome Hall.

Sam Morrow, a member of the Welcome Hall for many years, wrote the following tribute to the work of the Welcome.

The Old Welcome Hall

The Old Welcome Hall has been taken down
Which has stood for seventy years,
Where many have the Saviour found
With broken heart and tears.
And many have been obedient
And answered the Saviour's call
And went out to serve as missionaries
From the Old Welcome Hall.

The Old Welcome Hall has served its time.
They have built a new one in its place,
But many souls still live and shine
As trophies of God's grace.
Because they learned at Sunday School
When they were children small;
The wondrous love of Jesus
That was taught in the Old Welcome Hall.

If the Old Welcome Hall could only speak
What a story it would tell,
Of sinners who did the Saviour seek
When He saved their soul from hell.
They enjoyed sweet peace and fellowship,
And many times I recall,
When the Lord came down and blessed us
In the Old Welcome Hall.

Chapter Seven

ThE IroN HalL ASSEMBlY

There is an interesting historical connection between the Iron Hall and the infamous St. Bartholomew's Day Massacre in France. When Protestantism was introduced to France between 1520 and 1523, many members of the nobility, the intellectual classes, and the middle class accepted its principles. At first the new religious group enjoyed royal protection, but the rise in the number of French Protestants excited the alarm and hatred of the French Roman Catholics. The religious hatred was intensified by political rivalry between the house of Valois, then in possession of the French throne, and the house of Guise. Civil war broke out between 1562 and 1598 and bitter battles were fought between the French Roman Catholics and Protestants during those years.

The Protestants were being severely persecuted. On St. Bartholomew's Day, August 24, 1572 the Queen Mother and the King ordered thousands of Huguenots to be massacred in Paris and in other parts of France.

Many found life in France intolerable under the ensuing persecutions and because of the evaporation of religious liberty hundreds of thousands of Huguenots fled to England, Germany, the Netherlands, Switzerland, and the English colonies in North America. The total emigration is believed to have been between four hundred thousand to one million, leaving one million Protestants in France.

In this dispersion the "Le Pere" family moved to England and settled there. To ease their integration into English life the family changed their name to Lepper. The Leppers soon blended into English society and established a prosperous company which imported tea from India and Ceylon.

Mr. Charles Lepper, a descendent of the Le Pere family, was born in the middle of the nineteenth century. His father descended from the French Huguenot line and his mother was of Scottish descent.

When he was a young man Charles Lepper's father sent him to Trinity College, Dublin, to study Law. It was there in Dublin that he felt a very real and deep impression of the Spirit of God to begin to work in his heart.

From the time when Mr. Lepper came to a saving knowledge of the Lord Jesus Christ as his own Saviour at the age of nineteen he felt a deep constraint to serve his Lord. When he heard his Master's call he devoted his zeal and energy, and his love and eagerness to the service of the Lord.

Mr. Lepper got a job as a Tea Merchant in Belfast and moved to the North of Ireland. He and his wife bought a house in outskirts of Bangor and they attended the new Brethren Assembly which met in the Victoria Rooms in Belfast. His uncompromising fidelity to his Lord and unswerving loyalty to the Word of God made him a great witness for the truth of the gospel. His radiant testimony and generous heart made him appreciate and enjoy fellowship with all who owned Jesus as Lord, and he always loved to respond with overflowing liberality to every appeal from those needing assistance.

Charles Lepper employed all of his talents to spread the knowledge of his Saviour. He wrote several books which were widely circulated in the early twentieth century and through his instrumentality many were brought from darkness into light and from the power of Satan to God.

During the 1880s Charles Lepper felt constrained to become involved in the evangelistic outreach from the Victoria Hall into East Belfast. He commenced a Sunday School in the Mountpottinger Orange Hall to reach the many children of the area. He was encouraged by this endeavour and with the interest that was shown. The work diversified when Mr. Lepper and some others organised gospel meetings for adults. God blessed both works, and many people were converted by the grace of God. Soon there was a regular programme of weekly meetings and an encouraging number attended the services.

As the work grew and others got saved Mr. Lepper felt led of the Lord to purchase a piece of ground at the corner of Thorndyke Street, on Templemore Avenue in March of 1890. On this site he erected a building which became known as the Iron Mission Hall. Undoubtedly the hall earned its name because portions of the structure were made of corrugated iron.

Mr. Lepper was eager to evangelise the lost, but as the Mission grew he ensured that the work followed sound principles of Scriptural truth. Devoted and capable servants of the Lord ministered the Word of God, and soon the Iron Hall became the spiritual home for many believers. The work was carried on with apostolic fervour and made a telling impact on the densely populated Albertbridge Road community. From its conception and throughout its history the Iron Hall maintained a very strong emphasis on biblical ministry.

The early work developed so quickly that the early brethren felt it was necessary to call a full time evangelist to lead the work. The first person appointed to the position by the elders was Mr. Driver. Little information is available about this servant of God or about the dates of his ministry.

In 1909 Mr. Robert Graham followed Mr. Driver as the pastor of the hall. Many of his congregation worked on building the Titanic at the nearby Harland and Wolff Shipyard. In 1916 Pastor Graham was constrained to leave his ministry in East Belfast and went to work with the Glasgow City Mission.

Charles Lepper adopted the Iron Hall as his spiritual home. He continued to have a burden for the souls in that area. His love for and understanding of Christian literature was reflected by his own literary skills of which he left a rich legacy in the form of songs of hope and cheer for weary hearts. Several of his poems were dedicated to the work of the hall.

He dedicated one such poem/song based on Psalm 23 "to the little flock of 800 at the Iron Mission Hall, Mountpottinger." He wrote other songs for days of intercession at the Iron Hall during the closing days of the Great War in 1918.

Written for the Day of Intercession at the Iron Hall, April 17,1918. (Psalm XLVI.)

Oh God, our Refuge and our Strength,
In trouble we would humbly bow;
We here engage in earnest prayer,
To cry for help; we need it now.

We will not fear though mountains quake,
Though waters roar and troubles rise
The river from the Throne above
Will bring us gladness from the skies.

The City of our God is safe,
Supplied from never-failing springs;
The people purchased by the blood
Are quite secure beneath His wings.

We never can be greatly moved
While in the midst our Saviour stands;
He is our help 'gainst all our foes,
And keeps us safely in His hands.

The Lord of Hosts with us abides;
God is our refuge and our peace;
Omnipotence is on our side,
And shall make cruel wars to cease.

He breaks the bow, He cuts the spear,
The chariots He burns with flame;
He speaks the word "Be still, and know"
That Gideon's God is just the same.

On a visit to the Portstewart Convention in 1918 he mused at the great sea breakers rolling from the North Atlantic and put pen to paper and wrote:

In a Storm at Portstewart.

"What are the wild waves saying?"
The One who knoweth best,
Has likened them to sinners
Who cannot be at rest.

"The mighty waves," says Jesus,
"Have all gone over Me
That I might quell their raging
And find a calm for thee.

I plunged into deep waters,
I sank in miry clay,
That I might rescue sinners
Who drifted far away."

If waves arise He speaketh,
They all obey His will,
And His blest voice commandeth
The wildest waves, "Be still."

Oh, what a calm He giveth,
Our troubles all shall cease
When once the voice of Jesus
Proclaimeth peace, sweet peace.

An insight into the zeal and depth of dedication Mr. Lepper was reflected in another poem he wrote in which he expressed the conflict he experienced in Christian service.

The Conflict

Now is the time to serve Him,
Here in the battlefield;
Let saints put on their armour,
And fight with sword and shield.

A conflict is before us,
But we have nought to fear;
Our Captain has assured us
That victory is near.

Then lift your heads, ye soldiers,
And sing along the road;
Proclaim in simplest language,
"Salvation is of God."

This is the hour of trial,
Temptations may be strong,
But soon the morning dawneth
For which we've waited long.

We hear the Master's footsteps,
He starts upon the way,
To end this night of sadness
With one eternal day.

Look up, ye blood-bought children,
The hour is drawing near,
When every ransomed sinner
In glory shall appear.

Those who had the privilege of enjoying Mr. Lepper's personal friendship and profited from his godly influence felt a keen sense of loss when he was called into the presence of the Lord on 1st November

1923. His widow remained associated with the Iron Hall until her home call years later.

The brethren at the Iron Hall extended an invitation to Mr. Tocher to become the full-time evangelist at the Iron Hall. Mr. W. E. Tocher had come to Northern Ireland as an evangelist, commended from the Brethren movement near Dundee. He and his wife travelled throughout Ulster in a horse drawn caravan conducting evangelistic meetings in many isolated rural areas.

He accepted the invitation and commenced his ministry in the hall around 1916. He was a very competent minister of the Word, and crowds flocked to hear him. Over eight hundred people attended Tocher's meetings at the Iron Hall.

Seemingly nothing daunted Tocher. During the General Strike of 1919 some locals tried to force him to cancel the meetings at the Iron Hall. Employees from the shipyard and the other great industries of East Belfast, downed tools with workers all over the British Isles. They were demanding a reform of the standard working week from fifty-four hours to forty-four hours. "Work no more 'til forty-four," was their slogan. In accordance with the strike's organisers, households were obliged to turn all lights off— gas and electric. Mr. Tocher was determined, strike or no strike, the Lord's work must go on. At the regular time the lights at the Iron Hall were lit as usual for the mid-week evening meeting. A deputation of burly union men arrived at the door of the meetinghouse and told the preacher in no uncertain terms, "Put your lights out or we will put them out for you!" Tocher was not to be intimidated, and although he complied with their directive he sent word to all the people in the locality to bring their oil lamps to the meetings in future until the strike was over. The meetings continued unabated.

During Tocher's early years of ministry at the Iron Hall Ulster's renowned evangelist, W. P. Nicholson, conducted several evangelistic missions in East Belfast at which hundreds of people were converted. Many of these converts found their way to the corrugated iron building at the corner of Thorndyke Street to enjoy the powerful and effective preaching of W. E. Tocher.

Mr. Tocher also reaped an abundant harvest of converts through his own preaching and soon The Iron Hall was packed to capacity and at times it was bursting at the seams. To be sure of securing a seat it was necessary to arrive at the hall at least half an hour before the service began.

Such growth meant that the Hall had to be enlarged. The corrugated iron sides of the building were removed and replaced by brick walls which were built to the outer perimeter on both sides of the site. Soon afterwards the front and rear of the Hall had to be extended to their maximum also. With these renovations the corrugated iron, which gave the hall its name was discarded, but the name Iron Hall remained.

When Mr. Tocher terminated his ministry at the Iron Hall he was succeeded by Mr. Cooke who commenced his pastorate at the Hall in 1935 and remained there in that position for the next three years.

During the vacancy that followed Pastor Cooke's departure great responsibility fell on the elders to minister the Word of God at the Iron Hall while they prayed about a replacement. It was during a visit from Mr. Alexander Marks, a blind Jew who was invited to minister to the congregation for a period of six weeks that the answer came.   Mr. Marks informed the elders that Mr. T. E. Evans was returning home to Wales from missionary service in India and might be interested in the pastoral ministry.   Upon this recommendation the leaders of the Iron Hall approached the former missionary about the matter, and Mr. Evans perceived that the Lord was opening a door for him in East Belfast.

In 1939 Mr. and Mrs. Evans moved to Belfast to engage in this new sphere of ministry at the Iron Hall. Pastor Evans ministry was more of a personal nature rather than on the public platform. He had a warm disposition and regularly visited the hospitals and prisons. He called upon many homes in East Belfast to meet people surrounding the hall. He was more of an evangelist and missionary than a Bible teacher and was a keen soul winner. His bright Welsh disposition shone through in his preaching and he would suddenly burst into song in the middle of his sermon and sing as only a Welsh man could. He was a very caring pastor and was loved and appreciated by all.

Pastor W. E. Tocher

Dr. Henry Montgomery

Amy Carmichael

William Gilmore

Street visitation

Personal work

Poverty and drink - twin evils of the Shankill

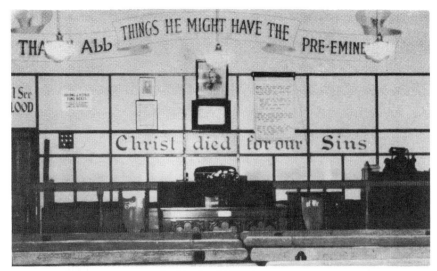

Inside the Old Welcome

Typical Shankill scene outside the Berlin Arms, c. 1900

The Iron Hall destroyed by German bombs in the 1940s

The Coalmen's Testimony Band March of Witness 1950

Ormeau Road Gospel Hall

The New Welcome Building

Kilburn Street City Mission

Olivet Hall

Ebenezer Gospel Hall, Oldpark Road

Kimberley Street Hall

Foundry Street Mission Hall

Apsley Hall

The early part of Pastor Evans' ministry was during the Second World War. He guided his congregation through this difficult time of great danger and catastrophe. The infamous German Blitz brought enemy aircraft over the city raining down their deadly bombs on the helpless population. In the space of a month in 1941 Belfast suffered three devastating air raids. On Easter Tuesday 745 men, women and children were killed, the highest casualties in any one raid outside London. Whole streets of terraced houses and quiet suburbs were destroyed. In all 950 people died in the raids. Tragically Thorndyke Street took a direct hit from a German bomb and most of the houses were destroyed with a heavy loss of life.

Pastor Evans visited the bereaved families bringing the comfort of the Scriptures to many broken hearts and shattered homes. The Iron Hall building suffered extensive damage and had to be virtually rebuilt. Just as the local population showed great resilience in the face of these hostilities, the believers at the Iron Hall rallied round to rebuild their church for the preaching of the Word of God.

At the end of the war a handful of men gathered together in the Iron Hall with the desire to sing hymns with music especially written for male voices. From this embryo the Iron Hall Gospel Male Voice Choir began. Over the succeeding years the choir developed their mission to one of gospel outreach—singing, testifying and preaching the Word of God. They travelled to Scotland and Southern Ireland in their ministry for the Lord. To be a member of the choir it was necessary to be able to testify to the saving and keeping power of the Lord Jesus Christ. The choir is still in existence today.

The Coalmen's Testimony Band was making a considerable impact throughout Belfast, and many people were converted at their first mission at Skipton Street Mission Hall. Pastor Evans attended these meetings and invited these Christian workmen to conduct an evangelistic mission at the Iron Hall. Night after night the coalmen sang the gospel, testified of God's grace in their lives and preached the Word of God in the plain man's language. More than fifty people trusted the Saviour during this mission which lasted for one month.

In 1952 Mr. Muir, a famous herbalist from Glasgow, conducted a children's mission for two weeks at the Iron Hall. This was a great time of blessing with over six hundred boys and girls attending each night.

Several years later two workers from Child Evangelism Fellowship, Mr. Sammy Seymour and Raymond Lunn, both from Kimberly Street City Mission, conducted another children's mission. Sammy Seymour arrived every night with a small attaché case with a bushy tail hanging out from one end. The curiosity to know what was in the case enthralled the children. He threatened to open the case each night but kept their suspense going throughout the two weeks. Sammy was a bright and happy worker and called the Christian boys and girls Glowing Smilers. Raymond played the accordion every night and composed a chorus for the occasion.

The meetings attracted more than one thousand boys and girls each night. The impact on the district was phenomenal and even the Belfast Telegraph sent a reporter to write a feature article on the "Glowing Smilers" at the Iron Hall. Scores of children professed faith in Christ, and a great follow-up programme ensued after the mission.

In the mid-fifties the former "The Iron Hall Mission," was reconstituted as the "Iron Hall Assembly." New elders were appointed as trustees of the property. These were Mr. Alexander Campbell, Mr. Jack Kane, Mr. Bertie Campbell, Mr. Billy Hinds, and Mr. Neil McCloy.

A wide variety of speakers were invited to preach at the Iron Hall. Jock Troop came from the Tent Hall in Glasgow. Mr. Callaghan, Mr. Reggie Squires, Mr. Leech and Mr. Michael Perrot all travelled from Dublin to minister at the Iron Hall. Dr. Herbert Lockyer from the United States spoke at special conferences. Pastor Evans invited Pastor Tocher to preach at the Iron Hall before Mr. Tocher died in 1956.

After twenty-three years of ministry in East Belfast Pastor Evans due to ill health retired and returned to his native Wales in 1962. Amazingly Mr. Evans made a great recovery from his illness and was able to return to India for a year in the service of his Lord.

Mr. Evan's departure left a void and brought greater responsibility on the elders of Iron Hall, especially Alec Campbell and Jack Kane who were in leadership of the work.

As the church congregation prayed for guidance to find a man to fill the vacancy attention was directed to Mr. Jack Mitchell of Glasgow. The Mitchell family was well known to the members at the Iron Hall for Mr. Mitchell Sr. had frequently visited Easter Conventions as the guest soloist.

Mr. Jack Mitchell had been involved with Pickering and Inglis, an evangelical publishing company in Glasgow, for many years and was much in demand as a preacher in the Brethren movement throughout Scotland. He had developed good communication skills and had a tremendous gift as a Bible teacher. The elders at the Iron Hall were convinced in their hearts that Jack Mitchell was God's man for East Belfast and sent an invitation for him to be their pastor. Mr. Mitchell had a corresponding assurance that this was God's opening for him, and in January 1966 Mr. Mitchell commenced his pastorate at the Iron Hall.

Under his leadership the Iron Hall became a distinctive centre for a sound and solid Biblical teaching ministry. Mr. Mitchell's Scottish accent added warmth to his fluency as he preached on rich Bible truths on the Lord's day and at the Monday evening Bible study.   People from beyond the bounds of East Belfast were attracted to the ministry at the Iron Hall. It was recorded in City Week, 14th April 1966, that "under Mr. Mitchell large audiences are again a feature of the Iron Hall especially on Sunday and Monday evenings, and older members of the fellowship say that he reminds them of Mr. Tocher."

In 1967 Mr. Mitchell introduced Mr. Ronnie MacMillan, a fellow Scot, to the fellowship at Templemore Hall, just down the avenue, and as a result they invited Mr. MacMillan to become their pastor. The close friendship between Pastor MacMillan and Pastor Mitchell enabled them to lead Templemore Hall and the Iron Hall into an United Easter Convention which continues to this day.

Mr. Mitchell's ministry was in much demand throughout Northern Ireland, and frequent invitations came from his native Scotland and England to speak at prophetic conferences. Mr. Mitchell introduced many preachers to the Iron Hall for special occasions. These included Dr. Allister Noble, Andrew McFarland, Geoffrey Bull, Archie Naismith and Billy Strachan.

Pastor Willie Mullan conducted a great evangelistic mission at the Iron Hall during Pastor Mitchell's time there and over one hundred people trusted the Saviour in the meetings. The Hall was packed to capacity night after night. As the number of people grew each night some believers left their seats in the church to allow room for the unconverted. The galleries and upper room were filled, and additional seating was placed in the vestibule of the church to accommodate the crowd.

The Hall underwent a major refurbishment in the early seventies and this gave more room for the growing congregation. Mr. Mitchell's ministry continued to be blessed even though the agitation and disruption of the Troubles restricted people's attendance at many church services during the seventies and eighties. The Monday night Bible Study increased in numbers so much so that they had to vacate the small upstairs room and use the main hall to contain the crowds attending the Bible Class.

Jack Mitchell completed twenty-one fruitful and blessed years at the Iron Hall and concluded his ministry there in 1987. His contribution to the ministry of the gospel in East Belfast during that time is impossible to quantify. The dynamic and blessing of God's servant continues to be felt to this day.

Mr. Mitchell's pending departure drew the attention of the Iron Hall's overseers to a young man who was the pastor at Carryduff Baptist Church. Denis Lyle was born into a Christian home in Banbridge, County Down. After his training at the Baptist College Denis accepted a call to Carryduff Baptist Church where God greatly blessed his ministry for eleven years.

After prayerful consideration the oversight decided to call Denis to become their new pastor. Denis accepted the call and commenced his ministry at the Iron Hall in May 1987. He quickly developed capable teaching skills which enabled him to continue the strong Bible teaching emphasis which has been characteristic of the Iron Hall for many years.

Denis Lyle also manifested tremendous evangelistic zeal and organised several evangelistic outreaches. He conducted a mission for three weeks with George Bates as the evangelist and the meetings were blessed by the Lord.   In June 1989 the Iron Hall combined with Templemore Hall for an evangelistic campaign in a tent at Orangefield Park. The meetings were conducted during a good spell of weather and hundreds attended each night as Denis Lyle and Victor Maxwell shared the preaching on alternate nights while Jackie Brown of CEF conducted special meetings for the boys and girls earlier each evening.   Ulster evangelist Ivan Thompson conducted a very successful mission at the Iron Hall with great numbers in attendance and many souls trusted the Saviour.   Roger Carswell from Leeds preached for an evangelistic outreach for two weeks in 1992.

Over the years the effect of the Iron Hall's witness has been felt far beyond the shores of Northern Ireland. Alex Stewart and Alex Ireland were both recommended by the Iron Hall to the work of Sudan Interior Mission in Nigeria in 1925. They and their wives gave a lifetime to the Lord's work in Africa.

Betty O'Neill, a nurse, served the Lord in the former Belgian Congo with Unevangelized Fields Mission and was caught up as a victim of the infamous Zimba uprising in 1964. Several of her close colleagues were martyred including Ruby Gray, a fellow nurse from Dromara.

Eric and Ann Magowan served the Lord in Africa with UFM. Ann attended the Sunday School at the Iron Hall and her family were members in the fellowship. Gareth, their son, is currently a member of the Iron Hall and is in training to be a missionary pilot with the African field in view.

Sharon Gray serves the Lord with Wycliffe Bible Translators in West Africa and is a linguistic consultant within her mission.

David Legge completed his theological training at the Baptist College and is the assistant pastor at Portadown Baptist Church. The oversight and members of the Iron Hall have called David to be their pastor, this is a big step for a young man, but God has gifted David and more importantly called him to this work.

Denis Lyle's ministry attracted large crowds both on the Lord's Day and on Monday nights for the Bible Study. Several of the series

Denis completed in these Bible studies furnished the material for two books that were authored by Pastor Denis Lyle.

Pastor Lyle was invited to conduct evangelistic campaigns in churches throughout Ulster and in Scotland. He had the opportunity to travel to Romania and minister God's Word there immediately after the overthrow of Communism.

After Mr. Drew Craig showed slides of needy work in Romania further contact was made with a small assembly in Moreni which is in north East Romania. The Iron Hall assumed the role of a sister assembly and pledged to help build a hall from the brethren in Romania. The building was started in 1992 and completed in 1995 at a cost of £22,000 which was donated by the Iron Hall Assembly. In 1996 Pastor Lyle, Alex Campbell and Billy Brown travelled to Romania with Drew Craig and other friends for the opening of this church .

Denis Lyle introduced several well-known preachers to the Iron Hall pulpit. Dr. Sidlow Baxter conducted three notable days of Bible ministry for them in 1994. Dr. Lehman Strauss held a week of meetings at the hall in 1997. Other men of God who ministered at the Iron Hall during Denis Lyle's time included Mr. Geoffrey Fewkes from Wales and Dr. Rex Mathie and Harold Peasley from South Africa.

The church marked the centenary anniversary of the Iron Hall in March 1990. Dr. Dwight Pentecost of Dallas Theological Seminary was the guest speaker for a special week long series of prophetic meetings. Night after night he opened the Scriptures and expounded great prophetic themes. These meetings attracted large crowds every night.

Over the years the Iron Hall has been given strong and capable leadership by its various pastors. It has also been well served by its devoted elders and deacons who have given unstilted dedication to the work. Mr. Bertie Campbell has been a member of the Iron Hall for most of his Christian life and is a most genial treasurer. Alex Campbell, a well-known Christian businessman, has been the secretary of the Iron Hall for over forty years. He was converted in the Iron Hall in 1943. These are only two of the ten elders who govern the work of the hall.

In addition to the leadership of the Iron Hall there is a capable group of Sunday School teachers, musicians and Christian workers who make their contribution to the glory of God.

Over the course of Pastor Lyle's eleven years in the ministry at the Iron Hall he was approached by several Baptist churches to consider a move to their pulpit. Repeatedly he resisted these approaches, until finally an invitation came for him to consider a call to Lurgan Baptist Church. Torn between his commitment to the Iron Hall and the challenge of moving into another sphere of work, Pastor Lyle did not find it easy to know what the Lord would have him do. After much prayer and sharing with the oversight at the Iron Hall, Denis left East Belfast and moved to Lurgan in February 1998.

The leadership of the hall is currently under pressure to make several vital decisions which will greatly effect the future of the work which Mr. Lepper started almost one hundred and ten years ago. Not only are they praying and considering a replacement for Pastor Denis Lyle, but they are also in negotiation with the Northern Ireland Housing Executive about either rebuilding on their current site or relocating to another area in view of the proposed housing redevelopment planned for the near future.

A modern chorus says, "Little is much when God is in it." This has certainly proved to be true in the history of the Iron Hall. The St. Bartholomew's Day massacre sent the Le Pere family to England, and one of their descendants, Charles Lepper, moved to Northern Ireland. Through the work and witness established by Mr. Lepper thousands of people have come to know the Saviour.

Chapter Eight

KNOCKNAGONEY HALL

In the latter part of the 1950s while the United States and the Soviet Russia raced each other to put satellites and space rockets into orbit around the earth, Belfast was trying to re-house its expanding population in satellite housing estates around Belfast. Some of these housing developments were enormous and provided dwellings for thousands of tenants migrating from older houses in the inner city which were being demolished.

On the east side of the city the Northern Ireland Housing Executive built a small but neat estate of red brick houses. It was sandwiched between the main Belfast to Bangor Road and the Old Holywood Road, and it gained its name from the link thoroughfare which was called the Knocknagoney Road.

Many families from different backgrounds were brought together to form a new community. Robert and Nancy Cousins originally relocated to Belfast from Annalong. They were allocated a new house in Knocknagoney Drive. They had worshipped at Templemore Hall.

Bobby and Minnie Ross from Church Street East Baptist Church left their former home on the Albertbridge Road and moved into a new house in the Knocknagoney estate. Jim and Olive Dixon, formerly of Templemore Hall, uprooted their family from Canada to return home to Northern Ireland and took possession of a new house in this same estate.

The Lord advances the work of the gospel either by sending His servants to particular locations or scattering them. The Lord's Hand was evident in drawing these three families together in the new Knocknagoney estate. In the process of meeting and getting to know new neighbours they found that they shared a common bond in Jesus Christ as Christians. After some conversations they mutually agreed that in the absence of any church in the area they had a responsibility to establish a witness for Jesus Christ and view this new housing development as a veritable mission field.

They approached Child Evangelism Fellowship to set up an outreach to reach the children of the area who were without Sunday School or children's meetings. Roy and Mary Deddis from Rathmore Street Mission Hall answered the invitation and started a series of Good News Clubs in the respective homes of the three families. The meetings continued with a good attendance indoors in the winter and outdoors in the summer evenings.

The success of this effort constrained the three men to venture farther and start a weekly gospel meeting in a house on the edge of the estate. In 1962 they rented an old house on the Old Holywood Road and after some renovations by Bertie Scott from Templemore Hall, the house was ready as a meeting place.

Bobby Cousins worked as a Co-op milkman. He also was a dedicated Christian and an untiring and enthusiastic soul-winner. He and his colleagues visited every home in the estate to witness to his faith in Jesus Christ. Few people had cars in those days, but Jim Dixon, a mechanic by trade, provided transport to take people to and from the meetings. He became greatly involved in the children's work. Bobby Ross was a constant helper and was ready to do anything that would help further the work of the gospel in that area.

A large tent was erected in the summer of 1963, and the Templemore Hall Male Voice Choir conducted a gospel mission for several weeks. In spite of some adversaries trying to sabotage the evangelistic effort by cutting the ropes of the tent, the Lord blessed those meetings and several people trusted Jesus Christ as Saviour. As a consequence of this mission an appeal for help was made to the assembly in Templemore Hall where Jim Dixon and Bobby Cousins still worshiped.

One Friday night after the weekly prayer meeting at Templemore Hall Bobby Cousins was speaking to Ken Brown, a member of the oversight. Bobby was aware of Ken's preaching ability and said to him, "We could do with a man like you in Knocknagoney."

"Where is Knocknagoney?" Ken asked, betraying his ignorance. Ken was soon to find out where Knocknagoney was for he was invited to speak at the 8:30 p.m. gospel meeting at the old renovated house on the following Sunday night. The person who had been booked to preach didn't turn up so Ken was called on at short notice to fill the gap. Ken admitted that he had no preparation, but he had heard Ian Paisley preach a sermon from Isaiah twenty-eight the previous night and decided to adopt the same message for his meeting at Knocknagoney. The Lord greatly helped him and as a result a sixteen-year-old girl was converted than night.

Ken was invited back to speak at another evangelistic meeting and soon found himself becoming increasingly involved in this fledgling work. Little did Ken Brown know that these initial visits to Knocknagoney would shape his ministry for the next forty years.

As the meetings took on a regular pattern and the attendance continued to increase the Knocknagoney Mission Hall was formally constituted. A committee was formed which consisted of Robert Cousins the chairman, Ken Brown the assistant chairman, Mr. Francey the secretary, Jim Dixon the treasurer and Bobby Ross a committee member. The Lord continued to bless the enthusiastic efforts and witness in the district and adults and young people were converted.

Pastor Willie Mullan and Dr. Ian Paisley and other preachers gave great support to the beginnings of this work and would often preach at

Knocknagoney after church on a Sunday night or at the midweek meetings. The children's meetings in particular were very encouraging—up to one hundred and fifty boys and girls attended

The consolidating of this work constrained the committee to look around for a more permanent meeting place. The Mormons were keen to enter the area and set up a work. Someone mentioned that they had made an approach to a local farmer, Mr. Reid, who had some land to sell across the road from the estate. The farmer refused to sell to the Mormons but was keen to do business with the Knocknagoney Mission Hall. He offered them an acre of ground and a farmhouse for £1,600. Although the price was reasonable the newly formed mission hall had no money to pay for the deal. Furthermore, there were no wealthy people in the young congregation. Nevertheless, they prayed about the matter and decided to take some practical steps.

They consulted the manager of the Northern Bank at Strandtown about the property and the possibility of an overdraft. The manager, a devout Christian, encouraged them to go ahead with the purchase of the land. He assured them the bank would lend them the money providing they got twelve guarantors who would each give a security for £150. There was one other important stipulation made with the bank loan; a church building had to be completed on the site within three years.

The group at Knocknagoney felt this was the green light of approval they needed to proceed with the purchase of the property. They had no difficulty in finding twelve Christians guarantors. Templemore Hall immediately arranged a Saturday evening Praise Service to raise funds for the hall and Ian Paisley preached to more than six hundred people on that occasion. At the end of the meeting collection boxes were circulated to the congregation. They received a substantial offering that evening at Templemore Hall, and the assembly pledged their practical support for the new work in Knocknagoney.

The believers at Knocknagoney were overwhelmed by the response to their appeal for help. The combined generosity of many people, and the sacrificial giving of those closely involved in the work liquidated the debt to the bank in a short time.

The next priority was saving money to erect a suitable building on the newly acquired site. Again God provided for their need through the assistance of fellow believers. Mr. Marsh drew up the plans for the new church and gave his services free of charge. The men from Knocknagoney rolled up their sleeves and dug the foundations with a pick and spade. There were many blisters and sore limbs as a result of the manual labour—Ken Brown ended up with a strained back and spent twelve weeks in hospital. However, the fellowship was good and the teamwork greatly enhanced the fellowship and sense of co-operation in the hall.

Mr. Cyril Stevenson from Kilkeel donated three thousand cement blocks to the work. Another contractor sent several lorries to transport the blocks to the site. One bricklayer was employed to work on the building. After hours Hubert Brown, a bricklayer and a well-known gospel singer from Lisburn, came straight from his work every night and continued bricklaying until dark. The men at Knocknagoney mixed cement and carried bricks to Hubert. The roofing was contracted out to an outside firm. The combined force of voluntary and paid labour continued for almost two years until the building was completed.

During the two years of construction the meetings continued in the rented house on the Old Holywood Road. The founders of the work felt that it was time to change the status of the fellowship from a mission hall to a church assembly. In April 1966 the fellowship was registered as Knocknagoney Christian Brethren. Elders were appointed to the oversight of the hall on Sunday, 23rd April 1966. They were Robert Cousins, Bobby Ross, Ken Brown and Jim Dixon. The congregation was largely made up of those who had been converted through the witness of the hall during the initial years.

The new Knocknagoney Hall was opened in 1968 with a full day of Bible Conference. Those invited to attend the opening were representative of all who had helped in the ministry of the mission hall since its inception. Mr. W. P. Moore a businessman in Belfast, was the chairman on that opening day. Hubert Brown and Betty Young were the invited soloists. Pastor Willie Mullan, Dr. Ian Paisley, Rev. Bertie Cooke and Dr. Hamilton Moore preached the Word of God.

The opening of the new building gave fresh impetus for the work. Attendance greatly increased and the fellowship soon matured and consolidated. As well as the regular meetings at Knocknagoney Hall there were other opportunities for outreach. They held open-air meetings and went out on door-to-door visitation. In June of each year the members at Knocknagoney were responsible in organising a Bible conference in the Ballyveigh Orange Hall near Annalong. This developed into a special annual outing to the Mournes in the early part of the day and after they had eaten a meal, they would attend the conference meeting.

In June 1969 Bobby booked the preachers for the conference as usual and had organised the necessary arrangements for the outing. However, when the actual day for the outing arrived Bobby was not able to attend because he had not been feeling too well. Bobby went to the doctor and was referred to the hospital. They diagnosed Bobby Cousins as having leukaemia. Bobby and Nancy and their young family were stunned with the news. It was a major blow to the fellowship into which Bobby had poured all his energy. The Christian public in East Belfast rallied round to pray for this devoted servant of God, but the Lord had higher plans. Bobby Cousins went to be with his Lord on 2nd July 1969.

Hundreds of people attended the funeral. It was a fine summer day, and Mr. Paisley conducted the funeral service in the open-air outside Nancy Cousins home. This was followed by another service in the Knocknagoney Hall where Pastor Mullan and Mr. Paisley preached to a packed building and the overflow crowd spilled out onto Knocknagoney Road. The influence and impact of Bobby Cousins' life in and beyond Knocknagoney was immense. Although he was not a preacher Bobby won many for the Saviour. His life had been an example and a challenge. His enthusiasm for the Lord's work inspired others to continue the work Bobby had dedicated himself to.

The void created by Bobby's death made it necessary for Ken Brown to sever his membership at Templemore Hall and give his full attention to Knocknagoney. Jim and Olive Dixon likewise relinquished their place at Templemore Hall in order to fully commit themselves to the work at Knocknagoney Hall. Jim took full responsibility for the children's work and maintained that involvement for well over thirty years.

As the Knocknagoney Assembly settled down it became established as a family church. The original core of believers who caught the vision for the work in the estate continue in the work to this day. After Bobby Cousins' death his widow, Nancy, devoted her life to the work at the assembly with many other like-minded ladies. In addition to the rich fellowship enjoyed in the regular activities the members of the hall frequently go away on outings to different parts of Ulster and even have gone for holidays in England together.

The annual Prophetic Conference in October continues to draw large numbers of believers from all over the city. At these meetings Ken Brown and an invited speaker highlight the great prophetic themes from the Scriptures.

The Knocknagoney pulpit is best characterised as a teaching ministry. Several students of the Scriptures are in fellowship in Knocknagoney, and they are given the opportunity to employ their gifts in preaching and teaching at the hall and in other assemblies.

Knocknagoney is a work that was born out of the vision and zeal of a concerned group of believers. They did not set out to build an assembly. They simply wanted to witness where they lived. Through their witness many were given the opportunity to hear God's Word preached and accept Christ as personal Saviour. God blessed their endeavours and built the work.

Chapter Nine

ThE EmmanueL HaLL

Roslyn Street

D r. Hyman Appleman and a team of American evangelists came to Belfast in the spring of 1959 at the invitation of Mr. Earnest Allen of the Revival Movement to conduct special evangelistic meetings to mark the centenary of the great spiritual awakening of 1859. The meetings were held in the Wellington Hall in Belfast's city centre, and other evangelistic campaigns were organised throughout the city.

One of those accompanying the evangelist was a young Texan by the name of Johnny Bisanyo. Before his conversion Johnny had been the leader of a popular dance band and a solo trombone player of some renown in his native U.S.A. As a Christian Johnny formed part of Hyman Appleman's evangelistic team and used his talent on the trombone for the glory of God.

Dr. Appleman perceived that Johnny extended beyond his musical abilities. As a result, during Dr. Appleman's visit to Northern Ireland, Johnny was invited to conduct special evangelistic meetings at the Roslyn Street Emmanuel Mission Hall. Night after night Johnny played the trombone and preached the gospel.

Mr. John Proctor and friends at Roslyn Street Hall worked hard visiting every home in the Woodstock and Cregagh Road area to invite people along to the special meetings. The meetings were bright; the singing was enthusiastic, and the hall was packed with people of all ages. Amongst many that trusted the Lord as Saviour at those meetings was a young man whose name was Stanley Barnes. He lived only a few doors from the Emmanuel Hall, and he and his seven brothers had attended meetings at the hall throughout their childhood. That young man later went to Spain with his wife Ina as a missionary, and today Stanley is the minister of Hillsborough Free Presbyterian Church.

The evangelistic mission was a turning point in the life of Stanley Barnes as well as for the new evangelist, Johnny Bisanyo. As a result of God's blessing on his ministry in Roslyn Street Johnny felt constrained to embark on an evangelistic ministry. This eventually led Johnny into the pastorate of the First Baptist Church of Houston, Texas, and later he became the president of the Southern Baptist Convention of the United States.

In an amazing cycle of divine providence Stanley Barnes authored a book entitled "All for Jesus". It traced the ministry of William Patteson Nicholson whose preaching had a great bearing on the founding of the work of the Emmanuel Mission in Roslyn Street which in turn led to Stanley's own conversion.

In 1922 W. P. Nicholson conducted a very successful evangelistic mission at Newtownards Road Methodist Church, at the Albert Hall on the Shankill Road and in St. Enoch's at Carlisle Circus. The success of these missions prompted the Kirk Session at Ravenhill Presbyterian Church to extend a hearty invitation to W. P. To conduct an evangelistic crusade at their church.

The invitation was accepted and the mission commenced in February 1923. As was the custom at Nicholson's missions he held special Men's Only Meetings for the shipyard workers. Led by a Salvation Army Silver Band, a large body of working men who had just finished their day's work, marched from the shipyard to the church, but when they got to the church the gates were closed.

The Rev. John Ross recalled, "When the gates were opened, the crowd was so large that the men got wedged between the pillars, and so fierce was the struggle to get in that the central pillar was moved from its place." The men were eventually admitted into the building, and that night Mr. Nicholson preached with amazing power.

About halfway through his message someone threw papers over the front of the gallery. Mr. Nicholson enquired what this disruption was all about. The culprit was a notorious gambler and he replied, "These are gambling papers." That evening he was gloriously saved. More than one hundred other men passed through the enquiry room, and many of them made definite decisions for Christ.

On the following day one of the gambler's friends said to him, "You are a lucky fellow, the two horses you backed yesterday were winners."

"Oh," he said, "no more of that for me. I was in Ravenhill Church last night, and I put all I had on One Who is always a Winner—the Lord Jesus Christ." From that day on he lived an out-and-out life for Christ.

Many men from the shipyard were gloriously converted, and as a result Harland and Wolff Shipbuilders were obliged to open a large shed in which to store the tools and other items of property which had been stolen and were being returned. This large storage shed became known as the Nicholson Shed.

W. P., as he was referred to, received a letter from Messrs. Musgrave.

Dear Sir,

We beg to acknowledge the receipt of tools returned by one of our own men, who signs himself ex-worker, and we thank you for the good influence you have used in this particular case. It will gratify you to know that we have heard of other similar cases directly attributed to your good work.

John Proctor from the shipyard was also saved at the mission in Ravenhill Church on 23rd February 1923. His interest in the meetings was aroused after hearing the sound of the Salvation Army Band leading the men as they marched from the shipyard to the church. Out of curiosity he went along to see and hear for himself what was happening. On that night John's heart was arrested by the Holy Spirit and he was suddenly and gloriously won for Jesus Christ. The next evening his sister Ellen trusted the Lord as her Saviour. From the moment of his conversion John Proctor sought to know and do the will of God. John did not know then that God was already preparing a work for him in East Belfast.

Mr. Alfred F. Downham, a well-known Christian businessman who lived in Lennoxvale on Belfast's Malone Road, was a very active member of Great Victoria Street Baptist Church. He was anxious to serve the Lord in the Sandy Row area, and as a result of his outreach activities he built a mission hall in 1923 in Wellwood Street which runs between Sandy Row and Great Victoria Street. He named the hall Emmanuel Mission No. 1. The work in that hall flourished and many were saved. Encouraged with what God had done in this side of town he felt the Lord leading him to extend his outreach and the work of the mission to East Belfast.

Mr. Downham surveyed the area and made various inquiries about the work that already existed there. John Proctor was just a new convert at this time, and he heard of Mr. Downham's burden. The two men shared a vision to establish a work for God in the area. Very soon John Proctor was invited by Mr. Downham to preach in Wellwood Street Hall and other mission halls and churches in Belfast.

After some negotiations Mr. Downham purchased a plot of land in Roslyn Street on which he erected a wooden hall. On 1 October 1932, the hall was opened for the glory of God and for the preaching of the gospel. This new hall in Roslyn Street was called Emmanuel Mission No. 2.

Although John Proctor did not have the advantage of formal Bible School training, he was endowed with great spiritual gifts. He was an able Bible teacher and was a very talented communicator with boys and girls to whom he endeared himself so easily.

John Proctor was invited to become the pastor of the new Emmanuel Hall in Roslyn Street. He accepted the call and was inducted on the same day the hall was opened. Mr. Lipton, a converted Jew, was the guest speaker for the special occasion.

Mr. Proctor served there until he retired in 1987 and through the years of faithful ministry with his wife Margaret at his side, he had the joy of seeing hundreds of men and women and boys and girls won for Jesus Christ. He became a legend in the immediate district. Everybody knew Pastor Proctor and he knew just about every family on the Woodstock Road. Many sought his counsel in domestic situations. Young couples consulted him about their marriage plans, and he always had wise advice for them. He identified with the elderly and infirmed whom he visited regularly and was not afraid to put his hand into his pocket and help some needy family passing through hard times. John was so well liked that the Roslyn Street Emmanuel Hall became commonly known as Proctor's Hall—a tribute to the man.

The work in Roslyn Street flourished under John's leadership. A new brick building was erected in 1934. The same could be said of John Proctor as was said of John the Baptist, the forerunner of Christ, in John 10:41-42, "John did no miracle: but all things that John spake of this man were true. And many believed on Him there."

Throughout his years of ministry John organised many evangelistic missions such as the one Johnny Bisanyo conducted. John Proctor was steadfast in his work, in season and out of season, and he preached the gospel and reached the district surrounding the hall for the Saviour. Emmanuel Hall was always well attended and the Sunday School was packed to overflowing when Pastor Proctor was at the height of his ministry. Sunday School excursions required thirteen buses to transport the children and their parents to a nearby seaside resort. Before each bus left Pastor Proctor would step on board and pray with the children before they departed. He repeated this exercise at the end of the day before the buses returned to Belfast. His genuine and consistent godly influence gave great authenticity to the message he preached from the pulpit and was a great testimony to the Saviour Whom he served.

Mr. Proctor wanted to make himself available and accessible to the local people. He never learned to drive so he walked anywhere he needed to go. When he had to travel a distance he would use public transport, and on that he met people to whom he invariably witnessed of his Lord.

In 1987 the hall suffered a minor fire and had to be refurbished.

John Proctor retired from full-time work at the hall when he was eighty-eight years old, but he maintained an active interest in the work of the Emmanuel Hall until he died on 26 August, 1991. He was ninety-two years old. His two sons Albert and Noel survived him.

After his death a letter was found among his possessions. It was from the famous Tent Hall in Glasgow. Following the death of Jock Troop, the Scottish evangelist of great renown, the trustees of the Tent Hall wrote to John Proctor inviting him to be the superintendent of Glasgow's foremost evangelistic centre. Mr. Proctor graciously declined the invitation indicating that he felt his life's work was at the Emmanuel Mission Hall in Roslyn Street.

Mr. Ernie Stitt, a member of Roslyn Street for more than fifty years and currently the secretary of the hall, wrote of his beloved late pastor:

He was small in stature but as God's choice, he was humble, gifted and a loving man but above all a great man of prayer. He was always concerned about the spiritual welfare of the people in the area.

When Pastor Proctor became frail in mind and body the board of trustees of Emmanuel Hall had to make a painful decision—what do we do in this situation? They prayed for God's guidance and help to show them who would be a suitable replacement to lead the flock. Norman Stewart who for many years was Pastor Proctor's right hand man, suggested Jack Craig from Clifton Park Baptist be invited to pastor the Hall. Jack was already a trustee of the hall and this made it easy to explain the awkward situation. Pastor Craig fully understood and graciously accepted the responsibility as Pastor and always addressed John Proctor as 'our Senior Pastor' until his home call.

Pastor Jack Craig was inducted on April 1987. He brought with him all his warmth and enthusiasm for the work in the city. Jack Craig had to retire from the leadership of the Emmanuel Hall in October 1992 due to ill health.

Ernie Stitt wrote of Pastor Craig:

"Pastor Jack Craig took up the challenge of the work and he proved to be a worthy replacement for Pastor Proctor. He was a great Gospel speaker and singer, and I along with many others looked forward especially his reading of the Scriptures. It was so unfortunate that his wife Thelma did not enjoy the best of health and needed quite a lot of attention but to his credit he never complained. Unfortunately, heart problems resulted in Pastor Craig having to resign. We praise God that through surgery and rest he made a good recovery and still takes an active interest in the work of the Lord."

Eighteen months later they called Mr. William McNaughten to replace Jack Craig. Billy was converted under the preaching of artist/ evangelist and former President of Moody Bible Institute, George Sweeting, He and his wife, Myrtle, were originally members of Templemore Hall until he was called on to lead the work at Banbury Street Mission Hall. Billy, a very able man in the Word of God, accepted a call to the Emmanuel Hall and was inducted in February 1994.

Ernie Stitt commented, "Those who attended the Emmanuel as members and friends fully appreciate God's answer to our prayer. As a Bible teacher Bill McNaughten has no peers."

A short time later Ron Weare was appointed as a visitor to the aged and infirmed in support of Pastor McNaughten's work. Ron had previously been the pastor at Beersbridge Road Elim Church in the mid 1970's, and he and his wife Gwen brought invaluable Christian experience which they wisely employed at the Emmanuel Hall.

The Emmanuel Hall has also been blessed with a great body of faithful workers who have made a valuable contribution to the success of the work. They have been responsible for the Sunday School, the

Women's Fellowship meetings, and the children's outreach. Today the Hall continues under the wise leadership of Ernie Stitt, Norman Stewart and Albert Proctor as elders, the latter being former Pastor's son. Samuel Sloan and Samuel Craig are the faithful deacons that serve the congregation on the Woodstock Road.

The Emmanuel Mission Hall was born in a time of great blessing and revival. It has been an instrument of great blessing to many throughout almost seventy years of its history. Those who guide the Emmanuel Hall today pray and plan for continued blessing as they pass over the threshold into the twenty-first century.

Chapter Ten

RATHMORE STREET MISSION HALL

s a boy I was reared on the Donegall Road in West Belfast but during the War I lived at my Granny's house at the lower end of Rathmore Street on the lower Ravenhill Road in East Belfast. Urban Sociologists tell us now that the tightly compacted rows of small terraced houses were often the impoverished and disadvantaged districts of the city. As children you could have fooled us for we were as happy as the day was long. I still remember playing in the wide open spaces of the Ormeau Park and chopping down bushes for the bonfire in the Botanic Gardens - that is until old Rubber Neck the Park Ranger caught us.

My boyhood memories of life on the Ravenhill Road are vivid. The regular blackouts and the air-raid sirens howling their warning repeatedly night after night underlined the danger people faced because they lived near the shipyards and other great industries. I remember being warned to stay away from the large emergency water tank beside the prefabs at the corner of Shamrock Street, the smell of bread baking at the nearby Royal Bakery and Granda's carthorse called Barney. Added to all these boyhood recollections were a variety of children's meetings that I attended in the area and the notable characters that led these centres of evangelism.

Around the corner from Granny's house was the Boyd Endowment City Mission led by Billy Anderson who was an institution in himself. Up Rathmore Street Joe Wells was only half-way through his sixty-seven years as leader of Rathmore Street Mission Hall, and at the back of Granny's house was Ravenhill Road Evangelical Church where a new preacher had just arrived from up the country, Ian Paisley.

Rathmore Street, beginning at Shamrock Street coursed its way around a bend and up a hill for about half a mile to Cherryville Street. It was at the heart of a maze of small streets that formed a tightly knit community, which was bordered in a triangle by Ravenhill Road, Woodstock Road and My Lady's Road. The Rathmore Street Mission Hall sat neatly in the middle terrace of houses and blended in with the houses that were built just prior to the end of the nineteenth century.

The history of Rathmore Street Hall is rather vague as no records can be traced, although it is known that ladies from Victoria Hall had a Bible Study in Rathmore Street around 1890. But by word of mouth it was passed down through the generations at the Rathmore Street Hall that the mission was an outreach from Donegall Square Methodist Church. The early history of the work of the mission certainly had strong Methodist connections.

A small stone plaque above the door of the old hall indicates that the premises were for the B. B. C.—Ballymacarret Bible Class. Apparently quite a few of these establishments were erected about this time for the study of God's Word.

The Ballymacarret Bible Class continued to use the hall for some time until it was eventually sold to a Mr. Burns. He in turn rented the hall for the preaching of the gospel, the stipulation being that it did not have a morning service and that it remained interdenominational in character. He made this stipulation in order to ensure that people went to their usual place of worship in the mornings. The first known brother to lead the work in the rented hall was Mr. Hadden who, from all accounts, was highly respected in the neighbourhood.

It was in 1921 that the history of the mission took a decided turn at the arrival of a young man named Joe Wells who came from the Old Tent Evangel on the Beersbridge Road. At this time Joe was a Methodist lay-preacher and was anxious to serve his Lord and grasped the formidable task of becoming the superintendent of the Rathmore Street Mission Hall. It was a daunting but challenging assignment for a young preacher when quite often the congregation consisted of only three or four ladies who attended regularly.

Joe Wells was a gentleman. He became well respected in the area and was a fervent preacher of the Word of God. It was Joe Wells persistence, tenacity and faith that kept the hall going, and surely that faithfulness was amply rewarded as he had the joy of seeing the work expand and many, many souls saved.

Initially Mr. Wells retained his membership at the Old Tent Evangel, but some time later he became a member of Grove Baptist Church. In later years he was appointed to be an elder in the Grove even though he continued as superintendent of Rathmore Street. He and his wife Agnes lived in Isoline Street on the Castlereagh Road where they raised their two children Eric and Lila who they had the joy of leading to Christ. Mr. Wells remained at Rathmore Street for sixty-seven years, fifty-three of which were spent as superintendent and fourteen years were as an elder when the hall reorganised to become the Rathmore Street Evangelical Church, but in all of this time, he never received a salary. He laboured in an honorary basis and until his retirement, earned his living as a collector for Burke's, a famous store on the Newtownards Road.

During World War II the Air Raid Protection used the hall for their organisational meeting in the district. For this they paid an annual fee of £10.00. In the 1940s the members of the hall were given the opportunity to purchase the building. This was a big challenge to them as the asking price was £100 which was a vast sum in those days as was reflected in 1944 when the total annual income for the hall totalled

£47.50. Bravely the small congregation, which was made up of working class people, rose to the occasion by their sacrificial giving to the Lord and also by very generous interest free loans from friends of the work.

Rathmore Street Mission was not only a haven of Christian fellowship, it was also a spiritual rescue shop reaching men and women in the community with the gospel. Frequently evangelistic campaigns were organised. In February 1945 the Ravenhill United Testimony Choir led by Joe Thompson had a very successful mission, and many were converted in the meetings. Encouraged by their first mission the same Ravenhill United Testimony choir returned in August 1946 for a second evangelistic mission.

The Shankhill Baptist Male Voice Choir also conducted a very fruitful evangelistic mission at the hall which resulted in many spiritual conversions. This was followed by another gospel mission in 1949 conducted by Pastors Hugh Orr from East End Baptist and William Wilson from Grove Baptist.

The harvest of souls was very encouraging in these evangelistic efforts, and Mr. Wells invited the Coalmen's Mission Testimony Band for a special mission in June 1950. During these meetings at Rathmore Street the Coalmen went visiting homes in the area. At one home Sammy Spence spoke to a good-living woman who protested her innocence when it came to a matter of sin. Sammy stressed that we are all sinners, and all need salvation. The woman replied to Sammy, "Mister, my name is on the church roll, and that is good enough for me." To this Sammy replied in his usual manner, "Missus, you might as well have your name on a sausage roll as on the church roll. Without Jesus Christ you can never get to heaven."

Other great missions followed with the Shankhill Baptist Male Voice Choir and pastors James Armstrong and Jim Irvine, and all resulted in many conversions. Besides these missions and the ongoing work of the gospel in the hall, there were open-air campaigns and children's missions held at regular intervals.

With great numbers being converted following these evangelistic missions Rathmore Street experienced its most fruitful era during the fifties and sixties. The Hall was packed to capacity. The young people's meeting often had in excess of fifty youth attending. Mr. & Mrs. Wells were greatly given to hospitality and their home was an open door. After church on Sunday evenings the young people would crowd into their house and enjoyed supper and a rich time of unforgettable fellowship.

The Rathmore Street Mandolin Testimony Band was a great feature of Mission during the 1950 decade. Ten musicians from the hall played their instruments and sang the gospel. They were in great demand throughout east Belfast and many souls were led to Christ through their witness for the Saviour.

There was always a very keen missionary interest at the Rathmore Street Hall with missionaries from all around the world visiting the fellowship at regular intervals. In 1951 Ethel Baily was sent to Bible College and was subsequently supported when she married Norman Dudgeon and went to India in 1954. Lily Donaldson was another missionary who was greatly supported by the friends at Rathmore Street. Fred and Ina Orr visited the Hall before going to Brazil and Fred on every furlough made a point of conducting meetings at the Mission Hall. In 1964 Fred conducted special meetings for Christians at the Hall. The meetings were packed out every night. On the final night he gave his testimony and challenged young and old to rededicate their lives to Christ and His cause.

Above the door of the hall was a very small area where six young men were sitting. God spoke to them all. Four of those young men, David Adamson, Brian Cargin, John Birnie and Norman Gray, dedicated their lives to Jesus Christ. David became a worker in the Irish Republic with C.E.F. Norman went to Spain as a missionary supported by the Hall. Today he pastors a church in London. Brian Carrigan and John Birnie did their theological training at the Baptist College in Belfast and became Baptist pastors. John later returned to be secretary and lecturer at the same Baptist College. Also associated with the Rathmore Street Hall at that time was young Billy Reid who went on to do theological studies and then into the Baptist ministry.

Besides giving money to missions Rathmore Street was known for many years as one of the distinguished contributors to Dr. Barnardo's

Homes. Year after year they were presented with the Barnardo's Shield in recognition of their generosity to this worthy cause.

The work at Rathmore Street was very much a team effort with Mr. Wells encouraging the workers. John Birnie Senior was greatly used in leading the young people's fellowship. Tom Wells, Joe Wells' brother, was ever ready to preach and help give leadership in the Hall. Tom often quipped that his initials, T. H. P. Wells, were an acronym for "Ten Horse Power Wells." Certainly Tom worked as if he were driven by steam but all recognised the power of God on this humble servant. Eric Wells, Joe's son, taught the large Bible Class each week. Stanley McDermott, Gordon Greenlees, Jack Moffet and a host of other workers all played vital parts in the work of the Hall.

In 1971 the members at the fellowship organised a surprise programme at the Hall to mark the 50th Anniversary of Mr. Wells ministry in Rathmore Street. In the "This is your Life" they not only brought Joe's family but many who had been converted, challenged and blessed through the fifty years of abounding in the work of the Lord.

In the early 1970s the fellowship took another step of faith with the purchase of Mr. and Mrs. McGregor's house which was joined to the Hall. With the acquisition of this house and the renovations that followed to incorporate it as part of the main structure another important milestone was reached in the history of the Assembly. On the 1st January 1974 the Rathmore Street Mission was transformed into the newly constituted Rathmore Street Evangelical Church with full Assembly responsibilities.

Leslie Armstrong was invited to conduct an evangelistic mission at the Hall just about this time and it was accompanied with times of blessing. Leslie's warm and persuasive preaching touched the hearts of many.

With the unanimous consent of the members the Rathmore Street Evangelical Church recognised brothers Joe and Tom Wells as being the first Elders in recognition of their labours for the Lord in the Mission.

The first Diaconate elected at that time consisted of Robert Lynas, Stanley McDermot, Andy Hunter, Jack Moffatt and Gordon Greenlees

It was in 1988 that Joe Wells went to be with the Saviour. I had the privilege of officiating at his funeral from his daughter Lila's home before his remains followed to Rathmore Street where he had faithfully and fruitfully served his Lord for sixty-seven years.

With the housing redevelopment throughout Belfast in the 1970's the terraces of old dwellings in Rathmore Street and most of those in the surrounding district were demolished.   Negotiations took place between the representatives of the Hall and the Northern Ireland Housing Executive about replacing of the Hall which was an intrinsic part of the district.   The only conditions under which the N.I.H.E. would contemplate a grant were providing the Hall was available for the use of the community at large for bingo sessions or social activities. The leadership could not compromise and follow down this road so they established their Building Fund and trusted the Lord to supply their need in building a new Hall. The Church building still retained its old facade in stark contrast to the new housing. This situation challenged the members of the Church to give even more to their Building fund to replace the cherished one-hundred-year-old building.

It was a great step of faith but God honoured His flock at Rathmore Street and on 24th October 1992 they opened a brand new building worthy of the work that they have carried for over one hundred years. After a short service outside the Hall Mr. Jack Moffatt, one of the oldest members at Rathmore Street Hall, turned the key and declared the new building open to the glory of God and for the preaching of the Gospel. The old stone tablet with the letters BBC (Ballymacarret Bible Class) which was displayed above the original building was retained as feature of the old structure. Rev. Ronnie McCracken was the special speaker at the opening of the new Hall.

With the new building providing better and more comfortable facilities the leadership organised an evangelistic Mission with Pastor Ivan Thompson.   The two weeks of special meetings were very well attended and several people trusted Jesus Christ as Saviour. Special ministry and Bible Teaching meetings with Jack Mitchell from the Olivet Hall appropriately followed the evangelistic meetings.

Today Rathmore Street Evangelical Church is a beacon of light in the same area they have occupied for more than a century. Under the leadership of Gordon Greenlees, Andrew Hunter, Stanley McDermott and Tommy Nelson they intend to keep on brightly shining until the Saviour comes again.

Chapter Eleven

THE ALBERT HALL

The evangelical fervour that captured Belfast at the turn of the century was greatly enhanced by the visits of Dwight L. Moody and Mr. Alexander in 1892 as well as that of Dr. R. A. Torrey and Mr. Alexander who returned in 1903. One man whose zeal shone like a burning star on the dark firmament of dismal social and economic problems of those times in Northern Ireland was Dr. Henry Montgomery. He impacted Belfast and beyond with an influence that would outlast his own earthly life's span. He was a man with a huge capacity for work, a lucid vision of the lost and a burning passion for souls; he also was a multi-gifted man of commanding personality who did not suffer fools nor idle Christians gladly.

Besides ministering to the multitudes he was a motivator. When he was the minister of Albert Street Presbyterian Church Dr. Montgomery engaged a former seaman and recently graduated student from the Bible Training Institute in Glasgow as an assistant minister. That student and young preacher was William P. Nicholson. These two men made a rare pair which impacted Ulster for decades to come. By Mr. Nicholson's own admission he considered that Dr. Montgomery was one of the greatest influences on his life which under the sovereign hand of God was used to win tens of thousands for the Saviour both in his native Northern Ireland and across the world.

William Nicholson was greatly challenged by the extraordinary example of Henry Montgomery. The colourful and commanding Dr. Montgomery loved an audience, as did Mr. Nicholson. Often on the streets of the city he would borrow a box or chair from a nearby house; from the top of the box he urged his listeners to repent and believe; after he had broken the ice, he would tell William Nicholson to get up and speak. It was a daunting school in which to learn, but Henry Montgomery told William, "If you can't hold them, you haven't much of a message, and you are not fit to preach."

It was the same Dr. Montgomery who invited the teenage Amy Carmichael to work amongst the poor people on the streets of Belfast at the early part of the century. Amy started a Bible class for the Shawlies in the city. This class grew rapidly, and the end result was the setting up of the Welcome Hall.

Dr. Montgomery was also a tower of strength in the work of the Belfast City Mission of which he became honorary secretary, a position he held for forty-six years. For the City Mission he energetically raised much financial support, recruited and motivated many missionaries for the city and often engaged in extensive evangelistic outreach amongst the destitute and underprivileged families in Belfast. It was said of him that "he was able to tap a stratum of society that seemed to be out of reach of any Christian agency in Belfast.

On the 28th January 1895 Dr. Montgomery presided at a City Mission rally in Belfast's exhibition hall. He was grieved at the apathy amongst many professed Christians at that time. Although thousands were perishing for want of the Bread of Life, it seemed that the agency (The City Mission) which professed to bring heavenly manna to the multitudes was severely handicapped by lack of funds, simply because well-to-do church members did not care nor contribute to their work.

Addressing the matter Dr. Montgomery spoke out of the fullness of his heart and said, "I cannot help noticing the fact that recently there has been a great increase in the provisions for the entertainment of the people—a new circus seating, I believe, 4,000 and a new theatre accommodating 1,500. In addition, the corporation for still another theatre, seating perhaps 1,000 persons has passed plans. Facts like these no Christian minister in the city can afford to ignore as showing the trend of taste in the community and, moreover, as marking the great increase in the population and the consequently increased necessity for evangelistic effort in reaching a large portion of the industrial classes."

Dr. Montgomery continued with passion and set many thinking. "With regard to the problem of the masses all I can say is that if we do not reach the masses, the masses will reach us and in a way some may not like."

Henry Montgomery was minister of Albert Street Presbyterian Church from 1882. His ministry in that part of West Belfast had been instrumental in leading hundreds of people to personal faith in Jesus Christ. As a result of his endeavours and enterprise there was a great expansion of the membership of his congregation in the decade that followed. His zeal and burden for the lost and needy caused his ministry to spill over beyond the bounds of the immediate area of his church. Through his outreach not only did they erect new church premises in Albert Street, but also there was an extension of the congregation into nearby Percy Street where a wooden building was erected in 1895.

One Sunday in 1892, after his evening service in Albert Street, Dr. Montgomery walked across the Falls Road and up Northumberland Street unto the Shankill Road. He was astounded and shocked at what he saw. Besides the unbridled drunkenness and unashamed promiscuity which abounded on the Shankill he was also touched with the abject poverty and social deprivation evidenced in street after street. Children like little urchins carried pots of beer home to their parents. Ever a man of action and practicality, Dr. Montgomery determined to do something about it.

Solomon of old said, "What mine eye hath seen has affected my heart." Henry Montgomery might not have known it at the time but what he saw on that visit was not only to affect the rest of his life but would touch the hearts of countless numbers of Shankill people in the succeeding years.

Dr. Montgomery shared his concern for the people on the Shankill Road with his friends at the Albert Street Congregation and farther afield. As a result a public meeting was convened in the Ulster Hall to highlight the needs of the area. This meeting was chaired by Sir Robert Anderson, the well known Christian businessman and philanthropist who later became High Sheriff of Belfast in 1904 and Lord Mayor of the city in 1908. At the meeting Dr. Montgomery spoke eloquently and emotionally as he shared his burden for the Shankill people with the packed Ulster Hall. As a consequence of this meeting a decision was made to begin a work on the Shankill Road in conjunction with the Home Mission of the Presbyterian Church in Ireland.

The campaign for the Shankill began with a series of Evangelistic Tent Missions, a method well established since the 1859 Revival. In the summer of 1896 a large tent was erected on the Shankill Road on what was to be the future site of the Shankill Road Mission.

In the planned seven-week mission that followed, crowded congregations heard the gospel every night. The mission proved so successful that the tent remained on the site, and the meetings continued for almost a year. It was only when bad weather destroyed the tent that the twelve-month mission was finally terminated. By then hundreds of people had been converted to Jesus Christ.

In November 1896 a communion roll indicated the first twenty-three communicant members of the newly formed Shankill Road Mission. These new members not only included some who had been converted at the recent tent meetings but others who had originated from as far away as Armagh, Banbridge, Aughnacloy and Edinburgh.

A temporary wooden structure was erected on the same site as the tent had been, and this continued to be used until the new mission building was available in 1898. Architects were commissioned to draw plans for the new building which was to occupy a complete street block. When finished it was a most splendidly ornate building, which was typical of the late Victorian era. It rose five stories high and had a Minor Hall, which was used for weekday meetings. A large number of smaller rooms were designed for the Sabbath School. There also was a suite of offices for administration, dispensaries for medical consultations and other rooms where both food and clothing were kept for distribution among the poor.

The principal feature of the building was the main semi-circular auditorium with a horseshoe gallery which was fully wrapped around the spacious hall. The total capacity of the auditorium was in excess of two thousand people. The pulpit was positioned at the front of a large platform which spanned the breadth of the hall. This platform was flanked on either side with two beautiful windows, and at the rear of the platform the tall staggered pipes of the Binn organ rose majestically to make a most impressive backdrop to the pulpit and the choir stalls. The magnificent auditorium was capped with a splendid translucent dome which allowed daylight to filter through.

Including four shops in the building complex reflected Dr. Montgomery's practicality; these fronted onto the main Shankill Road. The immense undertaking to erect such a grand building in a socially deprived area reflected the scale of Dr. Montgomery's vision and enterprise for the Shankill Road.

Dr. Montgomery and his family lived at the Crescent near to Belfast's Queens University, and he was undoubtedly impressed with the erection of the beautiful Crescent Church outside his own home. The sandstone structure which had been designed by a noted Scottish church architect, rose high above the surrounding skyline and undoubtedly impressed Dr. Montgomery to the extent he also embarked on an equally imposing building on the lower Shankill Road. A foundation stone for his new building was laid on 23rd October 1897, and the construction was completed the following year.

It is interesting to note that at this time many other equally impressive church complexes had been built or were in process of construction: St. Enoch's (1872); Carlisle Memorial (1875); St. Patrick's (1878); Townsend Street (1878); Nelson Memorial (1896). Alongside these buildings construction was also underway at such civic structures as the Mater Hospital, the Belfast Opera House and the new Belfast City Hall. They all filled the city skyline as powerful monuments to Victorian enterprise.

Although the new Shankill Mission building was pretentious when compared to the surrounding deprivation, Dr. Montgomery brought his own practical trademark of Christian love and genuine concern. In a climate of hardship, destitution and general despair, he introduced radical and pioneering measures to the Shankill people, such as free medical treatment, free clothing, Christian education, direct food aid, money and free holidays. He also proposed a residential training home with accommodation for twenty students.

With Dr. Montgomery's untiring energy, enthusiasm and personal charisma he continued to carry on with the work in the Albert Street Church and the Percy Street outreach and lead the flourishing work on the Shankill Road until 1902. He was finally forced to forego his charge in Albert Street in order to concentrate solely on the Shankill Road Mission which became known as the Albert Hall.

Dr. Montgomery also embarked on the construction of a suite of halls in neighbouring Percy Street where there had previously been erected a wooden hall. This was a scheme of modest proportions and was soon handed over to the National School Board, but his grander vision of practical outreach through the Shankill Road Mission continued to flourish.

The famous evangelist Gypsy Smith conducted an evangelistic mission for Dr. Montgomery during his first visit to Ulster in 1905. Thousands came to hear the gifted gypsy evangelist sing and preach, and many were converted to Christ.

All departments of the work at the mission were growing, and the Albert Hall became a focal point for those who lived on the Shankill. Sadly, events were soon to shatter the smooth running of the mission. The slaughter of the 36th Ulster Division on July 1st 1916 at the battle of the Somme was followed by the influenza epidemic of 1918-1919. These catastrophes left the Shankill people stunned and dazed.

The sectarian violence of the early 1920s, the political and constitutional changes and challenges with the partition of Ireland and the establishment of the state of Northern Ireland, caused great unease and unrest among people of the Shankill. This, coupled with soaring unemployment heralded a time of traumatic change and deepened the sense of despair in the streets and homes that surrounded the Shankill Road Mission.

Dr. Montgomery could not resist participating in the political developments of the time and closely identified himself with the Unionist cause. He was a close ally of Edward Carson, and his name follows immediately after that of Carson on the signing of the brave Ulster Covenant.

Besides the ongoing ministry of a busy church, Henry Montgomery was forever enterprising and pioneering in his endeavours to provide relief for the impoverished people from the Shankill Road. Without doubt, among the most popular of the mission's activities throughout Dr. Montgomery's ministry were the trips to Bangor. The success of this work resulted in the formation of a Fresh Air Colony. These were homes which were sponsored and provided by various commercial companies in Great Britain to provide deprived children with an alternative to their drab surroundings.

A Holiday Home of Rest already existed in Bangor and was supported by A. W. Vance. It provided some ten thousand working girls with a holiday ranging from one day to one month. In 1910 a donation was received from a Mr. Crosby of Boston, Massachusetts, allowing Henry Montgomery to open a Holiday Home for Girls.

In 1923 the Shankill Road Mission made a further donation of £10,000 to a Home Mission enterprise to provide a unit for mothers and babies. This home was named, Sunnyside Villa and was dedicated in June 1928. A farmhouse was later acquired and made available to staff. By 1932 trains and trams transported thousands of children to and from Bangor where they enjoyed the excellent facilities provided at the Fresh Air Colony.

In the ensuing years, Bangor Village as the colony became known to Shankill people, not only provided days and weeks of rest and recreation but it also afforded a haven for spiritual and moral renewal. Many young lives came to a saving faith in Jesus Christ at the Colony.

With the passing of time there was a gradual shift in emphasis relating to the allocation of the facilities at Bangor. By 1949, the way opened for elderly ladies to occupy the cottages of Bangor Village on a permanent basis, and the Crosby Home was offered for the use of Presbyterian Church missionaries returning on furlough.

The late 1970s brought this recreational aspect of the mission's work to a close. A resolution to the general assembly in June 1980 proposed that the Bangor properties be transferred by sale to the Presbyterian Housing Association Limited and the Presbyterian Residential Trust. This was duly completed.

William Campbell and Noel Williamson speak eloquently of the ministry of Dr. Montgomery in their centenary booklet about the work of the Albert Hall. They say, "Any historical study of the Shankill Road Mission must inevitably be dominated by the figure of Henry Montgomery, and as a result, it will seem somewhat unbalanced to those looking at our work for the first time.

"This imbalance, however, is unavoidable, since he was the outstanding individual whose vision conceived and planned the work. His massive energy built its fabric whose evangelical zeal sustained the wide-ranging programmes of outreach for nearly half a century and whose name was really regarded as synonymous with the mission for all but the final year of his long life."

His strategy of evangelical tent missions was clearly very much in vogue and directly influenced by the style of the Moody and Sankey missions in Belfast. Dr. Montgomery's vision for a work that reached every age and class included a vibrant Sunday School with a great group of willing teachers. The founding of the 36th Company of the Boy's Brigade provided a great outlet for the youth as also did the Girl's Brigade later. There was also a boys' club to encourage physical exercises and sports. Similar activities were also provided for the girls.

The ladies had their weekly women's meeting which was very well attended. A similar gathering was arranged for the men who attended their weekly Bible Class.

Henry Montgomery's gifts were many and indisputable. Without a doubt he possessed a shrewd business sense, a creative flair and a driving enthusiasm that enabled him to build valuable contacts in the business and political world around him. All this was harnessed to a deep Christian commitment and burning compassion which brought great success to the mission and gave benefit to many thousands on the Shankill. Through him many hearts were touched and many lives transformed by enduring material, social and spiritual benefits.

Dr. Montgomery invited his former assistant minister, Rev. W. P. Nicholson to conduct an evangelistic mission in the Albert Hall. Nicholson had developed his ministry and was widely used of God in association with Dr. R. A. Torrey in many parts of the world. His return to Northern Ireland corresponded with a time of sectarian troubles, which plagued Northern Ireland with much bloodshed and loss of life in the early twenties.

The first meeting was held in the Albert Hall on the Sunday evening of 11th February 1922. Before Mr. Nicholson preached in the Albert Hall, he conducted meetings in two other neighbouring churches— Townsend Street Presbyterian in the morning and Agnes Street Methodist Church in the afternoon.

A report in the Belfast News Letter states:

> The Albert Hall was crowded with a most attentive audience and the sermon was a rousing appeal to church members. Every available corner of the Albert Hall was occupied, and many that could not find a seat stood throughout the entire service. In the forty-five minute sermon, "there was not a dull moment during its entire delivery, and many were profoundly moved.

A subsequent report in the Belfast News Letter speaks of the services being, "quite phenomenal in their character." Another report in the same paper commented that Nicholson's sermon produced "a deep impression on the congregation and that the after-meeting was crowded."

The report of the Shankill Road Mission Committee to the General Assembly of 1922 states: "The Rev. W. P. Nicholson conducted a very successful mission in the Albert Hall which was packed every evening with close to 3,000 people; 2,260 men, women and young people passed through the enquiry rooms, and nearly all these were led, it is believed, to a definite decision for Christ."

Many of those who trusted the Saviour in that mission went on to become Christian ministers and missionaries serving the Lord in distant lands. Two of these missionaries were Mollie Harvey and Margaret McKnight. The latter married William McComb later, and these three missionaries founded the Acre Gospel Mission in 1937.

The great preacher and philanthropist continued his work until his retirement in 1924. The Presbyterian Church honoured this champion of the working classes in 1912 by appointing him to be moderator of the general assembly of the church. While the Victorian church and clergy everywhere, displayed something of the "rich man in his castle, poor man at the gate" syndrome, the simple truth is that Henry Montgomery lived and died as a beloved and revered pastor.

The pressure of the work plus the ageing process must have taken a heavy toll on Henry Montgomery. He resigned as superintendent of the mission in 1924 when he was still in full flow of his work. He was then seventy-seven years old. This resignation was virtually only on paper for he continued active in the work of the Shankill Mission until the year before his death in his ninety-sixth year.

It must have been a most difficult task to follow a man who was legend in his own time. There seems little doubt that Montgomery's enormous work rate and dominating personality did create serious problems for those who followed after him and particularly so for his first three successors who still worked with him.

Henry Montgomery's first successor was the Rev. Fred Gibson who had been the minister of the Ormond Quay Presbyterian Church in

Dublin. He was installed as superintendent of the mission in 1924 and remained in the position until 1931.

Mr. Gibson faced considerable difficulties in succeeding Montgomery in the mid twenties. Mass demonstrations and rioting by the unemployed were commonplace. In January 1924 four thousand people demonstrated in Glengall Street and were addressed by Tommy Henderson and Joe Devlin, well known political figures in the city. In March 1925 the Rev. William Corkey, a manager of nine local schools in the Shankill area, led a protest against Lord Londonderry's Education Act of 1923.

Besides the difficulty of following in the footsteps of such a successful and charismatic figure as Dr. Montgomery, Fred Gibson's problems were increased by the fact that Dr Montgomery was still very involved in every aspect of the Mission's affairs and outreach. It is a fact that Dr. Montgomery chaired the Rev. Gibson's first mission committee meeting and welcomed the new minister to the meeting.

In 1928 the trustees of the Shankill Road Mission awarded Dr Montgomery exclusive use of all parts of the premises on two days of each week and allocated the congregation four days use of the Albert Hall and the remainder of the premises "not permanently required by Dr. Montgomery." Such a situation most certainly would not be tolerated under modern conditions.

In spite of these difficulties the Rev. Fred Gibson was a faithful preacher of the Word of God. Besides beginning home prayer meetings he conducted several evangelistic missions at which many people were converted. Most notable of these gospel campaigns was that conducted in a tent during the General Strike of 1926 which brought a great spiritual stirring to the Shankill district.

In 1931 Fred Gibson relinquished his role as superintendent of the Shankill Mission when the Presbytery appointed him as superintendent of the Irish Mission. This was a position he had been well prepared for by his experience of ministering in Dublin and then his work on the Shankill Road under the shadow of Dr. Montgomery. He remained as superintendent of the Irish Missions until 1953.

The Rev. Robert Montgomery followed Fred Gibson as superintendent of the Shankill Road Mission. He was a local man who had been nurtured in the Shankill Mission, but although his name was Montgomery he was no relation of his famous namesake and forerunner. Robert laboured faithfully to uphold the first principles of the Shankill Mission which were laid down by Dr. Henry Montgomery. In doing so he engaged in an evangelistic outreach, maintained a social witness and philanthropic ministry both to those living in the general Shankill area and further afield.

Like his predecessor Robert Montgomery soon discovered that his illustrious namesake, Dr. Henry Montgomery, still continued to dominate the administration and supervision of affairs in the Shankill Mission. On October 5th 1932 the commission approved a resolution that Mr. Robert Montgomery B. A. would "be a fit and proper person to become colleague and successor to Rev. Dr. Montgomery." Perhaps characteristically, there was no reference to Fred Gibson who had ministered for the previous six years at the mission.

No sooner had Robert Montgomery begun his tenure as superintendent at the Shankill Road Mission than serious disturbances broke out on the Falls Road at Albert Street. The riots soon spread to the Shankill Road. The Northern Ireland government was forced to impose curfews. This added to the difficulties that Rev. Montgomery encountered in ministering at the famous Albert Hall. Notwithstanding these problems, the new minister heartily applied himself to the work.

Robert Montgomery resigned from the Shankill Mission in 1938 to take up a new charge in Rathgar, Dublin. In his absence Henry Montgomery, at the age of ninety-one, was still committed to look after the mission's Christmas charity work.

The Rev. W. P. Hall replaced Robert Montgomery in 1939 from Greenisland Presbyterian Church. Like the Rev. Montgomery before him, the Rev. Hall was installed as the new superintendent who would be a "colleague and successor to the Rev. Dr. Henry Montgomery."

A gentle and compassionate spirit marked Rev. Hall's ministry right from the outset. These characteristics were in stark contrast to the external events surrounding his service as superintendent. Europe was plunged into a conflict which not only had universal dimensions but was also devastating in its local impact; civilians became defenceless targets of Hitler's strategy of indiscriminate bombing.

Shankill men and women were again keen volunteers to enlist in His Majesty's forces and many made the ultimate sacrifice and left the Shankill bereft of potential leaders.

The mission itself suffered directly during the Luftwaffe attacks on Belfast in 1941. A direct hit on an air-raid shelter in Percy Street killed forty-two people and injured many more. The glass domes of the Albert Hall were shattered in the same raid, forcing the temporary removal of the congregation to share with the Townsend Street Presbyterian Church for the following six months.

Blackout curtains, gas masks, torches, vigils and prayers characterised the dark years of the war. Through all of this the mission continued to minister to those in need.

On 17th February 1943, Dr. Henry Montgomery passed into the presence of his Lord in his 96th year. His death touched the hearts of the whole Shankill community. His funeral on February 19th brought the Shankill to a complete standstill. Businesses closed, and the blinds in shops and homes were drawn.

At his funeral several thousand sombre people lined the Shankill Road, and one newspaper reported that "as the coffin was borne from the Albert Hall on the venerable doctor's last great pilgrimage, many women were in tears." The long cortege made its way from the Albert Hall along the Shankill Road and down Northumberland Street. The horse drawn funeral carriages paused near to the Albert Street Presbyterian Church where the great man had ministered God's Word and then continued on its way to the City Cemetery. At the graveside service the Rev. Robert Montgomery and Dr. D. H. Maconachie gave the final word.

With the burden of a wartime ministry, Rev. W. P. Hall found the pressure of being in sole charge of the Shankill Mission an increasingly stressful burden. The death of Dr. Montgomery was the final blow that left him without the wise support, counsel and guidance he needed.

Although the Canadian evangelist Dr. Oswald J. Smith conducted a very fruitful evangelistic mission at the Albert Hall in 1947, the Rev. Hall found he could no longer cope with the wide-ranging demands the mission had always made on its superintendents. Because of this and deteriorating health, Hall requested the help of a full-time assistant for the Mission. The commission felt unable to meet his request, and as a result he tendered his resignation in 1948. The commission accepted it with "regret and surprise."

The vacancy created by Hall's departure was resolved by a meeting between the Rev. Duncan Campbell and the Rev. Andrew McNabb who was the minister of Shawlands United Free Church in Glasgow. Duncan Campbell had concluded a successful mission in the Albert Hall in August 1948 and suggested to Andrew McNabb that he apply to the Shankill Mission for the vacant post of superintendent.

His application proved successful, and he began his ministry at the Shankill on 3rd February 1949, as "colleague and successor to W. P. Hall."

Mr. McNabb's call was the first in the post-Montgomery era, and his decade of ministry embraced a period of post-war austerity, and a series of international crises beginning with the Korean war in 1951 and culminating in the Suez crisis of 1956.

Records of the Mission at this time show that the numerous activities of the mission were carried on successfully. However, Mr. McNabb did not prove to be an innovator in his tenure as superintendent, nor was his ministry considered to be successful. Of his accomplishments, the most instrumental was his assistance in changing the status of the holiday homes in Bangor which passed to the responsibility of the Presbyterian Missions.

His friend and fellow Scot, Duncan Campbell, was invited again to conduct special evangelistic meetings at a filled Albert Hall. Mr. McNabb himself was a compelling preacher but he did not seem to combine the necessary gifts of evangelism with the equally important administrative skills applied with firmness and compassion.

The advent and impact of the television on society had a decisive effect on attendance at worship services both at Shankill and other congregations throughout Belfast. This marked the beginning of a decline in interest in and support for church membership and activity.

By the time of Andrew McNabb's resignation in 1958 the mission was facing a great challenge. It was perhaps his resignation that caused the commission of the Shankill Mission to consider the difficulties of one person fulfilling the dual responsibility of being the superintendent of the mission with the dual roles of administration of the large philanthropic programme and being the minister of the church. No easy answer was found at that time.

It was into this somewhat unsettled and uncertain atmosphere in August 1958 that the Rev. Ivor Lewis was called to the work at the Shankill Road Mission. The Rev. Lewis had been the minister at Berry Street Presbyterian Church where he had a very successful ministry.

The commission had proposed that the superintendent would concentrate on all the mission programmes such as a psychiatric clinic, the healing centre, a Personal Problem Bureau, the training of evangelists, industrial evangelism, evangelistic services, youth work and the training of lay workers.

Mr. Lewis proved himself to be an energetic worker in carrying out his duties as superintendent. His warm evangelical faith led directly to a deep concern for individuals in any kind of social need and for social problems generally. He became a most effective advocate for the Shankill Road Mission, enlisting a devoted band of fellow-workers.

He was a gifted orator with great evangelistic gift. He showed particular concern for victims of alcoholism and drug abuse and involved himself deeply in personal counselling with people from a wide range of geographic and social backgrounds. His personal involvement with people, and his powerful evangelistic witness were outstanding features of Ivor Lewis' fifteen years of ministry at the Shankill Road Mission.

With the outbreak of civil unrest on the streets of the Shankill and Crumlin Roads in 1968 the neighbouring community to the mission was plunged into turmoil and sectarian conflict.

The Shankill gained infamous notoriety as the focal point of Protestant violence and a target of Republican vengeance. The Shankill Butchers and the Shankill bomb are only two of many tragic memories of the terrible atrocities perpetrated during the terrible years of vicious tit-for-tat violence.

For ten years Ivor Lewis was in the heart of the Shankill as a minister of the gospel and was a tower of strength to young and old alike. He offered help and counsel to all who were in spiritual and material need. The gifted preacher served the people of the Shankill well until he was called to be minister of Whiteabbey Presbyterian Church in 1973.

As on other occasions, questions were again raised during Ivor Lewis' time as to new approaches to ministry and restructuring of the mission and its future role in the final quarter of the twentieth century. It was felt that this recurring discussion required an urgent response.

Bill Jackson had been the minister of the neighbouring Townsend Street Presbyterian Church. He was also a member of the commission when he was appointed to be superintendent of the Shankill Road Mission in 1974. Bill Jackson brought to the mission a prayerful, pastoral concern which expressed itself in personal counselling, the fostering of small, local communities and an emphasis on renewal by the Holy Spirit. However, he was encumbered in his work by virtue of the fact that there still was no real distinction between the social and spiritual work of the mission.

Added to this difficulty was the depopulation of the Shankill as families moved to outlying housing developments. This resulted in many local churches losing scores of members. Although there were consultations of uniting various congregations the negotiations did not usually come to fruition.

Under the leadership of Rev. Jackson a major renovation scheme was undertaken at the Shankill Mission. This included the demolition of the famous Albert Hall, which had often echoed the voices of some of the great preachers of the last century and was the spiritual birthplace of thousands of sinners. The renovation was undertaken to make the outdated facilities more attractive to the present Shankill population. A drop-in centre which provided well-priced meals and a games room was also furnished for use by the local unemployed youth.

However, efforts of evangelistic campaigns, cross-community and inter-church programmes did not produce any significant increase in the spiritual interest or health of the Shankill Road Mission.

Mr. Jackson introduced the Action for Community Employment (A. C. E.) scheme to provide a door back into long-term unemployment. It sought to give a sense of hope and a possibility of a new beginning to some who felt betrayed by the State.

The main feature of Mr. Jackson's superintendence was the gentle and compassionate manner with which he treated everyone he met and manifested in all aspects of his ministry at the Shankill Road Mission. He retired from the work in 1990.

The mantle of leadership of the Mission as it passed into its second century became the responsibility of Bill Campbell who was formerly minister of the Legacurry Presbyterian Church near Hillsborough. He was called to the superintendence of the Shankill Mission in March 1990.

Mr. Campbell quickly proved himself to be not only a gifted preacher and teacher but also a highly competent administrator. His ability to oversee the many demands of the work enabled him to give a sense of purpose and direction on the work of the mission.

A very impressive and effective renovation scheme was carried out successfully, and this was mainly due to Mr. Campbell's vision and drive. He had great ability to attract major funding to the mission from statutory bodies and other sources which stabilised the mission and made it secure financially. This undoubtedly was due to him having built up many useful contacts in the local community and in the Province at large. The Rev. Campbell energetically taking the needs of the mission to the whole church and community achieved all of this.

Under his superintendence the A. C. E. schemes and hostel provision expanded significantly, while the five-fold increase of permanent staff posts under the sole control of the mission greatly consolidated the overall effectiveness of the work.

He was able to re-vitalise the mission complex, and this has resulted in an increase in use by the local population. The mission building now stands as an attractive base and platform for new and appropriate programmes and initiatives of evangelism on the Shankill.

Without the dedication and co-operation of many faithful and committed workers under the leadership of each succeeding superintendent, Dr. Montgomery's vision of a mission with the ability to reach the people of the Shankill would long since have evaporated. For more than one hundred years the Shankill Road Mission has played a strategic role in the Christian witness to the gospel on the Shankill Road and the vision continues.

Chapter Twelve

THE BRANAGH MISSION

For the first sixty years of the twentieth century Bridge End was one of Belfast's busiest roads. Leading out of the city centre on the east side of the Queens Bridge which spanned the River Lagan, it continued for half a mile to the beginning of the Newtownards Road. Bridge End began at Station Street which not only led to the County Down Railway Station but also to the main entrance of the Belfast Coal Quay and the then world's greatest shipyard, Harland and Wolff. The short thoroughfare finished at the entrance to Short Strand where the Sirocco Engineering Works occupied a huge area. Midway along Bridge End was an imposing railway bridge which spanned the main road and cast its sombre shadow over the whole district. Congested between these various industries was a road lined with a variety of shops which sold every thing from pig's trotters to a navy sergeant's suit and several pubs where men from the nearby shipyard frequently boozed.

Behind these shops was a tightly compacted triangle of short streets hemmed in by the railway station and shipyard on one side and the River Lagan and the large Sirocco Engineering Works at the corner of

Short Strand on the other. The tight network of rows of "two-up and two-down" terraced dwellings housed many workers from the surrounding industries. The entire district seemed to live under the shadow of the dominating and dark railway bridge which swathed through the heart of the area. It was under the shadow of this bridge and in the heart of this close community known as Bridge End that the Branagh Mission was born. Today the mission is better known as the Branagh Memorial Church.

Eddie Magookin was born and reared on the Belfast's Shankill Road. After leaving school Eddie went to work as a stonemason with McLaughlin and Harvey, one of Belfast's main building and civil engineering firms. Eddie remained with the firm all his working life and was a foreman in the company. Prior to his conversion Eddie Magookin was a prodigal who was addicted to gambling. So bad did the habit become that Eddie was even threatened with eviction from his family home for his wayward habits. It was at that low point in Eddie's life in 1927 that he was converted to Jesus Christ. His life, his heart and habits were completely transformed by the power of the gospel. Soon after his conversion, Eddie, who once was a slave to sin, dedicated his life to be a servant of Jesus Christ.

In his youth Eddie had learned how to play various musical instruments, and as a Christian he became part of the Mizpah Musical Messengers. This musical group of instrumentalists and vocalists also testified and preached the Word of God. They were greatly used to spread the gospel message and were the means of leading many to personal faith in Jesus Christ. The various invitations and engagements that flowed in for the group meant that Eddie travelled far and wide on his small motorcycle. In the course of these travels Eddie not only widened his sphere of friends and service but he also met and fell in love with Jean Salmon who hailed from Memel Street which was just off Bridge End.

Eddie and Jean continued with their musical ministry around the city and beyond. However, in 1952 some Christian women from the Bridge End district suggested to Mr. Magookin he should start a cottage meeting in one of their homes. For Eddie it was not quite a call from "a man from Macedonia," but he felt as sure as Paul in Acts 16 that God had called him to this work. With that assurance in his heart Eddie initiated those first cottage meetings in the home of Mrs. Bella McMillan.

God not only blessed the effort of those first weekly meetings but interest in the meetings grew so much that larger premises were soon required. In 1953 Mr. Magookin was able to procure the use of a small hall in the same street. The hall was under the railway bridge and was squeezed in between the gable wall of an end house and the pillars which upheld the bridge. The small hall accommodated about forty people. There was no natural light in the hall, and it's only entrance was a narrow doorway which was jammed up tight against the railway pillar. It was so narrow that people appropriately called it the "Hole in the Wall." During the meetings often the thunderous roar of a train passing over head either drowned out the enthusiastic singing or interrupted the vigorous gospel preaching. Those who gathered in those first meetings in that old hall found that the "hole in the wall" became a gate of heaven to their souls.

Eddie Magookin was fully committed to this work, and as a result he withdrew from the Mizpah Musical Messengers. He assumed the pastoral duties of the newly formed fellowship while continuing his employment with McLaughlin and Harvey who facilitated him in every way to make his ministry possible. God's Word was preached not only by Mr. Magookin but also by many invited servants of God; this resulted in many people coming to know Jesus Christ as their Saviour through the work of those early days. The Memel Street Mission continued at the "Hole in the Wall" for two years at the end of which it was bursting at the seams, and it was obvious to all that larger premises were needed.

In the providence of God Mr. Magookin met up with Mr. John Branagh during one of the latter's frequent visits to his native Northern Ireland. John Branagh was born in Ballinderry. Like many others of his time he emigrated to the United States of America to seek better employment. God prospered him, and he was able to establish his own building firm in California. As a Christian John Branagh felt he was a steward of the prosperity that God had given him and felt he wanted to make his earthly riches work for a heavenly investment.

The involvement with the Mizpah Musical Messengers brought Eddie Magookin into contact with John Branagh. In the process of ceasing his association with the musical group to devote more of his time to the work in his neighbourhood, Eddie had kept in touch with his friend John in the United States. One day during one of his frequent visits from California John Branagh asked Eddie about the progress of the work in Memel Street and was glad to hear of its progress. It was just at that time that the Hole in the Wall had become inadequate to house the growing fellowship.

In searching for larger premises it was learned that the former Laganview Street Mission Hall was up for sale. In earlier years the Laganview Mission had been an outreach from Donegall Square Methodist Church, but it had fallen on hard times, and consequently it was closed in 1950. The building was subsequently sold as a business property, but none of the firms that occupied the former mission hall seemed to meet with any success. As a result the old Laganview Mission Hall became vacant again in 1955 and was offered for sale. On learning of this John Branagh showed great interest in the hall being re-opened for God's work. After some inquiries and discussions John Branagh provided part of the finances for the purchase of the building to accommodate the growing congregation. This wise steward, although generous to God's work, gave to a worthy cause only when he was satisfied that the local church or fellowship would also give wholeheartedly towards a project.

Many from the fellowship worked tirelessly to help in refurbishing the newly acquired premises. One of the prominent features of the Laganview Hall was the central pillar which was the main support for the upper floor. There also was a coke boiler, which had to be stoked up to keep everyone warm during the cold winter nights. Understandably, seats near the boiler were popular. When the needed renovations were completed and the new hall was opened the onetime Laganview Street Mission adopted a new name and became The Branagh Mission Hall. The meetings in the new Branagh Mission Hall were greatly blessed by God right from the first days. Many people from the local area were converted to Christ and added to His church.

John Branagh maintained his interest and practical involvement in the Branagh Mission from the other side of the Atlantic until the Lord called him home. It was not only the Branagh Mission that benefited from John Branagh's generosity but also many other building programmes were completed because of the generosity of this great man. He truly was a Barnabas who lived to encourage others in the cause of Christ. Ironically John was on one of his visits to his native Ballinderry in 1960 when he became unwell and subsequently died in Northern Ireland. His widow who for years whole-heartedly shared John's vision, maintained her husband's association with the Branagh Mission and supported it until she also went to be with Christ some years later.

Besides evangelising the Bridge End area by the conventional means of visitation, Bible studies and evangelistic endeavours, Mr. Magookin took a particular interest in reaching young men for the Lord. Young people gathered around the street corners or kicked balls in the street; there was little for them to do; therefore, Eddie had to be innovative in his methods. After sharing his burden with others and making it a matter of prayer, he set up a local football team that just simply became known as Branagh Mission. Eddie Magookin and Jimmy Holmes who had formerly played for East Belfast's favourite team, Glentoran, began to coach some of the local lads who had previously loitered on the streets. Their team gained admittance into the Churches League. Soon the Branagh Mission became a formidable football team that won the hotly contested Diamond Cup in 1969 beating Lower Shankill in the final at Solitude. However, winning the Diamond Cup was incidental to Mr. Magookin and Jimmy Holmes who were even more interested in winning trophies of grace which were more precious and lasting—the precious souls of the young men who played in the football team.

Besides having a training programme, all the players who registered with the team were obliged to attend at least one of the weekly meetings at the Branagh Mission. It was not uncommon at the Thursday evening Bible study to have quite a few pews filled with young unsaved footballers listening to the Word of God.   This resulted in many of these players coming to know Jesus Christ as Saviour.

One of those won to Christ by his involvement with the football team was Roy Gordon who today pastors the Branagh Memorial Church. In 1965 Roy enlisted as a player for the Branagh Mission team. He dutifully attended the meetings as was required and often beyond his obligation; he willingly went to the hall several times per week. One Saturday in 1969 while playing local rivals Sparta, Roy broke his leg in collision with an opposing player. This injury put Roy out of the game for a prolonged period of time and as a result he had a lot of time on his hands. At the same time Roy felt confused; his heart and mind were in turmoil, and he tried to fathom what was wrong with his life. Roy wrestled with various issues facing him and finally concluded that the root of his problem was a constant and deep conviction of his sin. Finally, on Friday 6th February 1970, Roy called upon God for mercy and experienced the transformation of the gospel in his life. God truly works in mysterious ways His wonders to perform. In an amazing process a game of football and a broken leg not only resulted in Roy's conversion, but now he is the pastor of the very church he was attracted to by his interest in football.

Other young men who also followed into Christian work also were brought to the Saviour and nurtured in their Christian lives through similar works at the Branagh Mission. The Rev. Wesley McDowell who has been the minister of Limavady Free Presbyterian Church for more than twenty years was converted at the Branagh. The Rev. Harry Rea who has been a minister in Newtownards and Larne Congregational churches for more than two decades came to the Lord at the Branagh. Mr. Jim Clarke who originally started his Christian service at the Branagh Mission dedicated his life to the work of the Belfast City Mission.

God's work is not sustained by the energy of one man no matter how gifted he may be. Mr. Magookin was greatly assisted in his work by a fine body of Christian workers. Some of his own family inherited his musical talents and put them to good use to accompany the bright singing for which the Branagh has been known. Space here does not permit us to mention all the people who made sacrificial contributions to the growth and development of the work at the Branagh Mission.

Like other parts of Belfast the Memel Street district of the city came under the hammer of urban re-development and was designated to be transformed into an industrial site. The uprooting not only depopulated Bridge End but was also a very traumatic experience for many. With the demolition of the houses that had formed the tightly knit community for almost one hundred years families were scattered to various new housing developments on the outskirts of Belfast. Like a captain that refuses to leave his sinking ship Mr. Magookin made sure that the Branagh Mission Hall was the last building in the area to be levelled to the ground, and the mission functioned there until the very day in which the old building was finally demolished.

Prior to these changes the leaders of the Branagh Mission had been aware for some years of the possibility of the local population being disrupted and the peculiar character of the Bridge End retreat in the annals of Belfast's history. As wise stewards preparing for the event they set aside money every month for the possible relocation. When the impending demolition became a reality, a new site was urgently and prayerfully sought. The housing executive offered a site on the Ballymacarret Road at the lower end of the Newtownards Road where a redevelopment programme of housing had replaced the typical Belfast streets of old terraced houses.

The oversight at the Branagh was well pleased with the site and embarked on a building programme to erect a new church. Mr. Heak, a Christian building contractor from Tandragee, was contracted to do the work. He built it after the style of his home church, Tandragee Free Presbyterian Church that had been designed by its minister, the Rev. Frank McClelland. With removal to the new area the Branagh then adopted the name of the Branagh Memorial Church. The new construction was soon completed, and on Saturday 27th June 1981 the new church was opened. Pastors Jack Mitchell from the Iron Hall and Peter Smith from Dundonald Elim Church were the guest speakers at the afternoon and evening conference. Mr. Sam Scott from Newtownards and the Woodvale Quintet provided inspirational musical messages.

The move to the new location not only proved to be a new beginning for the work of the Mission but presented a whole new mission field on their doorsteps. The building programme throughout the area not only re-housed local families, but people from areas of Belfast also moved into the area. The workers at the Branagh were quick to seize the opportunity and embarked on an evangelistic enterprise to reach their new neighbours. Many of those who were converted during the following months continue in the work today.

In 1982 George Bates conducted an evangelistic mission at the new church, and over a dozen people trusted the Saviour. Some of these are in active membership of the Branagh Memorial Church today. The increased numbers of children at Sunday School and children's meetings plus the involvement in the Campaigner movement obliged the leadership of the Branagh Church to consider an extension to the premises to accommodate these juvenile programmes.

Prayer was solicited at the church about a building site which was adjacent to their new church building. The site had originally been allocated to Glasgow Rangers Supporter's Club. Besides the incompatibility of having such a club in close proximity to the church, Mr. Magookin was convinced this same site was the ideal site for a new church hall. God intervened and answered prayer. Providentially and unexpectedly the Rangers Supporter's Club forfeited their reservation on the site, and it was offered to the church for £6,000. The policy of the Branagh in deference of their Christian testimony was always to operate within their budget without incurring debt. The members and friends of the Branagh rose to the occasion and gave generously, and the piece of land was purchased.

Mr. Heak, the same building contractor who built the church was again engaged to construct the new building. The plans allowed for the new building and the recently built church to be included in the same enclosure consequently creating one church complex. When the new building was completed it provided a beautiful suite of Sunday School rooms plus a large assembly hall and modern kitchen facilities. Mr. Magookin's mother-in-law, Mrs. Jean Salmon, cut the ribbon to open the new hall.

Missionary vision and challenge which have always been part of life at the Branagh have been greatly enhanced at the church in recent years with the introduction of the annual Branagh Missionary Conference. This conference has resulted in more than £15,000 being contributed to the Lord's work overseas annually.

The Rev. Tom Shaw conducted a very fruitful evangelistic mission in 1991 on the tenth anniversary of the opening of the new church. Other evangelists engaged in special outreach endeavours periodically. The hall finally gained a full-time pastor in Roy Gordon who after his retirement from the Northern Ireland Electricity assumed the pastorate of the church and ably carries on the work of the Branagh Memorial Church. He is greatly assisted by his other elders, Joe Smith, Wesley Kane and George Neil.

The Branagh has come a long way from the Hole-in-the-Wall under the noisy and overshadowing railway bridge to the flourishing Branagh Memorial Church in East Belfast. This work is a testimony and reflection of the promise of the Saviour who said, "I will build my church."

Chapter Thirteen

ThE OliveT HalL

There was no more pleasant a walk on a Sunday evening after church than following the Cregagh Road beyond the tram terminus at Bell's Bridge and continuing towards the Hillfoot Road and the lower Castlereagh Hills. An alternative was to follow the path to the Castlereagh along Daddy Winker's Lane.

Soon after World War II the landscape on the upper Cregagh was to change dramatically with the development of Belfast's first Industrial Park at Montgomery Road and the construction of service men's houses near on the left hand side of the road. The building of the flat roofed houses of the new Cregagh estate soon followed the opening of the Industrial Park on the opposite side of the Cregagh Road.

As Belfast developed, the first high rise apartments were built at Bell's Bridge, and as the volume of traffic increased this was followed by the construction of a roundabout at the intersection with Ladas Drive, Cregagh Road and Mount Merrion Avenue. Mount Merrion Avenue was the link road from Cregagh to Rossetta and Knockbreda where an extensive housing development had also greatly populated the area.

In the sixties St John the Baptist Church of Ireland built a modern church facility on the opposite side of Mount Merrion Avenue from the Cregagh Estate while the Mount Merrion Free Presbyterian Church opened their building in the early fifties. The most recent church fellowship to make their home in Mount Merrion Avenue is the Olivet Hall.

At the close of this Twentieth Century the Olivet Assembly has little more than a dozen years of existence, and the hall is only seven years old. However the Olivet Assembly is a well established church fellowship making a significant contribution to evangelical life in East Belfast. It is well known for its keen emphasis on its Bible teaching ministry, its rich Christ-centred fellowship and their evangelistic fervour in the Mount Merrion district.

The Olivet Hall fellowship traces it beginnings to a number of believers who met for a Breaking of Bread gathering at the Park Avenue Hotel on 10th, May 1987. Following that meeting most of those gathered felt constrained to continue meeting as a body for mutual fellowship, Bible study, prayer and Breaking of Bread.

Rented accommodation was sought in East Belfast and was eventually found on the Cregagh Road. These like minded believers met and officially constituted a new Christian Assembly with a governing oversight made up of elders chosen from among the company. After much prayer and consideration they named the Assembly "Olivet."

Soon the believers established a regular programme of weekly meetings. Most noted amongst these was the worship service on Sunday morning. Mr. Jack Mitchell, former pastor of Iron Hall Assembly and an elder at Olivet, wrote of those early gatherings,

> The believers endeavoured to worship the Lord in the beauty of holiness. Many have been the spontaneous tributes paid to the sanctity of 'the worship meeting,' by accredited brethren. One well-known brother wrote, after his visit, '... on sharing my experience at Olivet with my wife, I had to confess that it has been quite some time

since I felt the Lord so near as I did on Sunday morning.'
Also, from our hired house we have shared with the people
of Cregagh the gospel of God concerning His Son Jesus
Christ, and some have been saved.

Jack Mitchell is a very gifted preacher of the Word, and his rich
ministry at Olivet was greatly enhanced by other brethren who also
ministered the Word of God in the assembly. Such ministry soon
attracted other believers to join with them in this newly formed witness
for Jesus Christ.

In addition to meeting for the internal fellowship of the believers a
small team of door-to-door visitors began to visit the homes in the
Cregagh and Mount Merrion neighbourhood. God greatly used this
outreach endeavour to further the work and witness of the Olivet
Assembly in a way that they could never have dreamed.

Although the believers had no permanent abode, the leaders of the
work soon set up Sunday School and Good News club for the boys and
girls. Several young people made the Olivet their spiritual home and
organised the Young People's Fellowship where some of the young men
expressed their own gifts of leadership in the work.   The Ladies'
Fellowship was also formed and played a great part in the over-all
witness of the assembly.

Mr. Mitchell further reports about the development of the work:

Hired premises, as Paul realised in Acts 19, are often
necessary, and can be useful, but they have disadvantages
also. Furthermore, such disadvantages can create
discouragement in some saints, and this was experienced
at Olivet and resulted in a few withdrawals from the
fellowship. Clearly, a permanent home for the church was
essential, and prayer was made without ceasing unto God
for this. A saint with a sanctified sense of humour once
said that God's phone number is JER. 333! (Jeremiah
33:3). That Scripture reads: 'Call upon me and I will
answer thee, and show thee great and mighty things which
thou knowest not.'

The believers in Olivet certainly 'knew not' where ground
for their desired home would come from; for the local
authority was sure that no such ground existed in the area.
However, the saints kept dialling Jer. 333, and one Lord's
Day God gave the first part of His answer.

As our young men were carrying out diligently their
ministry of house visitation; one of them engaged a
householder in conversation. The house-holder remarked
that he had been watching the Christians going to and from
their hired hall and advised the young brother that he,
the house-holder, owned a piece of land suitable for
their purposes which he would be willing to sell to the
assembly.

With great delight the news was conveyed to the elders of
the church.

When the parcel of ground was inspected by responsible
brethren, certain advantages and disadvantages were
obvious. Once it had been the site of a nursery; now it
was more like a jungle! It was extensive enough, however,
for a building of the size the assembly had in mind and
would allow also for some private car-parking facilities.
The major disadvantage, however, was that the area was
land-locked and bounded on one side by the River Loop.
In short, if a church were to be built there, an adjoining
piece of land would have to be purchased to provide access
to Mount Merrion, and the narrow River Loop would have
to be piped.

In spite of these hazards, the brethren were instructed by
the assembly to purchase the nursery site; after all, did
not our Lord once say to His disciples: 'If ye have faith as
a grain of mustard seed, ye shall say unto this mountain
remove hence to yonder place, and it shall remove; and
nothing shall be impossible unto you.' Also, do not
Christians often sing: "Got any rivers you think are

un-crossable?" Olivet would put God to the test, and God would put Olivet to the test.

An approach was made to the Local Authority to enquire about the access ground to the site of the former nursery. God answered prayer and after negotiation the God supplied the need to purchase of the expensive 'access' ground from the Local Authority. After completion of that transaction, a number of saints met on the site and gave public thanks to God for His goodness and guidance.

The next hurdle was to pipe the River Loop. As Mr. Mitchell remarks, "What the crossing of the Jordan was to Israel, the crossing of the Loop was to 'Olivet.' Another miracle had been witnessed at Mount Merrion."

Having cleared and made the site ready a Christian building contractor , Mr. Heake from Tandragee, was engaged to build the new sanctuary. Several brethren also from the Olivet Assembly gave of their time and considerable talents and rendered quality workmanship to the new building.

All through the building programme God met their needs in tremendous ways. Mr. Mitchell comments:

What an avalanche of gifts from near and far; both monetary and material gifts have been showered on the assembly by saints whose hearts the Lord has touched. The Communion table, an electric organ, two pianos, all the furniture in the vestry, the equipment for the crèche, money designated towards the lovely stained-glass windows and much more, have come to us from the Father of Light, with whom is neither variableness nor shadow of turning, by way of His people, and all of this, be it noted, amidst the worst economic recession the country has known for sixty years.

Upon completion of the new structure the Olivet Hall was opened on Saturday 8th May 1993 with overflowing numbers in attendance. Mrs. Mitchell unveiled a plaque in the vestibule of the hall to mark the special occasion. The plaque reads:

Great is Thy faithfulness—Lam. 3:23
Olivet Hall was opened for the worship of God and
the ministry of the Holy Scripture
by Mrs. E. Mitchell
on Saturday 8th May 1993.
The Word of the Lord endureth forever—1 Peter 1:25

Pastor Sam Carson from Banbridge was the guest speaker for the inaugural meetings on Saturday and Sunday. An array of speakers who had helped the young assembly during their years in the rented property were invited each night during the ensuing week to minister on the theme of the Lordship of Jesus Christ.

The Olivet Assembly is well established with eighty members in fellowship and strong leadership maintaining an effective witness to the gospel of Jesus Christ. Although located in Mount Merrion, the assembly borrows its name from another mount, the Mount of Olives just outside Jerusalem. It was there that our Lord Jesus often resorted in prayer. The foot of that Mount of Olives was the scene of our Lord's sorrow in Gethsemane. Further up the Mount of Olives Jesus Christ ascended into heaven. Christians note the promise and prophecy of Zechariah who reminds that when Jesus Christ returns His feet shall touch on the Mount of Olives. The saints today at Olivet at Mount Merrion worship the Lord Jesus Christ who in the days of His flesh, was often found on that eastern Mount. The opening hymn for their inaugural meeting in 1993 sums up the theme of their worship and witness still:

JESUS, the Name high over all,
In hell, or earth, or sky;
Angels and men before it fall,
And devils fear and fly.

Jesus, the prisoner's fetters breaks,
And bruises Satan's head;
Power into strengthless souls He speaks,
And life into the dead.

Oh, that the world might taste and see
The riches of His grace!
The arms of love that compass me
Would all mankind embrace.

His only righteousness I show,
His saving truth proclaim:
'Tis all my business here below
To cry, "Behold the Lamb!"

Happy, if with my latest breath
I may but gasp His name:
Preach Him to all, and cry in death,
"Behold, behold the Lamb!"

Chapter Fourteen

KESWICK STREET
MISSION HALL

Picture Anne Fraser, a missionary nurse for over thirty years with
WEC International, surrounded by crowds of needy Hindus in
Kashmir, India.   Imagine Edmund and Marie Norwood
pioneering with the gospel amongst the savage Indians in the steamy
Brazilian jungles.   Envisage Eddie and Sadie Young working in the
interior forests of Senegal, West Africa.   See Hazel Miskimmin
distributing Christian literature at the gateway of the central market in
Manaus, the capital of the Amazon.   Think of Jim and Doreen Smith
serving the Lord amongst Latin Americans in the Peruvian Andes.   Also
see Victor and Audrey Maxwell teaching seminary students in Bible
Colleges in Brazil.

Such an array of missionaries in distant and diverse places have
several things in common.   They are not only all Christian missionaries
from Northern Ireland, but all of them trace their early beginnings to a
converted wine store on the corner of a street on the Shankill Road.

Since its inception in January 1945 Keswick Street Mission Hall
not only made a great impact in the terraced streets of north Belfast, but

was diligent in sending its missionaries to the ends of the earth. This should not be surprising for the Keswick Street Hall originated with a missionary vision and genuine concern for the lost of the Crumlin and Shankill Roads

Tommy Spence was born at the latter part of the nineteenth century in the old Springfield Village. As a boy he attended the Mayo Street City Mission Sunday School and was converted there as a boy of fifteen years. Tommy became a builder by trade and soon developed the ability to turn his hand to anything to do with construction. After serving his time and working for different construction companies Tommy acquired his own clientele for repairs and renovations. However, Tommy was not only a builder by trade; he also was a diligent labourer for his Lord.

After his conversion Tommy became a member of Woodvale Presbyterian Church and eventually served as an elder in that church. Having been in the Boy's Brigade as a lad, Tommy became a leader in the local Boys Brigade Old Boys Association.

During the early part of the Second World War Tommy was appointed by his church as superintendent of the Woodvale Mission in Disraeli Street which at that time belonged to the Woodvale Presbyterian Church. Later the Woodvale Mission became the Disraeli Street City Mission Hall

One summer's evening in 1944 Tommy was driving his old car down Sydney Street West. A derelict shop at the corner of Keswick Street caught his eye. Ever looking out for an opportune renovation Tommy went back to have a look at the old building. As Tommy surveyed the structure he noted there were neither doors nor windows in the dilapidated structure. Everything had been vandalised and was wrecked. Only the original frame of the deteriorated building remained.

Speaking later of his first impression of the hall Tommy said, "As I stood there in that empty shell, God gave me the vision that this building would make an excellent mission hall. This is where God's Word would be proclaimed, where sinners would be converted, and where some would be commissioned to carry the gospel to far off parts of the world." Tommy's prayers and predictions about the hall could not have been more perfectly realised than what the subsequent history of Keswick Street Mission Hall reveals.

As Tommy Spence thought and prayed about the matter, he knew there were several other people who would also be interested in opening a gospel witness at the corner of Keswick Street. Tommy further related, "I knew several men who might be interested in joining me in this work. I had worked with some of them. Others were from the churches nearby. They were all sound evangelical men with a great desire to spread the gospel. It so happened that not long afterwards I was walking through the nearby Woodvale Park one Sunday afternoon when I met Mr. Jimmy Allen. I had known Jimmy for some time and took the opportunity to speak to him about my thoughts for the old house at Keswick Street. He listened attentively, and then expressed his sincere desire to join me in all I was proposing to do. Jimmy Allen, a painter by trade, was a Methodist and one of the lay preachers in his church.

At this time, besides being an elder in my church, I was also the superintendent in the Woodvale Mission. One of the workers there who was a great help and inspiration to me was Mr. Eddie Jackson. He was a Spirit filled man, a great preacher of the gospel and as well as that, a great singer. When I shared my vision with him he showed an immediate interest to have a part in this work.

The next man I approached was Mr. Bob Trimble, a member of a Brethren Assembly and a very godly man. Originally from Kilkeel, Bob came to work in Belfast where he was employed to lay the new footpaths in Belfast during the reconstruction of the 1930's. I often worked with him and we always had happy and friendly fellowship together. Mr. Trimble also gave me his wholehearted support in what I was planning.

There was another man whom we wished to have as a helper, Mr. Joe Anderson. Joe, who owned a small home bakery in Sydney Street West, was a member of Shankill Baptist Church where he taught a Bible class. One day we went to the bakery to talk to Joe about our plans, and he assured us of his support right away. The members of Woodvale Mission encouraged us greatly in the work; in particular Mr. George McCurry and my brother Albert Spence were a great help.

The next step was to contact the estate agent whose office was in Donegall Street. After revealing my plans to him, he promised to write to the woman who owned the property informing her of our proposal to convert the building to a mission hall and to ask her if she would consider giving us a three year period free of rent. We requested this because the building needed so many repairs. We had a very favourable reply from the landlady. All that we had asked for had been granted.

The plans for reconstruction were submitted to the City Hall for approval. At that time government regulations were still in force after the war. This limited us to a maximum of £100 for building materials. The renovation work began in October 1944, and by January of the following year we had the hall ready, which included doors, windows, floors and a pulpit; a small kitchen was also included although it had been intended for a prayer room. The total cost for building materials was £100.

Following the completion of the renovation we began our programme of visitation around the area and were well received by the people. Most of the people in Keswick Street were glad to see the building repaired, for it had been an eyesore to them. Next, we arranged the official opening in the same month, January 1945. Many people came, as well as ministers and pastors from the surrounding churches. It was a memorable service, with our little hall packed to capacity. The work of the Keswick Street Mission was launched.

There were meetings each Sunday night, and there were also some meetings during the week. A Sunday School was started, and it flourished. Mr. Tom McNabb, the pastor at Cliftonpark Avenue Baptist Church, was invited to conduct the first evangelistic mission in the newly renovated hall. Of that time Pastor McNabb wrote:

> Much preparation was made; special prayer meetings were held; the district was visited, and invitations were distributed. We began on Sunday evening following the usual church services; the meetings continued each evening (except Saturdays) for four weeks.
>
> From the very beginning there was a very marked sense of the presence of God; much liberty was felt in the preaching of the gospel, and it soon became evident that the Spirit of God was at work and prayer was being answered. A number professed faith in Christ as their Saviour; one I remember was Miss Doreen McFadden who later became a nurse and served as a missionary in Peru; she is now Mrs. Jim Smyth.

In the process of time a full quota of weekly meetings developed. There was the Sunday evening gospel service, Bible study on Tuesday evenings, a Thursday night prayer meeting and Saturday night Fellowship Hour. The ladies met once per month for a missionary knitting class. At this gathering they not only read letters from missionaries and prayed, but they prepared knitwear and other garments to send to distant mission fields.

In 1947 young Rev. Ian Paisley conducted one of his first evangelistic campaigns and the second evangelistic mission in the Keswick Street Hall. Mrs. Elizabeth Costley, a baker at Mr. Anderson's home bakery, suggested to Mr. Anderson that a young preacher who had recently arrived in Belfast from up the country and was the minister at her church, would be a good preacher to visit Keswick Street. Mr. Paisley was not only invited to preach he was also invited to conduct his first evangelistic mission at Keswick Street in 1947. Besides the small hall being packed to capacity each night, Mr. Paisley conducted lunch-hour meetings for workers in the surrounding factories. It was a great time of blessing and over forty people professed faith in Jesus

Christ at those meetings. Among those converted at that evangelistic mission was Hazel Miskimmin who later went to Brazil as a missionary. Her brother Jackie also became closely associated with the work.

The Keswick Street Mission was truly interdenominational. The responsibility for the meetings was shared with Tommy Spence a Presbyterian, Joe Anderson a Baptist, Jimmy Allen a Methodist and Bob Trimble who was in fellowship in a Brethren assembly. Speakers from all over Northern Ireland were invited to minister the Word of God.

Although Tommy Spence initiated the first steps that led to the acquisition of the Keswick Street premises, he was not a platform man. Added to this, his deteriorating health caused Tommy to lose his sight, and this curtailed his activities. Tommy was a faithful servant of the Lord.

It was after the inauguration of the hall that Joe Anderson took the administrative leadership of the work. He was largely responsible for introducing a very keen missionary interest in the hall. Besides his personal sacrificial giving to the Lord's work, Joe's nephew, Edmund Norwood who came home from Australia to live with uncle Joe and Aunt Rachael, eventually went to Brazil with UFM Worldwide.

Keswick Street's chief goals were evangelism in the immediate area and missionary enterprise to the ends of the earth. Accordingly Fred and Ina Orr conducted an evangelistic mission at Keswick before they left for Brazil. Less than six months later Ina gave her life for the gospel when she died of fever in the Amazon. Other evangelistic missions were conducted during the fifties by the Tramway Testimony Band and the famous Coalmen's Testimony Band. These evangelistic outreachs were followed by missions with Johnny Cupples and Dick McWilliams from the shipyard and Joe Kincaid, a former policeman.

Pastor Will Hibbert was a regular speaker at Keswick Street, and he conducted a very fruitful evangelistic mission in the hall. Malcolm Fenton held another gospel mission in the hall soon after he commenced his ministry in Newtownbreda Baptist Church. The Rev. Donald Giles from Agnes Street Presbyterian Church also was frequently invited to preach at Keswick Street. All these missions and meetings resulted in multiple conversions.

Many of those who attended the meetings in the hall during those days spoke of how the meetings in the little hall were so well attended and of the warmth of the fellowship in Keswick Street. One lady spoke of how people had to arrive early in order to be sure of a seat in the meeting. Perhaps the greatest impact of Keswick Street could be measured in the fervent missionary prayer meetings, the missionary knitting class and the tremendous support Keswick gave to missions and missionaries. Undoubtedly this devoted missionary endeavour contributed to the large number of missionaries who went from the hall to the uttermost parts of the world.

There were many faithful workers at Keswick Street. Most of these were engaged in the Sunday School which had been a feature of the work at the hall right from the outset. Raymond Burrows wrote of the Sunday School:

> There was a Sunday School in those early days the superintendent of which was the late Mr. Jimmy Allen. After Jimmy Allen relinquished his place Mr. Geoff Black supervised the Sunday School. Geoff carried on for a number of years before handing the leadership of the Sunday School to Mr. Tommy Hood.

Mr. Raymond Burrows succeeded Tommy Hood and carried on the responsibility of leading the Sunday School until it ceased to operate around 1973 when he had to relinquish his leadership due to his employment. The Sunday School work was greatly enhanced by a full quota of faithful Sunday School teachers such as Mrs. Trimble, Mrs. Rachel Anderson, Mr. Geoff Black, Mrs. Peggy Black, Mr. Tommy Hood, Miss Annie Lindsay, Mr. Maurice Dorman, Mrs. Dorothy Dorman, Miss Mabel Jones, Miss Irene Cosby, Miss Sadie Cosby, Miss Hazel Miskimmin, Miss Evelyn Mitchell, Mr. John Wightman, Miss Lily Nelson, Mr. Norman McKeown, Mr. Tom Wright and Mrs. Molly Wright.

Many of these teachers eventually married and either moved away from the district or became involved full time in the Lord's work elsewhere. Consequently the Sunday School was greatly depleted of teachers. With the reduction of the number of classes and teachers Raymond decided that instead of discontinuing the Sunday School altogether he would organise an open school each Sunday afternoon.

In 1955, Mr. Anderson asked Evelyn Mitchell if she would be interested in starting a Young People's Bible Class as some of the youth had shown good interest in spiritual matters. After some consideration, Evelyn started a class for young ladies every Friday night. The class was a huge success and continued until 1958 when Evelyn left for Canada. However, before Evelyn left, she handed the class over to two senior girls, Audrey Smith and Rae Moles. The two young ladies kept the class going until 1960 when Evelyn returned from Canada and resumed her role in the class again. Audrey eventually left the hall to go and train at the Bible College of Wales and then on to Brazil to serve the Lord with the Acre Gospel Mission.

In the late 1950s Tommy and Mollie Wright rented the small flat above the Keswick Street Hall. Their close proximity to the work was a great blessing for they gave valuable assistance to the hall. Jackie Miskimmin was also a great worker at the Keswick Street Hall and a good helper to both Mr. Anderson and Jim Smyth until he went to live in England.

Invaluable in the work of the hall was the contribution made by Mr. Dick Bryans. Dick had been converted in the trenches during the First World War. A man who had taken Dick's place in the trench suffered a fatal direct hit from enemy fire. Dick often reminded his friends that another had taken his place on the Cross of Calvary. Although he worked at the shipyard Dick developed a very gifted Bible teaching ministry, and Mr. Anderson invited Mr. Bryans to be responsible for the Saturday evening fellowship meetings. Although Dick was to arrange for visiting speakers he was always prepared in case of a speaker defaulting. He invariably had a word from the Lord!

Besides Dick Bryans and Billy Quigg conducting a gospel mission at the hall, Mr. H. H. Murphy from Bethel Evangelical Church (now Bethel Baptist Church) had a very effective evangelistic mission with an emphasis on the Second Coming of Jesus Christ. These meetings not only challenged and thrilled the hearts of believers but were also greatly used to bring sinners to the Saviour.

Joe and Rachel Anderson were two mighty stalwarts for more than twenty-five years at Keswick Street. Yet, they were gentle and gracious people who lived for their Lord. Not only did Joe minister the Word of God on many occasions, but his favourite theme was the second coming of the Saviour. Perhaps the Text on the wall above the pulpit summed up Joe's expectation, "The coming of the Lord draweth nigh."

Following the meetings visiting speakers and friends were always treated to royal hospitality at Joe and Rachel's home in Tennent Street where the table was spread with many of the delicacies from Joe's home bakery. After the Saturday night meeting all the young people crowded into the Tennent Street house for a sumptuous supper and an even richer time of informal fellowship. Many testified that the fellowship at the Anderson's home was often like heaven on earth.

The warmth of fellowship at Keswick Street Hall touched many. Before Audrey Smith married and left for Brazil she often witnessed to Billy and Mary Gault who owned a small shop at the corner of Howe Street and Sydney Street West. That early witness resulted in Billy and Mary attending Keswick Street Hall and coming to know the Lord Jesus Christ as Saviour. Their contribution in later years would prove invaluable.

Joe Anderson died on 19th December 1971 and many thought the work of the Hall would fold up after his departure. His wife Rachel also went to heaven six months after her husband. Providentially just a short time prior to Joe's death Jim and Doreen Smith had returned from Peru where they had been working with the Regions Beyond Missionary Union. Because of ill health they could not return to south America and had settled down nearby at Snugville Street.

At Joe Anderson's invitation Jim had conducted many Bible Studies at Keswick Street. Following Mr. Anderson's death Jim felt constrained to offer leadership to the work. Although Jim maintained a job at the YMCA Sport's Grounds in south Belfast he accepted the challenge of leading the work of the Hall. Jim continued in this position until he retired from secular employment and moved to Magheralin.

The onset of the infamous "Ulster Troubles" nearby on the Crumlin Road and the redevelopment of housing resulted in a mass movement of population of the Shankill and Crumlin Road areas which became greatly depleted in residents. This brought a crisis to the members of the Keswick Street Mission. Could they continue through troubled times? Bravely they decided to tough it out and keep the door open for the witness of the gospel.

One Thursday night while Jim was leading the prayer meeting he heard the sudden and urgent call from a soldier outside the Hall, "Everybody on the floor quickly. There's gunfire!" Instantly every one dropped below the chairs and the meeting really did become a prayer meeting as the crack of gunfire whistled up and down the streets outside.

Because of employment Jackie and Edna Miskimmin were transferred to Gloucester and other workers got married and moved to provincial towns. These were costly losses to Keswick Street. However, just at that time Billy and Mary Gault offered to be responsible for the children's meeting. In an attempt to rally support for the Hall they also organised a series of Praise Services on Saturday evenings. Evangelistic Missions were organised at regular intervals with evangelists Jim Pedlow, W. P. Moore and Victor Maxwell engaging in several weeks of evangelistic campaigns. Although people were converted at these meetings numbers attending were not as great as in former years. In spite of the difficulties the workers at Keswick Street kept plodding. At the height of "the troubles" two young men stumbled into the meeting. They sat with their heads bowed during the duration of the meetings. Later it was learned that the two strangers were two of the "Shankill Butchers" who were under investigation at the time. They were in pursuit of spiritual help and subsequently both were converted before their conviction in the courts.

In 1981 the rented premises of The Keswick Street Mission were sold to the Tennent Street Housing Association without involvement of the members of the Hall. In the following year the leadership of Keswick Street were informed by the Housing Association that the building would have to be pulled down for redevelopment.

The members of the Hall met to discuss the crisis and to pray. God answered those prayers and brought about a change in the situation. Billy Gault had become a Belfast City Councillor and he with Mr. George Haffey of the Mustard Seed Mission Hall did much to influence the Association to have the Hall kept on for religious purposes. The Housing Association was sympathetic to the petition and decided to offer the Keswick Street Hall the opportunity of purchasing the property they had occupied for nearly forty years.

Trustees were soon appointed to oversee the affairs of the Mission. The £1,000 needed to purchase the building was soon raised.   On February 28th, 1983 the Hall became the legal property of the members of Keswick Street Mission.   Subsequently the Hall was renovated and modernised.

Even though numbers continued to decrease during the eighties Jim and Doreen Smith, Billy and Mary Gault, Howard White, Greta Parkes and Beatrice Stewart gave themselves unstintingly to the work. They continued to maintain a close link with the Spanish Gospel Mission, the Acre Gospel Mission, the Irish Evangelistic Band and the Dublin Christian Mission. Jim Smyth said that the greatest contribution of the Keswick Street Mission Hall during his twenty-five years of leadership was the immense contribution the fellowship made to missionary work around the world.

Not long after the Hall acquired freehold on the premises the fellowship at the Hall suffered a sudden and severe blow on the death of Billy Gault. Billy and Mary served their Lord in the area where they had lived and run a shop. They had impacted many lives.

Jim and Doreen Smith continued to keep the witness of Keswick Street Mission Hall shining in difficult times. Sadly Doreen fell into ill health.   Converted at Keswick Street in its opening days and having served the Lord in Peru for many years it was perhaps ironic that Doreen's home-call to heaven on 9th. March 1994 corresponded with the conclusion of the work at Keswick Mission Hall.

In the latter part of 1993 Jim Smith met Councillor Eric Smyth on the Shankill Road. Eric's dad had worked with Jim at the YMCA's sport's complex. After the initial conversation Jim mentioned about the work at Keswick Street being at a low ebb and he confessed they were praying for guidance whether the property should be sold or does the Lord have some one else to maintain the work and witness. Eric shared with Jim about the work of the Jesus Saves Mission in North Queen Street and offered to give some consideration to opening another branch of the Jesus Saves Mission in the Shankill area.

Eric returned to Jim in due course with a positive reply. The Trustees of Keswick Street unanimously agreed to legally transfer the property to the Jesus Saves Mission. Just weeks before Doreen Smith passed into the presence of her Lord, Dr. Ian Paisley who preached at one of the first missions in Keswick Street, was invited to preach at a special meeting marking the termination of the work of Keswick Street Mission Hall and the embarkation of the new venture of Jesus Saves Mission.

It has been said that in one apple there are many seeds but in each seed there is the potential of an orchard. Keswick Street Mission Hall never experienced hundreds attending their small hall. However, the seed of God's Word sown in the old converted wine store known as Keswick Street Mission Hall has resulted in a great spiritual harvest around the world.

Chapter Fifteen

THE JESUS SAVES MISSION

G eographically the steamy slums of Singapore are thousands of miles removed from the draughty and damp back streets of North Belfast. Culturally the Far Eastern city on the Malaysian peninsula is so far removed from Belfast's Tigers Bay that one would think they could have very little in common. Notwithstanding the geographical and cultural distance which may exist between these two localities, a sign above a church hall at the corner of Limestone Road and North Queen Street in Belfast reads, "Jesus Saves Mission," and it registers an association in Christian work between these two cities.

Over forty years ago Dr. Peter Ng, a minister of the gospel in Asia, caught a vision for the poor and needy who lived and slept on the streets of his native Singapore. Forsaking the conventional trend of securing a stable position in a fine church, Peter dedicated his life to helping these destitute people. Adopting General William Booth's policy of not preaching the gospel to a man who has an empty stomach, Peter gathered friends around him and raised funds to feed and clothe the poor; once they were fed and clothed, he would then preach the gospel to them.

As a result of this social outreach and personal evangelism so many of these street people were converted that Peter Ng recognised they needed premises where the converts could meet. In the providence of God he acquired a hall in down town Singapore that had previously been a meeting place for spiritists. They duly renovated and converted the hall and founded the Jesus Saves Mission.   Soon this vision, which was first born in the heart of Peter Ng, was imparted to other Christian workers around the world who started similar Jesus Saves Missions to the needy people in their respective cities. Within two decades the Jesus Saves Mission was represented on all five continents.

The Jesus Saves Mission came to Northern Ireland through the zeal and enterprise of Councillor Eric Smyth. Mr. Smyth has had a colourful background both in Christian work and in local politics. As Mayor of Belfast Eric welcomed President Clinton to the city during the Christmas festivities of 1995 and read the Scriptures to the thousands gathered to see America's first citizen. Even though he graced such high office Eric remained very much a man of the people with a heart to win people for Jesus Christ.

Born and raised in East Belfast, Eric as a teenager succumbed to the deception and contrivance of the American Mormon missionaries who acted as spiritual predators on vulnerable young people in the Cregagh area. Even though he had embraced a form of bizarre beliefs which are alien to the Bible, Eric still did not find peace and forgiveness. He tried to engage in Mormon activities to recruit others to the cult, but he wrestled with doubts and confusion in his own heart.

The bewildered young Eric was invited by Mr. Eric Moore to attend meetings at Everton Hall located at the top of the Cregagh Road. Although Eric was in the company of his friends from the Boys Brigade at the meeting that night, he listened attentively to Pastor Will Hibbert preach the gospel. In spite of the earlier resistance of his heart, by the end of the meeting Eric was broken, and he requested to speak to the preacher. After some counselling Eric knelt beside Pastor Hibbert and received Jesus Christ as his Saviour.

From his earliest days as a Christian Eric wanted to serve his Saviour. After he married Frances they set up home in Forth River Parade in the

Glencairn housing estate. Soon they opened their house for cottage meetings every week in a determined attempt to reach their neighbours for the Lord. This outreach proved to be successful and fruitful. Eric also became a deacon at the John Knox Free Presbyterian Church in Cliftonpark Avenue. Although he was busy for the Lord beyond his daily work he still felt constrained to devote more time to Christian work. It was a big step for a young married couple and their six children for the husband to opt out of secular employment. However, Eric felt there was a very definite conviction that God wanted him in full-time Christian ministry.

Because of this challenge in his heart he offered himself to the work of the Free Presbyterian Church. Initially Eric was designated by the Martyr's Memorial Free Presbyterian Church to be responsible for the Aughrim Street Mission Hall in Sandy Row, a work that had been founded by Alderman Duff many years previously.

Eric gave himself wholeheartedly to the work in Sandy Row, and within a short time he became well known in the district. Because of Eric's wide acceptability by the local people Councillor Billy Dickson invited Eric to become a candidate for the elections to the Belfast City Council in May 1981. After prayerful consideration Eric felt this was the right way ahead and he let his name go forward as the DUP candidate for the Sandy Row and Donegall Road ward.

Many people were surprised when Eric was elected because he was a relative newcomer to Sandy Row. For the first time he took his place as a Christian Councillor at the City Hall.

Contrary to the opinion of many at the time Eric did not find any conflict between his dual responsibilities as missionary and Councillor. He found he was able to make one role compliment the other. It was in the course of his council business that Eric learned from his fellow DUP Councillor who also was a Christian, Billy Gault, of the availability of a vacant house in Greenmount Street which would make a good point for opening a mission work in the heart of Tiger's Bay. The area, like other parts of Belfast, had been subject to much redevelopment and had also suffered greatly because of the on-going terrorist campaign. Eric immediately felt this opening presented a great challenge, and he told Billy that he would like to take time to think and pray about the matter.

After he had given the proposal some consideration in which he weighed up the pros and cons and spent some time in prayer, Eric informed Billy Gault that he would be interested in taking the house and to use it as a centre for gospel outreach in the district. Eric knew it would mean extra work, and whilst not wanting to desert Aughrim Street, nor his friends and constituents in Sandy Row, he nonetheless felt that God had led Billy Gault to approach him about Greenmount Street.

The first task was to transform the vacant house into a meeting place. Christians from the locality willingly helped Eric do some renovations to the property. When the house had undergone a radical conversion it was time for Eric and those who had so generously pledged to help him to introduce themselves and present the message of the gospel to the local residents.

Wesley Graham from Bangor was invited to conduct an evangelistic mission at the newly converted mission hall. Eric and his team systematically went from door to door throughout the whole area inviting the people to attend the special meetings, which began on 18th August 1981. At first the numbers were small, but by the middle of the second week thirty people were crammed into the small meetinghouse. As a result of those initial meetings four people came to know Jesus Christ as Saviour.

A new interest in a new hall had been generated in the North Queen Street area. New converts now needed instruction. Concerned Christians approached Eric about continuing the work as vital channels to the community had been opened during the opening mission.

Soon the Greenmount Street Mission Hall became a hive of activity. Children's meetings on Friday nights attracted children from all the neighbouring streets. Eric started a Christian Fellowship meeting on Tuesday nights. A prayer meeting followed on Wednesday nights. Very soon a Sunday School was established with seventy children packed into one-time bedrooms to learn lessons from the Scriptures.

As the work in Tiger's Bay increased, Eric had difficulty giving the necessary attention to the work both in Greenmount Street and at the Aughrim Street Mission Hall. However, he never ceased to attend the Sunday morning service at Dr. Paisley's Martyr's Memorial Free Presbyterian Church. One Sunday morning in 1982 Dr. Paisley invited Eric to meet with him in the vestry following the early morning prayer meeting. It was at that meeting that Eric was introduced to Dr. Peter Ng who was visiting Northern Ireland to preach and speak about the Jesus Saves Mission in Singapore.

Dr. Ng told Eric that he had heard from Dr. Paisley about Eric's outreach in a needy part of Belfast, and he invited Eric to bring the work under the banner of the Jesus Saves Mission. The two men shared their vision and spoke at length about the work. When Eric discovered that the Jesus Saves Mission operated on the very same principles as he had sought to establish in Greenmount Street, he agreed to explore the possibility of the new work in Tiger's Bay becoming another branch of the Jesus Saves Mission.

When he mentioned his conversation with Dr. Ng to his friends in Greenmount Street, they were delighted with the development. They wholeheartedly agreed to be affiliated to the Jesus Saves Mission. They felt this would provide the work in Tiger's Bay with a much needed identity.

Eric contacted Dr. Ng and informed him of the endorsement the friends at Greenmount Street had given to his offer of affiliation with the Jesus Saves Mission. From that point the work in Greenmount Street took on a new meaning. The workers felt their Asian friends were interested in helping them, and they were part of a worldwide team, all of who were united in the same kind of work.

Representatives from the founding church in Singapore made regular visits to Belfast to encourage, help and advise their sister work during 1983. For Easter the following year Eric was invited to Singapore to attend the annual convention of the Jesus Saves Mission on St. John Island near Singapore. It was there he met the international leaders of the mission and was formerly ordained as a minister of Jesus Saves Mission.

The new status of the growing work in Greenmount Street brought increased interest and enthusiasm for that work. Eric concluded that he did not have the physical nor spiritual stamina to continue dividing his loyalty and involvement to both the works in Sandy Row and Tiger's Bay. Reluctantly he finally relinquished his role in Aughrim Street to concentrate his energies to the work of the Jesus Saves Mission. However, just at the time when he made that decision a housing executive vesting notice was served on the Greenmount Street property. All the houses in the area were earmarked for demolition to make way for new housing.

Confronted with this new dilemma the Jesus Saves Mission committee applied to the housing executive for a new site. Initially their application was turned down. Another application was made to the planning office at the City Hall, and they were offered a far better site at a moderate price of £4,000. The new location was at the corner of the Limestone Road and North Queen Street, strategically and prominently placed to give the mission high profile and easy access.

However, to purchase the site was a big step for a small group of working class people. Added to the purchase of the site, a suitable building had to be erected and that was going demand a lot of faith, sweat and hard work. Eric and his friends were greatly encouraged by an initial gift of £4,000 from Singapore which paid for the site. The members at the Jesus Saves Mission worked hard and gave liberally, and within a year of purchasing the site they had raised a further £15,000 and began to build. In the middle of their construction programme they were all greatly encouraged when a medical doctor in Singapore forwarded an interest free loan of £72,000 for the completion of the work.

The new hall for the Jesus Saves Mission was opened on 23rd. May 1987. Dr. Ian Paisley was invited to preach at the special inaugural service which was packed to capacity.

The Jesus Saves work continues to grow and flourish. After the death of Eric's friend Billy Gault, Jim Smith, the leader of Keswick Street Mission Hall, invited the Jesus Saves Mission to take over their hall in 1994. Billy Gault had always been a good friend to Eric and had been one of the leaders at Keswick Street.

At the North Queen Street location a new Sunday School complex was opened on 28th October 1997 to accommodate over one hundred children on Sunday afternoons. Through the ministry of the Jesus Saves Mission Eric Smyth and his friends have witnessed the conversion of many people in Tiger's Bay including some former para-militaries and terrorists.

Having achieved the high rank as Belfast's Lord Mayor and being the first mayor to welcome an American president to Northern Ireland, Eric Smyth continues as a City Councillor. However, Eric's primary aim and passion is for the lost of North Belfast. His heart's desire and earnest prayer is that they all may know that Jesus saves.

Chapter Sixteen

PITT STREET METHODIST MISSION

Ballymacarrat was probably one of the tightest knit communities in Belfast during the first half of the Twentieth Century. Undoubtedly one of the main contributors to the sense of locale and affinity was the role of the church and especially the part played by the mission hall which offered a less formal atmosphere than the more refined church. The mission hall was the cement of the neighbourhood where friends met and exchanged news and views as well as receive spiritual food for their souls. This was certainly true of the Pitt Street Mission Hall.

Pitt Street was one of a labyrinth of short streets built over one hundred years ago at the lower end of the Newtownards Road and literally in the shadows of the gantries where the great Titanic was built at Harland and Wolff's shipyard. The mission hall was located halfway up the street and was bordered by Scotch Row and Pitt Place, short alleys adjoining Pitt Street, and was surrounded by hundreds of families who looked on the Pitt Street Hall as their spiritual home.

For almost seventy years the mission was one of the most productive Christian centres in east Belfast, not only in evangelism to the local community but also in providing many ministers, missionaries and Christian workers who touched regions all over the world.

The mission had its beginnings in the latter days of the 19th century (1893), when Mr. W. J. Dobson, then a young man living in East Belfast, was greatly interested in the spiritual welfare of the young people of the district. He decided to start a Sunday School which began in a house in Scotch Row. Soon the attendance was so great that more accommodation had to be found in Saunders Street National School nearby.

Mr. Tom Platt and friends from Mountpottinger Methodist Church helped Mr. Dobson as teachers, and Mr. Watkinson was nominated as the superintendent. The work continued to increase rapidly, and it was not long before it became obvious that a larger hall was required. The leadership at Mountpottinger Methodist Church gave full support to purchasing a site in Pitt Street, and soon the building of the mission began. The Pitt Street Methodist Mission was officially opened on 5th November 1903 and was dedicated to the Glory of God.

Although the Sunday School work continued to make progress, the activities of the mission were not confined to Sunday School work alone. Under the guidance of the Rev. J. C. Robertson, the work of the mission began to expand as the gospel was preached every Sunday evening by local preachers, Christian business men and ministerial students from the Methodist College. In future years a special evangelistic mission was organised, and Billy Spence from the Shankill was invited to be the evangelist. Billy was "a brand plucked from the burning" and he was wonderfully used by God to bring many to personal faith in Jesus Christ. This first mission was very successful, but it was only the beginning of even better days to come.

A Saturday evening gospel rally was introduced and so great was the response that extra seats were borrowed from homes in Pitt Street to accommodate the crowd. There was also a prayer meeting on Sunday mornings at eight o'clock. Many Christians like John McKay, who believed in the power of prayer, faithfully attended this prayer meeting to pray for the work of the mission. John was a true Christian gentleman, faithful in all the activities of the mission.

A Bible class was convened every Tuesday evening in which the members were encouraged to give their testimonies. Besides being a Sunday School teacher Mr. Dobson was also Bible class leader who had a great influence for good on all who knew him. Very soon a Men's Bible class also started and open-air meetings were held at street corners. Every Sunday evening before the mission meeting there was an open-air meeting at Scotch Row. Cottage Meetings also began in member's homes. One such meeting which was particularly well remembered was that of Mr. H. Cunningham of Thistle Street whose family have been in the Mountpottinger Methodist Church for six generations.

With the continual growth of the mission very soon more space was needed for the mission activities. Another decision was taken to build an extension to accommodate the various organisations. Mr. Tom Platt presented the site for the new hall to the mission out of his own generosity, and on 9th September 1924 the new building was opened and dedicated to the Glory of God. This new structure was named the Thompson Memorial Hall after the late Mr. Robert Thompson who had taken such a great interest in the work of the mission.

The Belfast Telegraph reported at the time:

> An interesting event in the history of Belfast Methodism took place on Tuesday evening when the new hall erected in connection with the Pitt Street Mission on the Mountpottinger circuit, at a cost of £2,600, was formally opened in the presence of a crowded congregation. The hall, which adjoins the building—in use for the last 21 years—is perhaps the best of its kind in the city, being splendidly finished and excellently ventilated and affording seating accommodation for 600 people. Apart from the local imporatance of the proceedings, the ceremony appealed to the wider Methodist public in that it marked the completion of the first of the schemes to be helped by the Forward Movement which aims at raising £100,000 chiefly for church extensions in Belfast. The scheme was of course in existence before the Forward Movement with the Pitt Street friends raising £1,000, but

the greater part of the balance will be provided by the fund, while the collection on Tuesday realised £65. Pitt Street Mission is the direct descendant of the old Scotch Row Mission and represents one of the finest evangelistic and social efforts of the kind to be found anywhere. There is a Sunday School of 800 children which has had to meet in two sections owing to want of room, but with the old and new halls (which are linked together) this difficulty will now be overcome. The work is almost entirely voluntary, and the completion of the hall has given great joy to Messrs., Thomas Platt, John Dobson, John McKay and others who have for years given of their strength and time to the needs of the mission.

Mrs. Marion Jennings who was successful in bringing the young people into closer fellowship started a Band of Hope. They won first prize once at the Temperance Rally for the best slogan against alcohol. On their banner a drunken man depicted the degradation of the drunkard's home and above it a slogan read, "Great Bluff this Stuff."

Rev. George Watson, when a candidate for the ministry, was appointed to Pitt Street in 1928/29. During his ministry there he commenced the Christian Endeavour Society which continued to meet until 1971. Lifelong members such as Mrs. Christie, Mr. W. Gamble, Mr. F. Berry and Mr. James Weatherup successfully carried on the work of the society.

In 1929 James Dixon, an evangelist from the Grosvenor Hall was appointed to take charge of the work. As a good soldier of Jesus Christ he was dedicated to winning souls for the Saviour, and he led the Pitt Street Mission through the lean years of the 1930's. It was with much regret that he had to retire from the mission in 1940 because he was unable to travel about in the blackouts during World War II.

It is commonly acknowledged that "Methodism was born in song." The Christians at Pitt Street who loved to sing certainly proved that to be true. Their enthusiasm for singing was encouraged by the devoted service of choirmasters and organists such as Mr. Peter Taylor who served the mission in these capacities for many years. It is impossible to mention all who gave of their time and talents in this way but their influence has survived to the present day in the excellent choir at Mountpottinger Methodist.

The work among the women in the mission steadily increased under the leadership of the first deaconess, Sister Hannah Matthews who later became Mrs. Thomas. For many years Hannah did a wonderful work at Pitt Street. It is impossible to estimate how great was her influence on the members of the Mothers Meeting where she was also greatly helped by Mrs. Kelly of Mountpottinger.

The next deaconess was Sister Constance Bassett who laboured for many years in the service of her Master, accomplishing wonderful works in the mission. A Young Women's Fellowship was formed to do great work in supporting the mission's charities and other good causes. They were a happy family group. These leaders have all have gone home to be with Christ whom they loved and served so faithfully. The good work continued under the leadership of Mrs. Malcolm Skillen and others right up until the mission closed its doors.

During the earlier days of the mission the Sunday School outings took the form of a tram-ride to Boyd's Field at the end of the tramlines at Belmont. Ropes were suspended from trees for swings; races were organised with prizes for the winners, and many other games were played. Refreshments were provided in the shape of mugs of tea and paper bags of buns and were much enjoyed. These were very happy occasions and as time went on the outings went further afield to Bangor, Warrenpoint, Whitehead and Portrush.

Later, Mr. W. Dobson took on the responsibility of organising the outings, known as "Dobson's Trips" on the 14th or 15th July when massive crowds attended. This holiday time was known as "The Wee Twelfth" in Ballymacarrett. It was an inspiring sight to see the procession marching to the railway station headed by the Sirocco Silver Band and the Pitt Street Mission Banner.

Captain S. J. Platt who had been an officer in the Royal Irish Regiment formed the 39th Boys' Brigade Company in 1903. The 39th Company achieved many awards at Battalion level. In 1915, Sgt. C.

Shannon was the winner of the first King's Badge in Ireland. Sir William Smyth, founder of the Boys' Brigade, paid a visit to the Company in 1918 to present the Cross of Heroism to Cpl. A. Lappin who had rescued two persons from drowning at Donegall Quay.

When the First World War broke out in 1914, Captain Platt returned to active military service, and a number of the boys volunteered for the army. Some of these made the supreme sacrifice while others returned home to take up the work again.

The Junior Section of the Boys' Brigade, known as the 39th Lifeboys, consisted of boys aged between nine and twelve years who were led by officers drawn from the B. B. and helped by senior boys. They were a lively lot who enjoyed their games and outings. They also put on an interesting display of their work at the end of the year. Their leaders had outstanding patience, and this was rewarded by many boys graduating to the B. B. when they came of age, living up to the B. B. motto "Sure and Steadfast."

After the Boy's Brigade had been introduced to the mission, a special meeting was arranged for Sunday School teachers and the superintendent to discuss week-night activities for the girls of the mission to bring them more into Christian fellowship. At this meeting it was decided to start a company of the Girls' Life Brigade, a Christian organisation formed by the National Sunday School Union. The company was known as the 7th Belfast Co. and began in September 1928. It has continued successfully through all the days of the Pitt Street Mission with an unbroken record despite the troubles of the "Blitz."

The first captain of the G. L. B. was Miss Minnie Cowan who served the company faithfully for over forty years. Miss Cowan always looked on the members of the Brigade as "her girls." Miss Cowan, whose booklet furnished most of the detail of this history of the mission, had been a member of the mission since she was a girl of twelve. She joined the Sunday School in Saunders Street at the invitation of Martha Cunningham. When Minnie's family moved to Duncairn Gardens during World War I, she still travelled to Pitt Street every week. Besides being the Captain of the Girls' Brigade she was also active in Sunday School work all her life.

Some of the girls who passed through the ranks went on to lead the Company at Mountpottinger, and others went to different parts of the world and continued in Brigade work, proving faithful to the aim of the organisation. In 1968 the G. L. B. and G. B. were united and the former 7th is now known as the 9th Northern Ireland Girls' Brigade. When the mission closed in 1972 the 9th G. B. continued to function at Mountpottinger.

During the infamous Blitz when German bombers rained their destruction on Belfast, Newtownards Road Methodist Church took a direct hit and was destroyed. It changed the face of the Newtownards Road. Not only was the church and the nearby Baines' Bakery devastated by the bombing, but the adjacent graveyard at the rear of Newtownards Road Methodist Church also disappeared.

The homeless congregation from Newtownards Road joined with that of the mission and both worked harmoniously together for the next eleven years until the new Newtownards Road Methodist Church was rebuilt in September 1952. With the exodus of the their friends returning to their new church, the survival of the mission was in some doubt. However, the Lord opened up the way with the assistance of the friends of Mountpottinger, and the work of the mission continued under the ministries of the Rev. R. R. Sayers, Rev. F. McIvor, Rev. S. McCready and the Rev. A. W. Cooke, grandson of one of the founders of the mission, Mr. Kerr.

The mission was forced to close its doors in January 1972 because of the housing redevelopment of the area. Its closure was regretted by all who had enjoyed such wonderful Christian fellowship there for so many years.

On Sunday and Monday the 5th and 6th of November 1971, the last anniversary services were held. The special speaker on Sunday was the Rev. J. W. Young, a former superintendent of the circuit. As had been the custom each year, all the organisations marched in procession to Mountpottinger Church for the morning service headed by the B. B. Band. Mr. Joe Nabney, a former member at the mission and one of Ulster's best known gospel singers, was the soloist and the Comber Quartet also sang. Col. H. J. Johnston, who had been a great friend of the mission, was the chairman for the final meeting on the Monday evening when the speaker was the Rev. Trevor Kennedy. The service was also very well attended and the Youth Choir sang several items conducted by Miss M. McCutcheon.

The last parade of the 39th B. B. Company was held on 9th January 1972 when some 300 former members took part, and a former old boy, Rev. H. Kirkpatrick, a Methodist minister in Leeds, was the invited preacher. The 39th Boy's Brigade Company ceased to be on that date, but the 39th old boy's continues to this very day and has gained worldwide renown by producing some outstanding musicians.

The farewell services to wind up the work of the Pitt Street Mission were held on Saturday and Sunday, 22nd and 23rd January, 1972. At the Saturday evening service nearly 200 people met for tea followed by a public meeting in which many ministers, formerly associated with the mission's work, took part. They paid tribute to the wonderful work achieved by the mission amongst the boys and girls in the neighbourhood.

On Sunday evening around 700 people attended including the congregations of Bloomfield, Mountpottinger and Newtownards Road Methodist churches. The speaker was the Rev. A.W. Cooke who had been the minister for the last two years of the mission. Other ministers who attended were the Rev. E. Gallagher, Rev. E. R. Lindsay, Rev. T. S. Kennedy and Rev. E. Mason. Miss Sylvia Cooke and Mr. Joe Nabney presented musical items. In his address, the Rev. E. Gallagher spoke on Peter's words, "You are living stones" thus making the point that the mission would never die whilst its members lived.

Rev. A. W. Cooke at the close of the service urged everyone to remember the words of our Lord, "Lo, I am with you always, even unto the end of the world." Friends of the mission had travelled from near and far to this reunion and were happy at seeing one another once again. It was a date to remember for all those who were privileged to attend.

The old Pitt Street Hall was demolished but the work of the hall lives on in the hearts and labours of those who found Christ at the old mission and went to serve the Lord. W. Barr, D. Hill, T. Hartley, H.

Kirkpatrick, J. McKernan, B. Kingsmore, M. Weatherup, E. Patton, R. Good, T. Kennedy, S. Allen and W. McNaughten were all former members of Pitt Street who went into the Christian ministry. Alex Stewart and Alex Ireland went to Nigeria and spent their lives there amongst the Haussa people. Wesley Cunningham went to Columbia during the difficult days of persecution. S. Wright and R. Garrit also went to the mission fields. Because of these lives and those of many others the work of Pitt Street lives on in eternity.

Chapter Seventeen

THE OLD TENT EVANGEL

It was not a Mission Hall but it was a feature of East Belfast for many years and became the birthplace of many souls and for many servants of the Lord it expressed the passion to win the lost. Some people called it the Canvas Cathedral, and John McNeill of Scotland called it the "Cloot Kirk." It was the Old Tent Evangel which in concept was the forerunner of the tent meetings Frank Knox, the famous Brethren evangelist, conducted for many summers on the blitzed ground in High Street after the Second World War, although they were not linked

The Old Tent Evangel had its beginnings during 1922 and the opening months of 1923. God very graciously visited Ulster and its capital, and especially the East End of Belfast, with revival. Everywhere men and women were flocking to Gospel services, eagerly and earnestly seeking for God's way of Salvation. There were many evangelists at work, and God richly blessed and used them all.

God allowed Mr. A. T. Patterson, the noted Scottish evangelist, to visit Belfast at this time. He faithfully and fearlessly proclaimed the truth of God and was the means in God's hand of pointing several hundreds of people to the Lamb of God, which takes away the sin of the world.

It was during this visit that he first received the vision to venture into something that led to this great movement. For days and weeks prayer was offered that God would guide in this great forward enterprise in the interests of Christ's Kingdom. Soon the answering voice was heard, and the initial step of faith was taken and he divulged the secret burden of his heart. He wanted to establish a centre of evangelism in East Belfast each summer. If tents can be used each year at Keswick and at Portstewart for believer's why not a tent each year to reach the lost with the Gospel.

Mr. Patterson called around him a number of Christian workers representing all evangelical denominations. Mr. A. R. Allen was appointed as Chairman, Harry Geddis was appointed as Secretary and William J. Scott was the Treasurer. A strong Committee of eight other men, which included Mr. Joe Wells who became the Superintendent of Rathmore Street Mission Hall, surrounded these men.

Many other Christians stood with Mr. Patterson and believed with him it was God's will, and so a large marquee was procured with seating accommodation for 1,000 people, and in July 1923 the tent was erected on the Beersbridge Road where the Elmgrove Primary School now occupies the site. The motto being for the Evangel was "Not to proselytise, but to evangelise."

From the commencement the people were eager, enthusiastic, and sympathetic, the opening meetings being well attended. These continued until the end of September, and many more souls found peace in believing. The tent was then stored for the winter months, and each summer since it has been erected for the preaching of the Gospel. Many evangelists and ministers have laboured under its roof.

In other places outside Belfast the Committee raised the Canvas Cathedral" for the proclamation of the old Evangel of God. The Committee were so overwhelmed by the many and varied answers to prayer that they were convinced He wished them to enlarge their borders and strengthen their stakes and in faith believing it to be His will, they purchased another large marquee with seating accommodation for about 600 people. The purpose of this marquee was to visit the provincial towns of Ulster during the summer months and make known that Jesus Christ came into the world to save sinners.

In 1927 Pastor Frank Forbes wrote of the Old Tent Evangel's Motto:

> The business of every believer, as of every body of believers, is to evangelise; and the business of any believer or any body of believers is never to proselytise, hence the Old Tent Evangel has been carrying out its business in a most consistent manner; consequently the Lord has been able to bless richly the efforts that have been put forth by this independent, and yet dependent, organisation.
>
> As one would with unprejudiced mind follow its career from its inception, there is but one conclusion to be arrived at, and that is that every energy has been concentrated upon the seeking out of the lost, for whom Christ died, so that they may be made to know the need of their souls and led to receive Him who alone can meet their need and save their souls, all this being done without any attempt to dictate where those who have been thus blessed should henceforth worship.
>
> This knowledge has come to the writer through direct and indirect contact with the work under review. If any age needed such a work, surely the age in which we live is a needy one. Notwithstanding the existence of the many churches, chapels, halls, and meeting-places, there are thousands in our loved land who have never heard the story of God's redeeming love in simplicity.   It is for these that the Old Tent Evangel exists.
>
> Soon our precious Lord shall come, and the opportunity for all of us to serve here shall have gone forever. What if we today should have to look back upon the service that we have sought to render Him, and not be able to look

forward to any further service on earth! Would satisfaction or disappointment, or a mingling of both, fill our breasts? In His mercy and love He may spare us, and tarry yet a little. Should this be so, let us rise to our responsibility, grasp every opportunity, and enjoy every privilege of co-operating with Him and His for the salvation of sinners.

Proselytising is not only a waste of time and talent, but also a weakening of trust and trustworthiness. Evangelising is a God-glorifying work, and also a gain in godliness to those who engage in it. The Old Tent Evangel meets a urgent need, so its need should be met with prayerful sympathy and financial support.

John and Robert Fraser, the noted Scottish evangelists, were frequent visitors to the Old Tent Evangel. After one visit John wrote:

For a number of years the Old Tent Evangel has been the scene of wonderful meetings. The Committee, culled from a variety of churches, has no religious fads to spread before the people and no set building to house the converts. The summer effort is true to their motto- 'Not to proselytise, but evangelise.'

It has been our favoured delight to have gospel fellowship with the people of the Tent Evangel, and they remind us of a well-oiled axle - smooth to work and difficult to friction. Vast throngs owe their spiritual uplift to the efforts of these well-saved men who, at personal sacrifice and amid opposition, have carried the battle to the gate. Horace said, "I hate the common herd and keep them at a distance;" but the canvas tent is a testimony that Christ loves the sinner. Plato said, "I am glad I was born a Greek, not a barbarian; a philosopher, not a common man;" but the canvas tabernacle pulpit's God became man to reach man the ungodly. Cicero complained that Homer taught the gods to live like men; but the teaching that is broadcast from the tent platform is that God desires men to be duplicates of Christ.

Long may the tent herald by its presence the attraction of the Cross, the glory of the Christ, and the rainbow beauty of the Bible. One old master said, "God has three sorts of servants: the slave, serving from principle of fear; the hireling, serving for wages; and the son, serving under love's influence.

The Committee of the tent, impelled by God's love, driven by the need of the unsaved, and overwhelmed by the thought that it is better to lose the smiles of men than the souls of the people, and that it is better to suffer for speaking the truth than that the truth should suffer by wicked silence, annually erect the great tent for gospel preaching. Its door of invitation calls to all people and to people of all distinction praise God for the welcome tent, the godly Committee, and the precious Evangel preached by many lips.

Trust no lovely forms of passion,
Friends may look like angels bright;
Trust no custom, school, or fashion
Trust in God and do the right.

Some will bate thee, some will love thee,
Some will flatter, some will slight;
Cease from man, and look above thee
Trust in God and do the right."

Besides the three months of meetings every year on the Beersbridge Road the Committee used the Canvas Tabernacle for evangelism in many provincial towns. One of the most notable campaigns outside Belfast was that conducted under the auspices of the Old Tent Evangel in Ballynahinch in June 1925. Mr. Edwin Patterson gave and account of those meetings:

A band of Christian workers, then known as the Mission Hall party, had been praying and looking to the Lord for revival. It was during the earlier campaigns of the Rev. W. P. Nicholson that our eyes turned to this honoured servant as the one who, if the Lord willed, would be the means of moving our town. After much prayer a move was made to secure a building large enough to accommodate the crowds which were sure to come. In this we failed. The largest and only church that would have been of any use not being available. It looked as if it wasn't to be our town that was to have the opportunity and privilege of hearing Mr. Nicholson.

However, when it became known that Mr. Nicholson contemplated a second campaign for those places not visited during his first tour of meetings, we again were on our knees praying for the way to open, and it did. Hallelujah Four brothers called to interview Mr. Nicholson in Bangor, in September 1924, and after hearing our case he promised to come. To put it in his own words, "Boys, I would like a month down in that wee half-damned town of yours."

The difficulty of housing was overcome in this way. We were to hire a tent to seat 1,200 or so, and the Mission was to be in June 1925. How we praised God that evening to think that, after all, the devil was to be defeated and hundreds of souls born into the family of God. It is easy to sit at a Committee meeting and arrange to hire a tent, but it is another thing to plan the seating and erection. In this we would have made a big mistake.

A contract was about to be signed for a big old tent with no seats, when the Secretary of the Old Tent Evangel (Harry Geddis), who was in Ballynahinch on business, heard of our Mission and called with me to offer their tent, with seats, platform, and lamps included. Of course our committee agreed at once, and the necessary arrangements were made.

During the last week in May the tent was erected by the Old Tent Evangel Committee with the help of locals and what a rough week it was. The rain came down in torrents and the wind blew. The ground inside and outside the tent was just mud. On the Friday evening Mr. Nicholson came to meet our Committee and make final arrangements, and no one will ever forget the prayer he offered. How he asked the Lord to bottle up the clouds and let us have dry weather for the month of June. That prayer was answered in a wonderful way during the campaign, which lasted five weeks. Not one meeting was hindered by rain.

For five Sundays one side of the tent was taken down so that the crowds who were unable to get into the tent could lie on the hillside on the grass and take part in the service, and not once was there any danger of a break in the weather. Best of all, over 500 souls passed through the inquiry room and professed conversion. To God be the glory, great things He has done.

During the Mission the Old Tent Evangel Committee came often to give their help, and we believe they too shared in the blessing. The work in connection with the Mission Hall got a great push forward, and now we are known as the Ballynahinch Christian Workers' Union. Perhaps sometime in the future our Belfast friends will he asked to stand by us, and we know they can be trusted.

Fired on by the blessing in Ballynahinch the Fraser brothers under the auspices the Old Tent Evangel Committee, were able to erect the Tent in Banbridge at the end of May 1926, to conduct a four weeks' evangelistic campaign.

A report of that Mission also indicates great blessing:

Although then unknown personally to anyone in Banbridge, they soon gathered round them a band of willing helpers and a splendid choir drawn from the different churches-the musical part being a special feature of the Mission. The attendance steadily increased from the very first night of the Mission, until there were almost a thousand people present some nights. The evangelists gave of their very best. They faithfully preached the old gospel, telling the old, old story of undying and redeeming love with such pathos and power that hearts soon began to melt and yield to the claims of Christ, and believers were built up.

A feature of the Mission was the early Sunday morning prayer meetings, which were attended by teachers from the various Sabbath-schools. There are many in Banbridge today who look back to the Fraser Brothers' Mission here as the time that they met with Christ and decided to become His followers; and others as a time when they had new visions of Christ and the joy of service. To God be the glory."

Beginning in July right through until September the tent was erected on the Beersbridge Road. Mr. A. T. Patterson, the founder of the work, frequently conducted meetings at the tent. Peter Connolly, a converted gang leader from Sunderland and great evangelist, also engaged in great campaigns at the canvas tent as did other evangelists such Mr. John Thompson, Mr. R. S. Bakewell and Mr. A. E. Shakesby.

The site became the property of the Education Board and was requisitioned by them for the building of the new School. This plus the onset of war in 1939 brought the era of the Old Tent Evangel to a close. It came to the Kingdom for a very definite time and thousands of souls are in heaven today because of the first vision of Mr. A. T. Patterson and the faithful workers who rallied around him.

Thinking of the Motto of the Old Tent Evangel, "Evangelise not proselytise," Pastor Frank Forbes wrote:

Give us a watchword for the hour,
A thrilling word, a word of power
A battle-cry a flaming breath
That calls to conquest or to death;
A word to rouse the Church from rest,
To heed the Master's high behest.
The call is given: Ye hosts arise
Our watchword is "Evangelise!"

The glad Evangel now proclaim
Through all the earth in Jesus' name.
This word is ringing through the skies,
"Evangelise, Evangelise!"
To dying men, a fallen race,
Make known the gift of Gospel grace;
The world that now in darkness lies,
"Evangelise, Evangelise!"

Chapter Eighteen

AnD WhaT ShalL I Say MorE?

In recounting the history of Belfast's Halls of faith and fame time and space fail me to tell of:

The Mustard Seed Mission Hall. If ever there was an appropriate name for a Mission Hall it has got to be this one. Just around the turn of the twentieth century Mr. John Govan and his wife arrived in Ulster from his native Scotland. John was a full cousin of Mr. John Govan who founded the Faith Mission and a good friend and colleague in the gospel who shared the same concern to win the lost for Christ. Although it was secular business that brought Mr. Govan to our shores yet he had other business interests beyond providing for his family's material and physical needs. John Govan was busy in his heavenly Father's business.

Belfast's population was growing and the housing programme was expanding after the city obtained it's Royal Charter from Queen Victoria in 1888. Mr. Govan had taken up residence on the Crumlin Road and was soon struck by the spiritual needs of the surrounding community. Ever a man of action, Mr. Govan, motivated by his concern for the lost, decided to do something to reach the people with the gospel. He approached the landlord of two terrace houses in Vistula Street, just off the Crumlin Road end of Tennent Street, and took a long lease on the two properties. The houses were duly converted into a meeting place and plainly furnished. It was there that the first meetings were commenced in the Mustard Seed Hall almost a hundred years ago.

Even though he was a busy man Mr. Govan led the work of the Mission with zealous passion to win sinners to the Saviour. His mustard-seed faith in a great God resulted in much blessing on the community and scores of neighbours were brought to Jesus Christ. The Hall became a refuge for fellowship and a centre for evangelism throughout almost six decades of Mr. Govan's leadership. The Mustard Seed Hall also invested generously in missionary interest and unstinting support for the Lord's work in other places. The Govan family were life long supporters of the Worldwide Evangelisation Crusade and good friends of Mr. William Weir who often preached at the Mustard Seed. The Munn sisters and Lily Boal were also frequent visitors to the Mustard Seed.

Mr. Johnny Govan succeeded his Dad in the leadership of the Mustard Seed Hall. With the same spiritual aims and enterprise as those pursued in the first forty years of the Hall, Johnny Govan continued to lead the work in Vistula Street. Alas, Johnny died while yet a young man and was followed in the leadership of the Hall by Mr. and Mrs Jenks, Mr. John Govan's daughter and son-in-law. In the fifties the Mustard Seed Hall was a centre of evangelical activity with many young people attending the meetings and the work was greatly blessed by the Lord.

The fame of the Mustard Seed Hall attracted believers from areas beyond Belfast to engage in outreach to the local community. Alex and Anna Todd lived in Railway Street, Lisburn and although they were very active in Christian service in their hometown, they also attended the meetings at the Mustard Seed Hall. Besides a Bible bookshop adjacent to their home Mr. & Mrs. Todd conducted a "Soul-winning Clinic" in Lisburn and for many years they were associated with an American soul-winning organisation known as "Christians in Action."

In spite of the leadership given to the Mission by Mr. Mitchell and Mr. Clarke and the great help of Mr. McEneny, the Mustard Seed Hall took a bit of a slump in the early sixties and the numbers attending the meetings diminished. Added to this discouragement, the lease was due up on the property and a group approached the landlord with a view of purchasing the property for use as a Bingo Club.

Mrs. Todd rose to the challenge of this crisis. She sold the shop in Lisburn and raised the capital to purchase the Hall. She introduced some of her student soul-winners to the Mustard Seed. Principal among these was Marie Smith from Mountcashel Street. Anna Todd with Marie maintained her emphasis on personal evangelism and every Monday night she conducted a soul-winning clinic at Marie's Smith's home in Mountcashel Street before the group ventured to evangelise the district with gospel tracts.

Often Anna and Marie would embark on a "Faith Trek." which was an exercise of dedicated shoe leather to win the lost. Armed with an abundance of gospel literature they set off on a trek either to different parts of Ulster or down to the Republic of Ireland and even at times to towns and villages in England. In all these places they did door to door evangelism winning the lost for Jesus Christ. God not only blessed them with the salvation of the lost but often they recruited other Christians for this evangelistic work. One such recruit was Mr. George Haffey from Lisburn.

Alex and Anna Todd had known the Haffey family since their evacuation to county Armagh during the Second World War but had lost contact with them in the process of years. On a "Faith Trek" in the Lisburn area in 1969 Anna met George again and invited him to help at the Mustard Seed Sunday School.

Armed with a company of workers and soul-winners the work at the Mustard Seed started to grow again. An adjoining property to the Mustard Seed was acquired and this expanded capacity of the premises. Soon after the acquisition of this extra property redevelopment began to change the landscape of the neighbourhood. Soon the Mustard Seed Hall was the oldest building left in the immediate community.

During the long history of the Mustard Seed special evangelistic missions were not top priority even though Derick Bingham led a children's mission in 1980. The leadership at the Hall considered evangelism to be their on-going responsibility and much of this done by door to door visitation and personal evangelism.

After Mr. Todd passed away in 1984 and Mrs Todd in 1993, the responsibility to provide leadership for the work at the Mustard Seed fell on Miss Marie Smith and George Haffey. Times have changed and society today finds no priority for Church or Mission Hall as formerly was experienced on the Crumlin Road. However, the vision lives on - to win the lost for the Saviour. Through the ministry at the Mustard Seed there have been hundreds of outstanding conversions both at the Hall and for many others that were contacted at their homes on the door-to-door visitation programme. Even in recent times some former terrorists have been led to Christ through the witness the Mustard Seed Hall.

Mustard-seed faith is what motivated John Govan one hundred years ago when he arrived on the Crumlin Road and by that same faith the workers at the Mustard Seed Hall still endeavour to bring in the harvest for the Saviour.

Find out what God would have you do,
Perform that service well;
For what is great and what is small,
'Tis only He can tell.

The Bethel Mission, Whitewell. This independent Mission Hall was located at the rear of terraced houses on the Shore Road near Whitewell. Although the Mission has ceased to exist in its time it made a great contribution to Christian life and witness in the Whitewell and North Belfast area and sent missionaries to the ends of the earth. Many people remember with fondness Miss Lily Boal who served the Lord with WEC in India and Emma and Janet Munn who served the Lord with the same Mission in West Africa. All these ladies identified with the Bethel Mission.

The work at the Bethel began in 1946 when some believers from Longlands in Whitehouse conducted open-air meetings at the Mill Road at the Whitewell village. During the meetings many people sat on the sea wall listening to the preaching of the gospel and testimonies of saving grace. Because of the interest created at these meetings Sammy McGarry and Mr. Tate rented a hall from Whitehouse Silver Band for fifteen shillings (£0.75) per week. The initial response to these meetings was very encouraging and after several months larger accommodation was required. Due to this growth the meeting moved to the nearby British Legion Hall which was a little bigger than the band hall. Eventually the fellowship was able to purchase a former Billiard Hall at Whitewell and this became the permanent home of the Bethel Mission.

In the first three years of the work fifty people came to know the Saviour as a result of faithful witness to the gospel. Various preachers from different denominations were invited to preach at the band hall and the British Legion Hall. The Coalmen's Testimony Band were regular visitors to the Bethel. Adults, young people and children continued to be converted at these meetings including Mrs. Brennan and her eight children. Such blessings brought great joy and growth to the meetings

Missionary interest was also fostered at the Hall and resulted in sending and supporting missionaries in many distant countries. The fellowship at the Bethel Mission was rich and the leadership introduced a Sunday morning worship service which helped establish the Bethel Mission as the spiritual home of many saints in the Shore Road area.

For many years Sammy McGarry, Mr. Tate and Percy Moore led the work and maintained a bright witness for their Lord in this neighbourhood. The work finally closed down in 1975 because of the shift of population and industrialisation of the York Road district.

A noble life is not a blaze,
Of sudden glory won,
But just the adding up of days,
In which good work is done.

These noble servants of Christ did well for their Master.

Tamar Street Baptist Hall.   Although our Lord had no place to lay His head in that He did not own a house, yet it is an interesting study to find how many homes were put at His disposal. He often resorted to Bethany with Lazarus and the two sisters. In Galilee Peter's mother-in-law not only gave him hospitality but also as the day lengthened it must have seemed that her home resembled a hospital out-patients clinic as all the sick and infirmed gathered at her door to meet the Great Physician. I wonder how the owner of the house felt when determined men who could not edge their way in by the door started to tear up the roof to lower their friend into the house. That took a lot of tolerance. There was an unknown man who not only provided a colt for our Lord's entry to Jerusalem but also furnished and prepared the room for our Lord to transform the Passover Meal into the Remembrance Supper. Even after His ascension to heaven various homes were still made available to those who gathered in His name.

Today that tradition continues and many Mission Halls and churches had their beginnings in a house that was open to the Lord and His servants. Back in 1906 Mr. and Mrs. John Galway made their home at 51 Tamar Street in East Belfast available to Mr. Alex Jardine to conduct "cottage meetings."   This "Wee Meeting," as it was affectionately known, continued in the same house for over a year until renovations were carried out to the Galway home and the property became known as Tamar Street Mission Hall. Evangelistic and fellowship meetings were conducted at the Hall on Wednesday and Friday evenings.

When Mr. Jardine was called to be the pastor at Grove Baptist in 1915, Tamar Street Mission Hall became an outreach of Grove Baptist Church with the Church responsible for appointments at the Hall. After Mr. Jardine left to be pastor the work continued to make steady progress under the leadership of Mr. Sam Edmonds who remained the Superintendent for almost thirty years. Mr. Edmonds was known and greatly loved by all in the Tamar Street area. He was greatly helped and encouraged in the work of the gospel by workers such as Jack Graham, Bob McCaskey, Billy Hodden, Agnes Burns, Barbara Murray, Annie Kennan and Mary and Bob Glendenning.

In 1923 Bob and Mary Glendenning took their leave of Tamar St, when Bob accepted a call to be the Pastor at Knockconny Baptist Church near to Ballygawly in County Tyrone. At their Farewell Services at Tamar Street Hall on 23rd August, a neighbour, Mrs Kitchen, was led to saving faith in the Lord Jesus Christ.

As the work progressed it became obvious that there was the need for larger premises. Eventually some ground was purchased from the Railway Authority and this is the same site occupied by the Tamar Street Baptist Hall to this day. A wooden structure, which was purchased from the Bangor Hospital, was erected on the site in 1934.

Shortly after the erection of the wooden structure on the newly acquired site Mr. Tom McLearnon started to attend the hall to assist Mr. Edmonds. He arrived just at the right time for in 1938 Mr Edmonds was called home to be with the Lord after thirty years of faithful service at Tamar Street. Mr. McLearnon was appointed to succeed Mr. Edmonds as Superintendent

On the terrible night of the Blitz in May 1941 the Hall was severely damaged from the intense bombing near to the Shipyard. However, this did not unduly hinder the witness in Tamar Street as the work continued in a nearby Band Room on Dee Street.   The meetings continued in the borrowed Hall until 1947 when in the goodness of God, a new brick building was erected on the original site. The total cost of the new building was £1450. The war damage grant amounted to £1050 so the balance was raised by the members and adherents at the Hall. The new building was officially opened on 2nd August 1947.

Tom McLearnon faithfully led the work at the Hall through the war years and until his retirement in 1952. In the same year Mr. Bobby Maxwell came from Grove Baptist Church and had the responsibility to lead the work for the next two years.

At Tamar Street temporary positions and appointments have had a strange way of lingering longer than expected. Mr. George Wilson, who was a member of Bloomfield Baptist Church and also a Sunday School teacher in Tamar Street Hall, followed Bobby Maxwell. Initially George was asked to be the interim Superintendent until Grove Baptist

Church could appoint a permanent replacement. That temporary position continued for the next twelve years. George Wilson had to finally relinquish his leadership responsibility when his family moved away from the area to live at Dundonald after George's retirement.

In 1957 the organist, Ella Wilson and her sister Betty, emigrated to Canada. Mrs Maxwell, wife of Bobby Maxwell, the former Superintendent at the Hall, came to replace Ella at the organ for two weeks only. Over forty years later Mrs. Maxwell is still at the organ and is a faithful worker at Tamar Street.

There have been many evangelistic missions at Tamar Street. Most notable of these was the mission when Mr. Currie Brennan was the evangelist. Not only was the Hall packed to capacity but also people sat on window ledges and attentively listened to God's servant. Many people trusted the Lord as a result of those meetings. In 1971 the Dromara Musical Messengers with Mr. Francis Corry from Ballykeel Baptist Church conducted two weeks of evangelistic meetings at which several people came to know the Saviour. Philip Campbell of The Evangelisation Society also conducted two weeks of evangelistic meetings in 1990. Again these meetings were very well attended and greatly blessed by the Lord.

After George Wilson's retirement from the Hall there were another two short term Superintendents, Mr E Scott and the late Mr. Jack Johnston. One young man who assisted Jack Johnson was Lawrence Lindsay. In 1960 while he was a member at Grove Baptist Church, Margaret Kitchen invited Lawrence to assist in the Sunday School at Tamar Street Hall. Lawrence readily agreed and soon he became greatly involved in the work at Tamar Street. He not only assisted Mr. Jack Johnson but when Mr. Johnson relinquished his position, Lawrence Lindsay was appointed as Superintendent of the Hall in 1967.

For almost thirty-three years Lawrence has led the work at Tamar Street through difficult years of "The Troubles" and the urban redevelopment programme that has scattered the local population. Many other Halls in the Ballymacarret area have closed because of these factors but the work at Tamar Street continues and much of this is due to Lawrence's leadership.

What used to be known as "Tamar Street Mission Hall," is now the "Tamar Street Baptist Hall." The Hall now has its autonomy as an independent fellowship and in August 1992 they added a Sunday morning Worship Service to their weekly programme.

Helen Keller was asked if she knew anything that was worse than being blind. She replied. "Worse than being blind is to have eyesight and have no vision." Solomon taught, "Where there is no vision the people perish." Thank God for those who almost one hundred years ago had the vision to start the "Wee Meeting" in John Galway's house in Tamar Street and for the vision and faith to keep that work going for almost one hundred years.

Banbury Street Mission Hall. William Patteson Nicholson conducted an evangelistic Mission on the Newtownards Road in 1923. Over a thousand people professed faith in Christ as a result of these meetings. Amongst the converts were five young men from Ballymacarret. Before those meetings Jimmy White, Tommy Hunsdale, Jimmy Scott, Sam Hewitt and another pal all played cards on a plot of spare ground in Banbury Street. After their conversion Jimmy White led the same five chums in serving they Lord. They acquired the spare ground in Banbury Street for a witness to the Gospel in the Dee Street and Mersey Street area. The young men erected a wooden hall which was a forerunner of the more permanent brick building that was constructed some years later.

Although Jimmy White pioneered the original work in Banbury Street he was later succeeded by Mr. Stanley Gillespie who led the work for over forty years until his death in the mid eighties. He maintained the emphasis of reaching to the immediate area with the gospel of Jesus Christ. Mr. Vitty who had been a constant worker at the Hall replaced Stanley Gillespie and continued with same zeal as that shown by his predecessor. Mr. Billy McNaughten, a member at Templemore Hall who often preached at Banbury Street, was invited to follow Mr. Vitty in 1988. Billy McNaughten, an able Bible teacher, led the work until he received a call to pastor the Roslyn Street Emmanuel Hall early in 1994.

Under the leadership of Mr. Stanley Rollins, the work in Banbury Street Mission Hall continues in accordance with the first aim of those five young men converted at W. P. Nicholson's meetings.

Fret not because the place is small,
Thy service need not be,
For thou can'st make all there is
Of joy and ministry

The dewdrop, as the boundless sea,
In God's great plan has part
And this is all He asks of thee;
Be faithful where thou art.

Foundry Street Mission was one of many Mission Halls in the heart of industrialised Ballymacarrat. It was founded in 1917 by Frank Dinning, a local Insurance agent, acquired an old rag store at numbers 86 and 88 Foundry Street and converted it into a Mission Hall. Frank led the work through many years greatly assisted by friends from East End Baptist Church. Fred Curragh, Sammy Chapman and Jimmy McQuilken were right-hand men to Mr. Gillespie in the work.

Besides the large Bible Class and the full quota of meetings each week Frank also invited many preachers from all denominations to help in the evangelistic outreach from the Hall into the surrounding neighbourhood. The old Foundry Street Hall became a source of great blessing to local Christians and the place where many people were converted to Jesus Christ. Sammy Spence and the Coalmen were regular visitors at Foundry Street. Charlie Simpson and a testimony band which consisted of converted Roman Catholics, conducted an evangelistic mission at the Hall and in the late fifties Rev. Ian Paisley also held special meetings at the Foundry Street Hall at which many people were converted.

Missionaries frequently visited the Hall and a special interest was shown in the Poona and Indian Mission for many years. Although the Hall no longer exists the missionary interest cultivated in Foundry Street

Hall continues to this day in special missionary prayer meetings in private homes.

The Foundry Street Hall had many characters who not only helped in the work of the Hall but also engaged in open-air activities and soul winning at the local pubs on Friday and Saturday nights. Most notable amongst these was Tommy Hutton who led a band of outreach workers. After Mr. Gillespie died Mr. Porter and Jim Wilson with others continued to carry on the work through until 1973 when Foundry Street came under the redevelopment hammer. The local houses were demolished to make room for new dwellings and the old Mission Hall was forced to close. From the converted rag store sounded out the gospel for fifty-six years. It is not success that God blesses but faithfulness in doing His will.

Felt Street Mission Hall maintained a strident witness for the gospel for many years in the Sandy Row and Donegall Road areas. It was not only a centre of evangelism but also was known for its keen missionary interest and support. It closed in urban redevelopment in the early seventies.

The Matilda Street Hut was a wooden structure on a patch of land at the rear of Matilda, Bentham and Mabel Streets, where believers gathered to worship and serve the Lord. Like other halls it fell victim to the movement of population and urban redevelopment.

Cupar Street Mission Hall, located between the Shankill and the Falls Roads, was a great centre for evangelism right on the political divide between the Shankill and the Falls Road. In the years prior to the troubles the workers were able to reach out to both communities. It fell victim to the troubles of 1969 and then the displacement of population with urban redevelopment.

Skipton Street Mission Hall Like the nearby Tamar Street Mission Hall the Skipton Street Mission originated as an outreach from Grove Baptist Church on the lower Newtownards Road. Mr. & Mrs. Tommy Meaney laboured with others in the area for many years. After the Hall was closed due to urban redevelopment Mr. & Mrs. Meaney, at a mature age, went to serve the Lord in Papua New Guinea with New Tribes

Mission. Not long after they arrived on the mission field Mrs. Meaney fell victim to a terminal illness and subsequently died. Recalling the former days at Skipton Street her son Peter wrote the following lines:

The Old Mission at Skipton Street

In the East End of Belfast
There's a place that stands tall
It's known by the locals
As the 'Skip' Mission Hall

Many people have sat there.
Many answered the call
From the hundreds of preachers
At the Old Mission Hall.

The Meaneys, The Gearys,
Pastor Wilson and all
How many years service
In the Old Mission Hall?

Many parties we've had there
The Socials were a ball
Sticky buns and sweet tea
In the Old Mission Hall.

The Street had more characters
Than a Soap Opera call
But they'd still enter the door
Of the Old Mission Hall.

With School on a Sunday
And kids wall to wall
Everyone was happy
In the Old Mission Hall.

Folks have gone to Peru
To New York and all
But our hearts are still with you
In the Old Mission Hall.

Now the night has arrived
For us all to recall
The great time we've had
In the Old Mission Hall.

The bulldozers will arrive
To knock down the wall
But the Spirit will linger
Of the Old Mission Hall.

Northumberland Street Mission Hall. This hall no longer exists but for the first part of the twentieth century it served the Shankill community with great distinction. Besides being a gospel beacon on the Shankill it produced missionaries such as Fred Wright, one of the "Three Freds," martyred by the Kayapo Indians of the Amazon in 1937. Fred's brother Joe Wright and his wife Amy also served the Lord in Brazil with U.F.M. Violet McGrath went out as a missionary and spent a lifetime in Japan. Willie and Margaret McComb, having served the Lord with U.F.M. in Brazil returned to the Amazon with Mollie Harvey to found the work of the Acre Gospel Mission. Willie McComb's brother, Joe McComb, also served the Lord in Brazil with U.F.M. The old Hall has gone but its influence still lives on. Some one has well said that the church is a place for gathering sinners in and sending the saints out. That was the story of Northumberland Street Mission Hall.

Aughrim Street Mission Hall was founded and developed by Mr. Albert Duff, commonly known as "Da Duff" in the Sandy Row area where he endeared himself to the hearts of the people. In his early life Mr. Duff was a salvationist with the Salvation Army in county Armagh. When he came to Belfast he joined the Belfast City Missionary and worked as a Missioner in the city for several years before his involvement with Aughrim Street. The work in Aughrim Street flourished and Mr. Duff was so encouraged he opened a similar work near Brown's Square on the Shankhill Road. Besides his very fruitful work at the Mission Hall he also maintained involvement in local politics and served for many years as a Belfast City Councillor for the Sandy Row Ward. Mr. Duff became an Alderman of the Council and was also nominated as a Justice of the Peace. After Mr. Duff's death the Aughrim Street Mission

Hall became an Outreach Mission of the Martyr's Memorial Free Presbyterian Church and continues as such unto this day.

Everton Hall. A top BBC programmer was recently invited to make his selection of 'Desert Island Discs'. Recalling the days of his early childhood he said he had been greatly influenced and taught many values at the Sunday School at Everton Hall in Belfast.

Everton Hall, located at the top of the Cregagh Road, has been a witness to that area since 1934. Several Christians from the immediate neighbourhood felt constrained to establish an evangelistic thrust to reach the growing community on the edge of Belfast's south-eastern boundary. Mr. McKeown from the nearby Hillfoot Road and Mr. Fred Backley teamed up with Robert Simpson, Bryce Smith and Robert McLarin to lay the basis of an undenominational witness in the upper Cregagh district.

They acquired a site in the new housing development that bridged the Cregagh and Mount Merrion communities. A new hall was erected and soon the work was established. The Everton Hall was not designed to replace any church and for that reason no Sunday morning service was arranged until later years. It was essentially an evangelistic outreach with a range of regular meetings, children's meetings and Sunday School. Initially the work grew until the outbreak of the Second World War when many people were evacuated to more rural localities.

By the end of the War the congregation had fallen to very few people attending and it was even suggested that the Hall should be closed. Willie and Margaret McComb, founders of Acre Gospel Mission, returned from Brazil in 1946 and set up home nearby. Mr. McComb was challenged by the need of the area and he re-opened the Hall and pastored the work until he was invited to be Pastor at Castlereagh Evangelical Church in 1951.

Mr. Sam Simpson preached at Everton Hall and subsequently in 1951 he was invited to replace Willie McComb. He accepted the challenge and undertook to lead the small congregation in reaching the neighbourhood. Prolonged seasons of prayer saturated every department of the work and much blessing followed. Many souls were saved. After one memorable night of prayer fourteen people trusted the Saviour the following Sunday. Numbers began to increase and soon people had to arrive early to secure a seat in the small hall.

Sam Simpson continued at Everton Hall until 1960 when he accepted a call to be Pastor at Banbridge Baptist Church. He was followed in 1960 by Pastor Will Hibbert who remained at Everton Hall until he accepted a call to Castlereagh Evangelical Church in 1964. A vacancy prevailed for several years during which time Mr. Stanley Moore and friends did a sterling work at the Hall. His own son Eric with wife Jean went to Ecuador as missionaries with H.C.J.B.

Pastor William McGilton led the work at Everton Hall from 1969 until 1972 when he left for Dungannon Baptist Church. During these succeeding pastorates there was much blessing on the work and many people came to a personal knowledge of Jesus Christ.

Another long vacancy followed after the departure of William McGilton. Mr. Jim McAleese accepted the challenge to pastor the work in the mid eighties. Jim's tenure at Everton Hall saw the transition of Everton Hall being transformed into Cregagh Baptist Church. The work continues today with a full quota of meetings. A team of workers led by Mr. Nixon maintain the witness that was first established sixty-five years ago. The original leaders have gone to be with the Lord and this reminds us that the only generation that can reach this generation is our generation.

Ivan Street Mission Hall is a converted terrace house just off the York Road. The Hall was born in 1971 out of the zeal and vision of Mr. John McFeeters who was the leader of the Rathcoole Testimony Band. After John's conversion he was out and out for his Lord and bought up every opportunity to witness and help. Anxious to establish a gospel witness on the north shore area of Belfast he was informed that a terrace house was available at a very reasonable price. With his son David, John put a £100 deposit to secure the purchase of a terrace house in Ivan Street. Immediately the men of the Rathcoole Testimony Band rolled up their sleeves and renovated the old house and made it habitable for meetings.

The Ivan Street Mission Hall with a capacity for sixty people was never designed to take the place of church, or Sunday worship. There still are no Sunday services in the Hall. The meetings are still conducted in the style of the old "cottage meetings" of former years. On Monday evening there is a Good News club for the boys and girls and a Gospel meeting follows this. The small hall is frequently packed to capacity. On Saturday night the believers gather for prayer meeting in respect to the outreach.

John McFeeters pioneered the opening of this work but in less than a year after its opening in 1971 John went to be with Christ. The Rathcoole Testimony Band led by Mr. Alex Young continues this bright witness for the Saviour in the York Road.

I think it was C. T. Studd who said, "I do not want to live within the sound of church or chapel bells."

The Old Forge Mission Hall. When Queen Elizabeth was crowned in 1953 Bobby Moore caught the vision for a witness to be raised in the upper Ligoniel area. Bobby worked in the Belfast Power Station and was part of a group of zealous Christians who wanted to serve the Lord. Bobby was challenged by one friend who left Northern Ireland to serve the Lord in Rhodesia (Zimbabwe). One Sunday afternoon while Bobby was walking up the steep hill at Ligoniel just at the edge of the city boundary he noticed a small wooden Hall and thought it would make a fine place for a gospel witness.

After inquiry about the property he was able to rent the former Unionist Hall at Wolfhill Lane, and helped by friends and family they established a programme of meeting to reach the district for the Saviour. They named it the Old Forge Mission after the former metal workshop nearby. Having founded the work Bobby continued to lead the mission until his death when after which Mr. William Willis, Bobby's son-in-law assumed that responsibility.

After ten years renting the property in Ligoniel the mission moved to other rented premises in Loftus Street just off Agnes Street in the early sixties. After three years in Loftus Street they were able to purchase a shop at the corner of Glenfarne Street where on the 18th December 1982 they opened a new hall.

The mission continues as an outreach of the gospel in the district as well as a haven of fellowship for older saints. The Old Forge Easter Convention is a feature of their yearly programme. During the course of its history the Old Forge has had many evangelistic campaigns with the Coalmen Testimony Band, the Emmanuel Male Voice Singers, Pastor Ivan Thompson and other evangelists. They reached out to factories, mills, hospitals and to the boats in spreading the message of the gospel. That work and witness continues to this day.

Witnessing for Jesus Christ is not winning arguments but winning souls for Christ. That work and witness of The Old Forge Mission continues to win souls for the Saviour.

• • •

It has been truly said, "There is properly no history, only biography." Behind every movement God uses men. Our Saviour promised "I will build My church and the gates of hell shall not prevail against it." That promise is being fulfilled every day as God moves across our world in the gathering in of the redeemed. In the fulfilment of this assurance God still uses men, men of vision, men of passion and faith.

When Paul wrote to the Philipians he recalled three important days in the history of that church. "I thank my God upon every remembrance of you...For your fellowship in the gospel from the first day until now; Being confident of this very thing, that he which hath begun a good work in you will perform it until the day of Jesus Christ: (Philippians 1:3-6)

There was the first day of city evangelism when he and his company entered Philippi and saw the first converts at the riverside, on the street and in the jail. There was the then present day ten years later when the flourishing church continued to grow and be blessed. Paul then referred to that final day when God shall complete His work in the church. Paul expressed his confidence and faith that God who began the work, will continue to work and one day will complete His work in the church.

Other books connected to the events or personalities in this book

All For Jesus - *The Life of W. P. Nicholson*
by Stanley Barnes

Angel of the Amazon - *A Thrilling Story of Compassion and Faith*
by Dr. Bill Woods, OBE with Victor Maxwell

As Our Heads Are Bowed - *Lives Transformed Through the Ministry of Ian Paisley*
by Noel Davidson

The Authentic Servant - *In Mark's Gospel*
by Victor Maxwell

The Awesome All's - *A Look at the All's of Scripture*
by Lehman Strauss

Crowned With Victory - *Four Forgotten Irish Firebrands*
by A. W. Tozer, Leonard Ravenhill, Helen Bingham & James Grubb

D. L. Moody - *Soul Winner*
by Chester Mann

Found Faithful - *Studies in Bible Characters*
by William Gilmore

First Citizen Smyth - *From the Heart*
by Noel Davidson

Gipsy Smith - *An Autobiography*

The Good, the Bad and the Lukewarm - *A Relevant Approach to the Seven Churches in Revelation*
by Denis Lyle

Goodbye God - *Twelve Stirring Messages from W. P. Nicholson*
Compiled by Stanley Barnes

Great Conversions - *From Augustine to Helen Roseveare*
by Frederick S. Leahy

The History of Presbyterianism in Ireland - *From St. Patrick to the 1859 Revival*
by Thomas Hamilton

The Holy Spirit - *Who He Is And What He Does*
by Reuben Archer Torrey

The Invitation - *365 Devotions from John's Gospel to Help You Find Your Place in God's Plan*
by Derick Bingham

Joy In Shared Tears - *Christian Testimony in Romania*
by Drew Craig

Just The Way I Am - *The Ivan Thompson Story*
by Noel Davidson

The Life and Times of Henry Cooke
by J. L. Porter

Sankey - *The Singer and His Song*
by Helen Rothwell

Singing We God - *Fifty Years with The Woodvale*
by Victor Maxwell

Sweet Believing - *Eight Character Studies of the Scottish Covenanters*
by Jock Purves

This Is For Real - *Life was a Total Hell on Earth Until he Discovered the Power of Heaven*
by George Bates with Noel Davidson

The Titanic's Last Hero - *A Story of Courageous Heroism and Unshakeable Faith*
by Moody Adams

Treasures of Worth - *A Pioneer Missionary*
by Mollie Harvey

With Flaming Zeal - *A Look at the Lives of Eight Great Missionaries*
by Lionel Fitzsimons

With Hearts on Fire - *The Story of Robert and Ivy Milliken*
by Chris Clement

The Year of Grace - *A History of the 1859 Revival*
by William Gibson

Available from your local Christian Bookshop
or direct from Ambassador Publications